HEIDEGGER'S INTERPRETATION OF KANT

Heidegger has a reputation for reading himself into the philosophers he interprets; his interpretation of Kant has therefore had little uptake in Anglophone Kant scholarship. In this book, Morganna Lambeth provides a new account of Heidegger's method of interpreting Kant, arguing that it is more promising than is typically recognized. On her account, Heidegger thinks that Kant's greatest insights are located in moments of tension, where Kant struggles to articulate something new about his subject matter. The role of the interpreter, then, is to disentangle competing strands of argument, and to determine which strand is most compelling. Lambeth traces Heidegger's interpretive method across his reading of Kant's *Critique of Pure Reason* and situates Heidegger's reconstruction of Kant's best line of argument against other post-Kantian readings. She finally shows how Heidegger's deep engagement with Kant sheds light on Heidegger's own philosophical views.

MORGANNA LAMBETH is Assistant Teaching Professor in the Cornerstone Program for Liberal Arts, and Affiliated Faculty in the Department of Philosophy, at Purdue University. Her research has appeared in *The Cambridge Heidegger Lexicon* (Cambridge, 2021), *History of Philosophy Quarterly*, *Inquiry*, *Journal of Aesthetics and Art Criticism*, and *Kant Yearbook*.

HEIDEGGER'S INTERPRETATION OF KANT

The Violence and the Charity

MORGANNA LAMBETH

Purdue University

Shaftesbury Road, Cambridge CB2 8EA, United Kingdom

One Liberty Plaza, 20th Floor, New York, NY 10006, USA

477 Williamstown Road, Port Melbourne, VIC 3207, Australia

314–321, 3rd Floor, Plot 3, Splendor Forum, Jasola District Centre, New Delhi – 110025, India

103 Penang Road, #05–06/07, Visioncrest Commercial, Singapore 238467

Cambridge University Press is part of Cambridge University Press & Assessment, a department of the University of Cambridge.

We share the University's mission to contribute to society through the pursuit of education, learning and research at the highest international levels of excellence.

www.cambridge.org
Information on this title: www.cambridge.org/9781009239233

DOI: 10.1017/9781009239271

© Morganna Lambeth 2023

This publication is in copyright. Subject to statutory exception and to the provisions of relevant collective licensing agreements, no reproduction of any part may take place without the written permission of Cambridge University Press & Assessment.

First published 2023
First paperback edition 2025

A catalogue record for this publication is available from the British Library

ISBN 978-1-009-23925-7 Hardback
ISBN 978-1-009-23923-3 Paperback

Cambridge University Press & Assessment has no responsibility for the persistence or accuracy of URLs for external or third-party internet websites referred to in this publication and does not guarantee that any content on such websites is, or will remain, accurate or appropriate.

To Chad

Contents

Acknowledgments	*page* ix
List of Abbreviations	xi

	Introduction		1
	1	Fundamental Ontology	4
	2	Human Finitude	5
	3	Receptivity	6
	4	Time	7
	5	Main Sources	8
	6	Chapter Overview	11
1	The Two-Strand Method of Interpreting Kant		15
	1	Heidegger's Reconstructive Interpretation of Kant	17
	2	Attributing Error to Preserve Kant's Insight	25
	3	Heidegger's Theory of Error	27
	4	Heidegger's Later Retraction of the Kant Book	36
	5	Conclusion	39
2	The Receptivity and Spontaneity of Cognition		40
	1	Heidegger Contra the Neo-Kantians	43
	2	Heidegger's Opening Discussion of Intuition	49
	3	The Spontaneity and Receptivity of the Imagination	60
	4	The Imagination and Time	66
	5	Conclusion	72
3	A Common Root: Heidegger's Foundationalism		73
	1	Heidegger's Insistence on Human Finitude	75
	2	The Promise of a Homogeneous Root	82
	3	The Perils of a Homogeneous Root	86
	4	A Heterogeneous Root	92
	5	Conclusion	103
4	The Metaphysical Deduction and Schematism		104
	1	The Metaphysical Deduction and Schematism in Context	107

	2 Anticipation: The Metaphysical Deduction	109
	3 Ground: The Schematism	113
	4 Conclusion	131
5	**The Transcendental Deduction**	133
	1 The Two Strands of Argument	135
	2 The Synthesis of Apprehension	140
	3 The Synthesis of Reproduction	144
	4 The Synthesis of Recognition	147
	5 The Unity of the Three Syntheses	155
	6 Conclusion: Heidegger's Interpretive Strategy Revisited	158
6	**The Form of Time and Self-Affection**	160
	1 Heidegger's Temporal Idealism	163
	2 Convergence with *Being and Time*	167
	3 Progress beyond *Being and Time*	180
	4 Conclusion	190
	Conclusion	192
	1 Metaphysics	192
	2 Discursivity	195
	3 Conceptualism	197
	4 Idealism	199
	5 Historicism	201
	6 Concluding Remarks	204
	Coda	206
	Bibliography	208
	Index	214

Acknowledgments

This book was developed from the dissertation that I defended at Northwestern University in June 2018. Therefore, I must first thank my dissertation committee for their support of this project: my advisor Cristina Lafont, as well as committee members Rachel Zuckert and Mark Wrathall. Each committee member provided invaluable feedback on the project, and I thank each of them for the time, energy, and care that they took in mentoring me throughout my study. I thank them especially for grilling me on Heidegger's interpretive method during my dissertation defense, a conversation that provided the germs for this book project. I would also like to thank Rachel Zuckert for her generous and careful feedback as I reformulated the dissertation into a book, and especially for her extensive and insightful comments on many drafts of the first chapter.

I would like to thank Georg Bertram, who hosted me as a visiting researcher at the Freie Universität Berlin during my final year of graduate study, as well as the financial support of the Deutscher Akademischer Austauschdienst, which funded the visit. I thank colleagues at the Freie Universität, Humboldt Universität, and within the DAAD program, who provided feedback and conversation during this critical year of research. I would also like to acknowledge research funding from Northwestern University and from the Deutsches Literaturarchiv Marbach.

I am thankful for the financial support of Purdue University, which funded the postdoctoral scholarship that enabled me to write this book. I owe a great deal of gratitude to the chair of the philosophy department, Christopher Yeomans, who provided an incredible amount of encouragement, support, and feedback on the project, from reading chapters to advising me on the book proposal to giving me the opportunity to teach a graduate seminar on the book. I would also like to thank the graduate students who attended that seminar (during the summer, no less!): Jiusi Guo, Xuechen Guo, and Daniel Linford. I thank also my colleague at Purdue, Jacqueline Mariña, who provided extensive feedback and encouragement on this project.

I am grateful to Kate Davies, Colin McQuillan, Karin de Boer, and Jeffrey Kinlaw for their insightful commentaries on chapters of this study. I would also like to thank my interlocutors at the venues where I workshopped chapters: the 2019 Workshop for Pre-Tenure Women in Philosophy, the Heidegger Circle, the Central and Pacific Meetings of the American Philosophical Association, and the North American Kant Society. I am grateful to Mark Alznauer, William Blattner, Cristina Carrillo Cañas, Andrew Cutrofello, Penelope Deutscher, Amy Floweree, Elise Frketich, Jeffrey Gower, David Johnson, Pierre Keller, Hao Liang, Can Laurens Löwe, Carlos Pereira Di Salvo, Richard Polt, Simon Truwant, and Chen Yang for conversations, dispatches, and feedback contributing to this study. Special thanks go to Lauren Leydon-Hardy, whose friendship and incisive philosophical feedback has been an invaluable source of support for this project.

I thank Hilary Gaskin and the Syndics of Cambridge University Press for their support of the project, as well as the two reviewers for the Press who provided careful and productive feedback on my manuscript. I also thank the University of Illinois Press for allowing me to republish material in the first chapter of the book. A version of Chapter 1 was first published as "A Tale of Two Faculties: Heidegger's Method of Interpreting Kant," in *History of Philosophy Quarterly* 38.1 (2021): 57–80.

Finally, I thank my family: my first and best editor, Dan Lambeth; Susan Lambeth, who convinced me that I could be anything, even a philosopher; and Chad, whose support, patience, and humor carried me through the many upsets and labyrinths of this work.

Abbreviations

Works by Heidegger are referred to in the text and notes according to the list of abbreviations below. I include also the volume number of the original German text in Heidegger's *Gesamtausgabe*. Since the development of Heidegger's thought is important to the present study, these works are listed in the order in which they were published or (in the case of lecture courses) presented.

PRMP   "The Problem of Reality in Modern Philosophy." Translated by Philip J. Bossert and John van Buren. In *Supplements*. Edited by John van Buren. Albany: State University of New York Press, 2002. 39–48. [1912] [GA 1]

Logic   *Logic: The Question of Truth*. Translated by Thomas Sheehan. Bloomington: Indiana University Press, 2010. [1925–1926] [GA 21]

BPP   *Basic Problems of Phenomenology*. Translated by Albert Hofstadter. Bloomington: Indiana University Press, 1982. [1927] [GA 24]

BT   *Being and Time*. Translated by J. Macquarrie and E. Robinson. Malden, MA: Blackwell Publishing, 1962. [1927] [GA 2]

PIK   *Phenomenological Interpretation of Kant's Critique of Pure Reason*. Translated by P. Emad and K. Maly. Bloomington: Indiana University Press, 1997. [1927–1928] [GA 25]

KPM   *Kant and the Problem of Metaphysics*. Translated by Richard Taft. Bloomington: Indiana University Press, 1997. [1929] [GA 3]

EHF   *The Essence of Human Freedom*. Translated by Ted Sadler. London: Continuum, 2002. [1930] [GA 31]

IM   *Introduction to Metaphysics*. Translated by Gregory Fried and Richard Polt. New Haven, CT: Yale University Press, 2014. [1935] [GA 40]

WT	*The Question Concerning the Thing: On Kant's Doctrine of the Transcendental Principles.* Translated by James D. Reid and Benjamin D. Crower. London: Rowman and Littlefield, 2018. [1935] [GA 41]
N1	*Nietzsche*, vol. 1. Edited and translated by David Farrell Krell. New York: Harper and Row, 1979. [1936–1937] [GA 43]
CP	*Contributions to Philosophy (of the Event).* Translated by Richard Rojcewicz and Daniela Vallega-Neu. Bloomington: Indiana University Press, 2012. [1936–1938] [GA 65]
N3	*Nietzsche*, vol. 3. Edited by David Farrell Krell. Translated by Joan Stambaugh, David Farrell Krell, and Frank A. Capuzzi. New York: Harper and Row, 1991. [1939] [GA 47]
PWM	"Postscript to 'What Is Metaphysics?'" In *Pathmarks*. Edited and translated by William McNeill. Cambridge: Cambridge University Press, 1998. 231–238. [1943] [GA 9]
KTB	"Kant's Thesis about Being." Translated by Ted E. Klein, Jr., and William E. Pohl. *Southwestern Journal of Philosophy* 4.3 (1973): 7–33. [1961] [GA 9]
HJC	Martin Heidegger and Karl Jaspers. *Heidegger-Jaspers Correspondence.* Edited by Walter Biemel and Hans Saner. Translated by Gary E. Aylesworth. Humanity Books, 2003. [1920–1963]

Introduction

In 1781, Immanuel Kant, after ten years of muted scholarly output, published the *Critique of Pure Reason*. In this groundbreaking work, he sought to answer questions about the shape of reality by inquiring, surprisingly, into the shape of human cognition. He suggested, that is, that investigating *how* we human beings know allows one to draw conclusions about *what* we can know – the basic form of objects, as we human beings experience them. Kant likened his inquiry to the Copernican Revolution, where Copernicus was able to explain his astronomical observations not by studying the movement of the stars in isolation but by considering the standpoint of the observer (who, it turned out, was actually the one in motion). Similarly, Kant hypothesized that one could explain the basic regularities in our experience not in reference to the objects we experience themselves but in reference to the perspective that we bring to those objects. Kant revised and published a second edition of his work in 1787, in addition to rounding out his so-called critical period with two more critiques: the *Critique of Practical Reason* (1788) and the *Critique of Judgment* (1790).

Almost 150 years later, Martin Heidegger, fresh off the success of his own groundbreaking work *Being and Time* (1927), taught a lecture series on Kant's first *Critique*. In this series, Heidegger followed through on his conviction that Kant "must be discovered completely anew" against the backdrop of the German Idealist and Neo-Kantian interpretations that had dominated the reception of Kant's work (HJC 86).[1] It turns out that Heidegger's new discovery of Kant was related intimately to his own philosophical views; as he declared at the end of the lecture series, he

---

[1] With the exception of *Being and Time*, I cite Heidegger's works in reference to the page numbers in English translations, as provided in the List of Abbreviations. That list also provides the corresponding German edition of these works in Heidegger's *Gesamtausgabe*. For *Being and Time*, I cite the marginal page numbers reflected in Macquarrie and Robinson's English translation, which matches the German pagination.

had found in Kant "a crucial confirmation of the accuracy of [his own] path" (PIK 292). The book that he published just one year later, *Kant and the Problem of Metaphysics* (1929) – his so-called Kant book (*Kantbuch*)[2] – attributed to Kant many of the questions and ideas that animated Heidegger's own philosophical work.

Heidegger's interpretation of Kant was and remains hugely controversial. The controversy can be summarized neatly by the marginalia that Heidegger's one-time mentor Edmund Husserl scrawled in his own copy of Heidegger's Kant book: "is this Kant?" (Husserl 1997: 442). Many readers have answered this question in the negative. Indeed, Heidegger is widely seen to be reading his own views into Kant, cherry-picking textual evidence that resonates with Heidegger's views and disregarding those claims that diverge. Heidegger is thought to admit as much when he acknowledges the "violence" of his interpretive technique – a technique, in Heidegger's own words, that sought to "understand [Kant] better than he understood himself" (PIK 2), "wring from what the words say, what it is they wanted to say" (KPM 141), and occasionally "go way beyond Kant" (PIK 243) – and certainly when he later "retract[s] the overinterpretation" of the book (KPM xviii), offering a more modest reading of Kant in the 1930s. While Heidegger's violent interpretation of the late 1920s has gained some purchase in the Continental European reception of Kant,[3] the book has had little uptake in Anglophone Kant scholarship,[4] reflecting the widespread view that Heidegger's purported interpretation tells us more about Heidegger than it does about Kant.[5]

In this book, I seek to clarify Heidegger's method of interpreting Kant, which I believe has not been appreciated fully. Heidegger's apparently selective use of textual evidence can be explained, I argue, by what I call his *two-strand interpretive method*. Heidegger suggests that Kant's greatest insights can be located in moments of tension, where Kant struggles to articulate something new about his subject matter. However, to isolate

---

[2] Heidegger adopts this abbreviation, for example, at KPM p. xvii. For the sake of brevity, I also adopt the term, as well as the more general "Kant interpretation" to refer to Heidegger's interpretive works on Kant in the late 1920s.
[3] See McQuillan 2017 and Dahlstrom 2010 for summaries of this reception.
[4] There are some exceptions, though: see, for example, de Boer 2020 and Longuenesse 1998, who both mark their convergence with some of Heidegger's conclusions, while offering their own arguments to motivate them.
[5] Extended studies by Sherover (1971), Schalow (1992 and 2014), and Engelland (2017) use Heidegger's interpretive works on Kant to shed light on Heidegger's own thought. Weatherston (2002) does attempt to evaluate Heidegger's interpretation but rejects it as a potential reading of Kant, arguing that Heidegger reads his own questions into Kant and that his analysis is philosophically flawed. My arguments to follow will depart from Weatherston's assessment.

those insights, Heidegger suggests, one must differentiate between two strands of argument: one that is informed by traditional accounts of Kant's subject matter, and another that offers an innovative and phenomenologically compelling take on it. This method of interpretation is grounded in a conception of the philosophical enterprise, where tradition serves as a necessary crutch for framing one's inquiry, but philosophical breakthrough relies on surpassing that tradition and experiencing the phenomena in question anew. Therefore, rather than seeking a consistent Kant, Heidegger dives into Kant's text looking for a Kant who is radical – and one, moreover, who is right. Heidegger's interpretation is oriented toward isolating that compelling strand of argument, differentiating it from the strand of argument that is informed by tradition, and explaining why the former strand most convincingly answers Kant's leading questions in the *Critique of Pure Reason*.

In the chapters that follow, I spell out Heidegger's distinctive approach to reconstructive interpretation, and trace this interpretive method across the major moments of his Kant interpretation. Working out Heidegger's interpretive method over the course of his Kant book yields results in two directions. First, as the received view of Heidegger's Kant interpretation predicts, we will make discoveries about Heidegger's own thought. However, I argue that Heidegger is more deeply engaged with Kant's thought than is typically recognized. Kant does not offer Heidegger a distorted mirror in which he can see only himself. Rather, Heidegger's interpretation is tethered firmly to Kant's own work. Therefore, we will learn, surprisingly, that when Heidegger marks convergences between his own thought and that of Kant, he marks real convergences; Heidegger shares affinities with Kant's thought that have been underappreciated. In particular, I will argue that Heidegger does not overemphasize human passivity or openness to the world, as some commentators have suggested. Rather, he recognizes with Kant the fundamental role of human spontaneity in organizing our experience. Further, I will argue that Heidegger's Kant interpretation does not defend a realism about time (where time is derived, say, from the real structure of the world) but develops with Kant a temporal idealism.

Second, in tracing Heidegger's method through his Kant interpretation, we will learn more about Kant and the complex of philosophical issues that preoccupied Kant and Heidegger both. In particular, we will see Heidegger develop a strand of argument that offers an answer to one of Kant's own questions: how two distinct human capacities come together, our capacity to receive information about the outside world (in sensibility) and our capacity to organize that information conceptually (in understanding). In Heidegger's view, Kant's attempt to unify these two capacities – primarily, in the Transcendental Deduction – is hindered by a strand of argument that figures the faculty of understanding as atemporal, or removed from the condition of time. This strand of argument creates a "rupture" between sensibility (as we sense things in time) and understanding (which is apparently atemporal) (PIK 242). However, Heidegger thinks that Kant's occasional hints that understanding is related to time – its concepts comprising our expectations for the future – offer a strand of argument that allows one to appreciate the unity between the two capacities in the fundamental, temporal structure of the imagination. To elaborate on this strand of argument, I will introduce four themes that are prominent in Heidegger's interpretation. After introducing these themes, I will discuss the primary sources for the present study, and preview the chapters of the study.

1 Fundamental Ontology

Heidegger coins the phrase "fundamental ontology" to describe his own inquiry in *Being and Time* (BT 13). In that work, he raises the question of Being – or the question of the meaning of Being – that inquires into the implicit understanding that allows us to differentiate easily between beings and nonbeings. Heidegger inquires therefore into an *ontological* understanding: an appreciation of the basic criteria that qualifies something as a being. Heidegger argues that we can discover the basis for this ontological understanding by inquiring into one kind of being in particular: the human being, or Dasein. We are the foundation for ontology in that we are beings who are able to understand the world in light of an ontology, taking up an understanding of Being. Without beings such as us, there would be no ontology, no understanding of being. But, moreover, our ontology – the sort of beings that *we* are – shapes the sort of ontologies that we can form. For example, because we have a temporal structure, we find a temporal structure in every other being we experience. This inquiry into the ontology of the human being, explored precisely as a basis for other ontologies, Heidegger calls *fundamental ontology*.

Heidegger suggests that Kant's first *Critique* can also be interpreted as a fundamental ontology (KPM 1).[6] While Chapter 1 in this book will

---

[6] This happens in the very first line of Heidegger's Kant book: "The following investigation is devoted to the task of interpreting Kant's *Critique of Pure Reason* as a laying of the ground of metaphysics and thus of placing the problem of metaphysics before us as a fundamental ontology" (KPM 1).

explore this claim more deeply, we can begin to appreciate it here by returning to the so-called Copernican Revolution that I mentioned above. Kant's basic program in the *Critique of Pure Reason* is to inquire into the human perspective – the basic structure of our cognition, the ways in which we are constrained to make sense of the world around us – in order to learn about the basic structure of that world. Kant inquires into what kind of cognitive capacities we have in order to discover what kind of beings populate our experience. While Kant does not label his inquiry into the human being an ontology – his overriding concern in the first *Critique* being the metaphysics of the natural world – he nevertheless maintains that inquiring into the kind of knowers that we are will provide a foundation for that metaphysics.

2 Human Finitude

Kant's inquiry into what kind of knowers we human beings are – that is, his critique of pure reason – has two sides.[7] On the one hand, Kant wants to know what can be securely established about the nature of our reality. On the other, he wants to "dismiss ... groundless pretensions" (Axi).[8] He wants to discover, that is, what we *cannot* know, what *cannot* be established as a metaphysical conclusion (even if previous metaphysicians thought otherwise). Kant researches both sides, offering the "extent and boundaries" of metaphysics (Axii), by inquiring into the capacities of human knowers and the limitations of those capacities. If we find that our cognitive capacities have certain contours – specific ways in which they take in and process sensible information – we can be sure that the objects we will experience will reflect those contours. The contours of our capacities are at the same time their limitations; if some being exceeds our capacities to sense and process what we sense, then we can be sure that being will never feature in our experience, and we must relinquish our "groundless" claims to know something of it.

In his interpretation, Heidegger emphasizes that Kant is interested in the constraints on our cognitive capacities. Heidegger names this point of

---

[7] He indicates both sides in his well-known description of critique: "reason should take on anew the most difficult of all its tasks, namely, that of self-knowledge, and to institute a court of justice, by which reason may secure its rightful claims while dismissing all its groundless pretensions" (Axi).

[8] When I cite the Critique of Pure Reason, I follow the common practice of citing pagination from the first (A) edition from 1781, and the second (B) edition from 1787. Otherwise, my citations of Kant's work reflect the pagination from the Akademie der Wissenschaft (Ak.) edition of his works, which are listed in the margins of English translations.

emphasis "finitude" (KPM 15f.), nominalizing an adjective that Kant uses to discuss limitations elsewhere.[9] Inquiring into the limitations inherent to human cognition, Heidegger suggests that Kant inquires into *human finitude*.[10]

Kant's account of the faculties that we bring to experience, and his account of what those faculties possess (i.e., how they are constrained to function) independently of experience – or *a priori* – figure into his account of those limitations. For example, Kant suggests that we finite knowers are constrained to make sense of the beings we encounter by way of concepts, which are general rules that range over many aspects of our experience. The concept "dog," for instance, ranges not only over the dog one has just perceived but also over other individuals that meet the criteria laid out in the concept. Further, Kant famously suggests that we possess certain concepts, such as the concept of substance and the concept of cause, a priori. We finite knowers are constrained to use this set of concepts – the categories – as the ground rules of our experience. For instance, we must conceive everything we encounter as causal (i.e., changing according to certain causal laws). The categories constrain the human capacity to actively organize our experience, which Kant also refers to as our *spontaneity*.

Beyond the constraints that limit human spontaneity in the way that we process what we sense, Kant argues that there are constraints also on the way that we sense the world around us, outlined under the next heading.

3 Receptivity

According to Kant, *receptivity* is our capacity to be affected by the world around us – to receive information about or sense that world. Heidegger too adopts this term in his interpretation of Kant, and emphasizes the novelty of Kant's account, which recognizes that receptivity is a fundamental component of human cognition. Heidegger believes that this innovation is lost on the German Idealist and Neo-Kantian interpreters who home in on Kantian spontaneity. While some commentators see Heidegger, in turn, as homing in on Kantian receptivity, I will argue that Heidegger attempts to recuperate Kant's insight into human receptivity, while also recognizing the contribution of spontaneity to human cognition.

---

[9] For example, Kant uses this term to consider the position that space is not infinite; rather, "the world is finite and bounded in space" (A428/B456).
[10] According to Colin McQuillan (2017), this emphasis on finitude is Heidegger's major contribution to the Continental European reception of Kant: these later thinkers likewise took Kant to be a philosopher of finitude, i.e., one who focuses on the inherent limitations of human experience.

On Kant's account, we are constrained to know the world only by receiving information about it, in *intuitions*. There is no extra-sensible intuition of empirical objects, such that we might divine an object in the next room out of sheer concentration; nor, as Heidegger elaborates, do we possess the infinite intuition that God purportedly has, where picturing some object brings it into being. What we know about the empirical world is obtained one and all through our sensibility.

Beyond the mere receptivity of our cognition, we are also constrained, on Kant's account, by the form of our receptivity. That is, we can only receive sensible information in a certain format; there are *forms of intuition* that we possess a priori, and from which we cannot deviate. First, we perceive objects external to us in space. All external objects are spatially extended, and spatially situated in relation to one another (side by side, to the left or to the right, and so forth). On Kant's view, then, we are incapable of receiving nonspatial information about the outside world; it is impossible for us to perceive an object that is not located in space.

While Heidegger acknowledges Kant's view of space, he is far more interested in the second constraint on our way of receiving sensible information, outlined under the next heading.

4 Time

On Kant's view, time is also a form of intuition. We are constrained to perceive objects in time; further, we order our own thought processes in time, making time the more universal form of intuition, as it applies both externally *and* internally. Whether external changes, or the flow of our own internal thoughts, everything occurs in time.

Heidegger is fascinated by Kant's position on time, which he flagged already in *Being and Time* as Kant's major insight (BT 23). Since time is a form of intuition for Kant, he is a temporal idealist: on his view, time is relative to the human standpoint – something we add to the world, through our way of receiving information about it. Whether Heidegger endorses Kant's temporal idealism has been the subject of much critical discussion, and it is a topic I take on in Chapter 6, where I argue that Heidegger further develops his own account of temporal idealism through his Kant interpretation.

While Heidegger admires Kant's view of time, he also thinks the view would benefit from further development. One of his chief complaints about Kant is that Kant provides disparate constraints on human cognition – a smattering of necessary concepts, two forms of intuition – without adequately explaining how these aspects of the human perspective come together. What unifies these elements; most pressingly, what bridges the gulf between our capacity to passively receive and our capacity to actively organize? What, fundamentally, is the structure of the human being?

Heidegger thinks we can answer these questions by recognizing that time is not just one constraint among others, but the foundational structure of human cognition. That is, developing the temporal dimensions of Kant's faculties – where sensibility takes in the present, understanding projects future expectations, and both faculties refer to a further ability to retain the past – shows how they hang together. Heidegger argues that these three temporal capacities make up the unified structure of human temporality, a concept for which Heidegger finds a placeholder in Kant's intriguing though (in his view) underdeveloped discussion of the faculty of *imagination*. This development of Kant's thought more satisfactorily explains how the (unified) human perspective generates the basic shape of reality, both intuitive and conceptual in form.

5 Main Sources

Heidegger comments on Kant in a number of works in the mid- to late 1920s, including the 1925–1926 lecture course *Logic: The Question of Truth* (Logic), the 1927 lecture course *Basic Problems of Phenomenology* (BPP), and Heidegger's 1927 monograph *Being and Time* (BT). While I rely on these sources in what follows, my primary points of reference are the two works that make interpreting Kant's *Critique of Pure Reason* their main goal, demonstrating the two-strand interpretive method at the heart of this study: Heidegger's 1927–1928 lecture course *Phenomenological Interpretation of Kant's Critique of Pure Reason* (PIK), and the 1929 monograph, *Kant and the Problem of Metaphysics* (KPM). I generally bracket later interpretations of Kant that are meant to correct what Heidegger came to see as a misguided interpretation: the 1935–1936 lecture course *Question Concerning the Thing* (WT) and the 1962 essay "Kant's Thesis about Being" (KTB). However, I do address the criticisms that the 1935–1936 interpretation contains, and explain why I think Heidegger is wrong to renounce the late 1920s interpretation, at the end of Chapter 1.

Since I focus on the late 1920s interpretation of Kant, I avoid the period that has preoccupied many recent discussions of Heidegger's thought and legacy: the 1930s, which saw Heidegger publicly join and celebrate the

National Socialist Party,[11] and privately (as we now know) record his anti-Semitic beliefs in his so-called Black Notebooks.[12] Though my study stops short of the 1930s, Heidegger's Nazism remains relevant to the era of thought that I consider here, the late 1920s. Some argue that Heidegger's disagreements with the Neo-Kantians have ideological or political undertones.[13] Others argue that Heidegger's work in the 1920s expresses philosophical ideas that would motivate Heidegger's turn to Nazism.[14] I will note, in what follows, when this political context is relevant to my discussion. Though I will offer a somewhat more positive appraisal of Heidegger's thought in the late 1920s, Heidegger's profound failures in the 1930s remain a concern for me, as they should any scholar of Heidegger. In the Coda, I briefly suggest how my work in this study may help to navigate the challenges posed by these failures, carving out an area for future research.

In what follows, I have taken it that Heidegger's interpretation of Kant in the 1927–1928 lecture course is largely consistent with his 1929 Kant book – that the former does indeed present the "essentials" of the latter, as Heidegger claims in the first preface to his 1929 book (xix). I support the view that Heidegger's reception of Kant is consistent during this period – in line, for example, with Chad Engelland's periodization of Heidegger's reception of Kant,[15] but contra Karin de Boer and Stephen Howard's claim that Heidegger substantially revises his position in the 1929 book. However, the work that follows does challenge their reason for finding a revision in the 1929 book. In particular, de Boer and Howard claim that Heidegger transitions from attempting to discern the unity of intuition and thought in the lecture series to taking "a more radical stance" in the Kant book that asserts the primacy of intuition for cognition (2019: 363). However, as will become apparent in later arguments, I believe that these two moves are compatible. In brief, the primacy of intuition for cognition

---

[11] Rüdiger Safranski provides a biographical account of this period in Safranski 1998. However, his assessment of Heidegger's anti-Semitism must be reconsidered in light of the Black Notebooks.
[12] These notebooks, spanning 1931–1942, were made public for the first time in 2014. For a summary of the controversy surrounding their publication, one may consult Farin and Malpas 2016: ix–xii. For a helpful list of sources, see Serafin 2015. For analysis of the passages expressing Heidegger's anti-Semitism, see Alweiss 2015.
[13] For discussion of this point, I am especially indebted to Truwant 2022: 5 n. 15. One may also consult Friedman 2000, Gordon 2010, and Krois 2004.
[14] For the Neo-Kantian Ernst Cassirer's iteration of this charge, consult Truwant 2022: 18. Perhaps the most prominent advocate for this view is Farías 1989. In my own treatment of this topic, I will (too briefly) discuss Karl Löwith's concern, more recently revisited by Jeffrey Andrew Barash, that Heidegger defends a political decisionism in the 1920s (Barash 2012; Löwith 1995).
[15] Though, for reservations concerning Engelland's periodization of Heidegger's reception of Kant, see Lambeth 2020.

is supposed to drive an inquiry into what unites intuition with the cognitive element over which it has primacy, understanding, leading us to discern the unity between them. Further, I find both moves in both sources (i.e., PIK and KPM), reflecting not only that the moves are compatible, but also a broad agreement between these sources.

Both the 1927–1928 lecture course and the 1929 Kant book focus on the first part of the *Critique of Pure Reason* – the Transcendental Analytic – while making only passing reference to the Transcendental Dialectic.[16] While I show in what follows that Heidegger responds to the major sections of the Transcendental Analytic – the Metaphysical Deduction, Transcendental Deduction, and Schematism – the Kant book does not proceed in the order that Kant does.[17] Heidegger proceeds in four parts (KPM 2). Heidegger first outlines his understanding of Kant's basic project (a "laying of the ground for metaphysics"). Then, Heidegger offers a preliminary interpretation, covering the Transcendental Aesthetic, and the sections of the Transcendental Analytic that I listed above. Heidegger next confirms his interpretation of those sections by focusing on the larger relationship between the faculties of sensibility, imagination, and understanding. Finally, Heidegger connects Kant's views to his own philosophical views and vocabulary in a "retrieval." It's fair to say that Heidegger proceeds in an elliptical manner; he does not offer a linear argument, but rather circles back to and deepens ideas developed earlier in the interpretation. For my part, I largely stick to Kant's headings when reconstructing Heidegger's interpretation, to facilitate comparison to Kant's text.

For quotations, I rely on the English translations that are in print: Richard Taft's translation of *Kant and the Problem of Metaphysics* and Parvis Emad and Kenneth Maly's translation of the *Phenomenological Interpretation of Kant's Critique of Pure Reason*. However, I adopt a few standard modifications. While both translations translate *Erkenntnis* as "knowledge," I translate the term rather as "cognition," in line with the translation of Kant that Guyer and Wood standardize in the Cambridge edition of the *Critique of Pure Reason*.[18] However, in my own prose, I do

---

[16] Heidegger does treat the Transcendental Dialectic, as well as Kant's practical philosophy, in his 1927 course, *Basic Problems of Phenomenology*, and in the 1930 lecture course that examines Kant's account of freedom: *The Essence of Human Freedom*. I use both sources, though sparingly, below.
[17] Dahlstrom offers a helpful chart tracking where Heidegger discusses each part of the *Critique of Pure Reason* (1991, appendix). See also his overview of Heidegger's interpretive works on Kant in Dahlstrom 1994: 293–299.
[18] I defend the practice of translating Heidegger in reference to standardized translations of Kant in Lambeth (2021a).

use "knower" to refer to one who has cognition, for lack of a better term. I also translate Heidegger's term *Hinnehmen* as "taking-up"; this translation reflects the root of the word (*nehmen* as "taking"), the directionality of *hin* (as "up"), while using a more apt expression than Taft's "taking-in-stride."[19] Finally, I translate Heidegger's term of art, *vorhanden*, as present-at-hand, or more briefly "at hand," to match the translation of this term standardized by John Macquarrie and Edward Robinson in their translation of *Being and Time*.

6 Chapter Overview

In Chapter 1, I provide an overview of Heidegger's method of interpreting Kant. I argue that Heidegger, like many reconstructive interpreters, takes up the main question posed by the first *Critique* and attempts to identify Kant's most plausible line of response to it, consulting the claims in Kant's text alongside Heidegger's own beliefs about Kant's subject matter. Because Heidegger seeks to attribute true claims to Kant, his method of interpretation resembles that of Donald Davidson and Hans-Georg Gadamer. However, I suggest that Heidegger improves upon their method, because he recognizes the methodological role of disagreement in coming to agree with some author, thereby making room for differences in view between interpreter and text. He argues that we should expect great thinkers to struggle with their subject matter, offering competing strands of argument as they attempt to work out their view. The job of the truth-seeking interpreter, then, is to isolate the most promising strand of argument, differentiating it from those strands that are not as compelling. Accordingly, Heidegger offers a two-strand interpretation of Kant that differentiates an insightful line of argumentation that prioritizes the faculty of imagination from a less promising line that prioritizes the faculty of understanding. Further, Heidegger offers a theory of error explaining why Kant struggles with his subject matter: Kant retreats to his less compelling strand of argument due to the anxiety he experiences in uncovering the fundamental structure of the human being.

In Chapters 2 and 3, I show that Heidegger's two-strand interpretation of Kant is informed by the successes and the failures of previous interpretations. Together, these chapters show that Heidegger does not bring idiosyncratic concerns to Kant's text, but rather carries forward an interpretive tradition that began with the German Idealists and continued

---

[19] Dahlstrom also uses this translation of *Hinnehmen* (2010: 386).

with the Marburg Neo-Kantians: an interpretive tradition, namely, that attempted to unify Kant's dual faculties of sensibility and understanding, and to therefore ground the metaphysical principles that depend on their unification. However, Heidegger improves on his predecessors by picking out a strand of argument that can better meet this challenge.

Heidegger sees the Marburg Neo-Kantians and the German Idealists as radicalizing the strand of argument in the first *Critique* that prioritizes understanding. As I outline in Chapter 2, the Neo-Kantians radicalize this strand by insisting that human cognition is understanding through and through; Kant was wrong to think we have a separate faculty of sensibility, for sensing is really only a kind of thinking. This interpretation erases the signature discursivity of Kant's position, the idea that two qualitatively different faculties are required for us to cognize. I show that Heidegger's interpretation, while it prioritizes the imagination, does not have this result. I argue that Heidegger's central thesis in his Kant book – that, on the best version of Kant's argument, the imagination has priority as the source of cognition – rests crucially on the claim that the imagination is both receptive *and* spontaneous. Thus, Heidegger's interpretation maintains Kant's discursivity thesis, while inquiring more deeply into the unified receptivity and spontaneity that characterizes the human being.

In Chapter 3, I turn to the German Idealists, who radicalize the strand of argument prioritizing the understanding in a different direction. In particular, they attempt to unify Kant's faculty psychology by uncovering a "common root" that is the source of sensibility and understanding. For the German Idealists, this common root is a homogeneous capacity that can generate the other faculties. Though the identity of this capacity shifts across the German Idealists – apperception for Fichte, intellectual intuition for Hegel, and so forth – the common root that generates the other faculties is, broadly speaking, a spontaneous capacity. Insofar as these interpretations rely on telling a causal story, where one faculty *causes* others to arise, they return to a precritical position that Kant would reject; on Kant's critical philosophy, we are precluded from extending categories like causality to our faculties for cognition, since such faculties do not appear sensibly in our experience. I argue that, while Heidegger also seeks a common root, he avoids this problem by insisting that the common root is heterogeneous. His common root – the imagination – is a unification of three basic capacities, rather than a single, deeper capacity that causes the others. Thus, I argue that Heidegger does not seek a foundation for metaphysics that is beyond the bounds of what Kant thinks we can know; he works with the cognitive capacities that Kant already identifies, but seeks to explain more fully the structural interrelationships between those capacities.

Chapters 4 and 5 trace Heidegger's two-strand interpretation across the major sections informing his reading of the first *Critique*. In Chapter 4, I reconstruct Heidegger's interpretation of Kant's Metaphysical Deduction and Schematism. In Heidegger's view, these two sections inquire into the source of the categories that human understanding possesses a priori. Heidegger's reading of both sections exhibits a characteristic move in his interpretive method, where he sees an innovative line of argument prioritizing the imagination emerge from a more traditional setup. My reconstruction also reveals some variety in how one can apply Heidegger's interpretive method to the different parts of a text. Heidegger suggests that the traditional strand of argument is more prominent in the Metaphysical Deduction; while Kant attempts to derive the categories from the atemporal logic of the understanding, his references to the faculty of imagination at certain critical junctures reveal the breakdown of those attempts. By contrast, the emerging, innovative line of argument is more prominent in the Schematism, which quickly surpasses its traditional framing in order to offer a phenomenologically compelling account of how the categories, as ways of interpreting time (as constant, unidirectional, and so forth), inform our perceptual experience.

In Chapter 5, I reconstruct Heidegger's interpretation of Kant's Transcendental Deduction and address the common objection that Heidegger's interpretation cherry-picks evidence from Kant's text, failing adequately to address counterevidence. I argue that Heidegger both acknowledges and addresses the counterevidence that critics have cited. Heidegger identifies that counterevidence as a component of Kant's traditional strand of argument and argues that this strand of argument is less compelling than other, more radical ideas in Kant's text. On the traditional strand of argument, Kant attempts to spell out the a priori contact between sensibility and understanding by identifying a form of atemporal self-consciousness, apperception, that uses concepts to actively unify our sense experience. Heidegger is critical of this argument because it remains unclear how apperception, construed as atemporal, can be unified with our temporal sense experience. How do two unlike things come together – time and not-time? Heidegger argues that one arrives at a more convincing account by developing the temporal dimension of apperception, where it holds up expectations for the future. This development helps one appreciate the deeper unity of our passive sensing of the present and our active anticipation of the future – a unity grounded in the fundamental, temporal structure of the imagination, three interlaced temporal capacities that characterize the human being.

In Chapter 6, I explore a significant thesis that emerges in Heidegger's reading of Kant: the form of time that Kant outlines – the linear, unidirectional time that shapes our engagement with the natural world – is dependent on another model of time – the human temporality comprising three interlaced temporal capacities. I argue that developing this thesis represents the central philosophical payoff of Heidegger's Kant interpretation, the way in which Heidegger attempts to develop his own thought through interpreting Kant. In particular, I argue that Heidegger goes to Kant to develop his own account of temporal idealism. In my view, Heidegger concurs with Kant that the form of time is relative to the human standpoint, but offers a deeper account of where that form of time comes from – that is, how it derives from the very structure of the human being. By deepening Kant's temporal idealism, Heidegger also develops his own argument for temporal idealism. While his argument for this position in *Being and Time* attempts to trace the characteristics of linear time back to the human being's temporality, his account of time in the Kant interpretation elaborates how temporality produces linear time. In particular, he outlines the process of self-affection, in which the interaction between the human being's three temporal capacities actualizes another model of time by interpreting the time that we ourselves are. I argue that this argumentative approach foregrounds a gap between the temporality of the human being and the interpretation of time upon which we arrive, suggesting that time could be otherwise interpreted. This finding sets the stage for Heidegger's "history of Being" in the 1930s, wherein he traces major shifts in interpretive frameworks across Western history.

Having worked through Heidegger's method of interpreting Kant, I use the Conclusion to step back and consider its results, locating Heidegger's interpretation of Kant among contemporary Anglophone interpretations. I show that Heidegger's interpretation is legible within the broader landscape of Anglophone Kant scholarship by charting its position on Kant's metaphysics, discursivity, conceptualism, idealism, and historicism. Heidegger offers us, I conclude, a live option for interpreting Kant.

CHAPTER 1

The Two-Strand Method of Interpreting Kant

Many historians of philosophy interpret texts reconstructively. That is, many historians of philosophy attempt to reconstruct the best or most compelling account of the subject matter that the author puts forth, rather than taking on every claim that a text has to offer; they leave aside the claims that are unconvincing or even in tension with the most promising account. Reconstructive interpreters, then, are guided by concerns that are both exegetical (what is said in the text?) and philosophical (what is true about the author's subject matter?). This method of interpretation is rightly called a charitable one because it takes seriously the author's attempt to discover the truth about some subject matter; reconstructive interpretation attempts to piece together that true account. Further, reconstructive interpretation opens up the possibility of learning from the text – that is, learning the truth about the subject matter under discussion, by reference to the author's most compelling account of it.

Despite the benefits of reconstructive interpretation, this method of interpretation comes with a risk. As Robert Brandom notes, interpreting a text in light of one's own sense of what is true runs the risk of "hermeneutic ventriloquism" – "when the author's lips move, but only the reader's voice can be heard" (2002: 90). Interpreting a text in reference to one's own beliefs about what is plausible might result in a reading where the interpreter fails to recognize meaningful differences between the views of the author and that of the interpreter; instead, the interpreter reads her own views into the words of the author. Hermeneutic ventriloquism undermines both of the benefits mentioned above: one is not being charitable to the author, as the author's views have fallen quite out of the picture, and one does not learn from the text, but articulates one's own beliefs.

Heidegger's interpretation of Kant's *Critique of Pure Reason* might seem like a prime example of hermeneutic ventriloquism. Indeed, the standard reception of Heidegger's interpretation sees him as reading his own views into Kant. Ernst Cassirer may have been the first to offer this line of criticism, suggesting in a 1931 review that Heidegger's *Kant and the Problem of Metaphysics* "penetrates ... by force of arms into the Kantian system in order to subdue it and make it serviceable for his problem" (1967: 149). Similarly, Dieter Henrich argues that the interpretation is motivated by Heidegger's own research program from *Being and Time*, having "little in common with the problems that determine the development of Kant's thinking" and "results [that] diverge from the explicit position of the Kantian text" (1994: 53).[1] Scholars of Heidegger have largely conceded this point. For example, Daniel Dahlstrom comments that Heidegger's "so-called 'thoughtful dialogues' often seem much more like rapacious monologues" (1991: 331).[2] Similarly, most book-length treatments of Heidegger's Kant interpretation examine the interpretation in order to shed light on Heidegger's thought, rather than taking it seriously as a way of interpreting Kant.[3] There is widespread scholarly agreement, then, that Heidegger's interpretation of Kant is more about Heidegger than it is about Kant; Heidegger engages not with Kant's problems but his own, resulting in a reading of Kant where Kant's doctrine looks remarkably similar to that of Heidegger.[4] Indeed, Heidegger's own admission that his interpretation of Kant is a "violent" one seems to vindicate this standard reading (PIK 247; KPM xx).

Heidegger certainly takes a reconstructive approach to interpretation – interpreting Kant in light of what Heidegger takes to be a plausible response to Kant's leading question – but, I will argue, and against the consensus view, that his approach differs from reconstructive approaches

---

[1] Cassirer criticized Heidegger's interpretation even earlier, in 1929, in his famous dispute with Heidegger in Davos (see KPM 193–207). For reception in a similar vein, see Barrett (1968: 357), Sherover (1971: 5, 13), Sallis (1987: 163–164), Waxman (1991: 15), Blattner (1999: 11), Friedman (2000: 61), Weatherston (2002: 35), Banham (2006: 127), Gordon (2010: 161), Golob (2013: 365), and McQuillan (2017: 84).

[2] Cf. Dahlstrom (1994: 299), though, which offers a brief defense of Heidegger's interpretive approach.

[3] As I mentioned in the introduction, these extended studies include Sherover (1971), Schalow (1992 and 2014), and Engelland (2017). Weatherston (2002) offers a negative appraisal of the interpretation as a reading of Kant but, like the previous commentators, takes it to shed light on Heidegger's thought.

[4] Recently, Frank Schalow has offered a twist on this standard reading, suggesting instead that Heidegger reads *Dilthey* into Kant: Heidegger imports Dilthey's concept of understanding (*Verstehen*) to "broaden" Kant's inquiry (Schalow 2016: 379–380; see also Schalow 2013). Schalow's suggestion leaves us in much the same place as the standard reading: we are getting a ventriloquized version of Kant. As I hope to show, such readings fail to appreciate Heidegger's deep engagement with Kant's text – both the problems that Kant takes up and the concepts that Kant uses to work out these problems.

that do run the risk of ventriloquism. While reconstructive interpreters like Donald Davidson and Hans-Georg Gadamer both seek widespread agreement with the authors who they interpret, Heidegger makes no such attempt. In fact, Heidegger claims to find a deep divide in Kant's text: two strands of argument in tension with one another. There is a strand of argument with which Heidegger agrees, which prioritizes Kant's faculty of imagination, and a less plausible strand of argument that prioritizes the faculty of understanding. Closely investigating the tensions in Kant's text, Heidegger avoids an interpretation of Kant where Kant simply says what Heidegger would like him to say.

Contrary to the standard reception of the interpretation, Heidegger's interpretation of Kant provides a model for navigating the dangers of reconstructive interpretation – that is, for avoiding the risk of hermeneutic ventriloquism. Interpreting Kant, Heidegger provides a model of charitable, reconstructive interpretation that nonetheless recognizes differences of view between interpreter and text. I outline Heidegger's interpretative method in Section 1 of the chapter, showing that Heidegger attributes error as he interprets. In Section 2, I illustrate Heidegger's interpretive method with an example: his interpretation of Kant's Metaphysical Deduction. In Section 3, I argue that Heidegger supports his attributions of error with a theory of error, based on his account of anxiety in *Being and Time*. Finally, in Section 4, I address Heidegger's later comments criticizing the violence of his late 1920s Kant interpretation, arguing that they do not provide compelling reasons to reject the interpretive method that he relies on therein. Together, these sections correct the standard reading of Heidegger's method of interpreting Kant and bring out Heidegger's contribution to the method of reconstructive interpretation.

1 Heidegger's Reconstructive Interpretation of Kant

Heidegger often contrasts his own, reconstructive interpretive style – what he calls a "thoughtful dialogue" (*denkendes Zwiegespräch*) – with a more scholarly interpretive style that he dubs "historical philology" (*historische Philologie*) (KPM xx; see also KPM xvii). This distinction is comparable, I argue, to Brandom's distinction between interpreting *de re* and *de dicto* (2002: 94–111). That is, the distinction hangs on whether the interpreter's own beliefs about the subject matter under consideration in the text inform her interpretation of it. In the philological or scholarly method of interpretation that Heidegger eschews (Brandom's *de dicto* interpretation), the interpreter's beliefs about the subject matter are to play no role in interpreting the author's claims. Rather, the interpreter attempts to interpret claims in light of other elements in the text (or the author's broader corpus). This is not a dialogue but a rather one-sided affair; the interpreter merely attempts to get the author's account right, bracketing her own beliefs about whether the account is a plausible one.[5] As Heidegger remarks in a note on the Kant book, "discovering 'Kant in himself' is to be left to Kant philology" (KPM 175).

By contrast, in reconstructive interpretation (Brandom's *de re* interpretation), the interpreter interprets in light of her own beliefs about the subject matter, consulting the claims that appear in the text in addition to her beliefs. This sort of interpretation is a dialogue: a conversation between author and interpreter about the subject matter treated in the text. Further, the dialogue is driven by a *shared* question. The interpreter enters into the dialogue because she is occupied with the same issues as the author; reading the text, she attempts to identify a plausible response to their shared question.[6] Therefore, the interpreter consults her own beliefs in order to ascribe *true* claims to the author. This is the interpretive style, I argue, that Heidegger takes up in his interpretation of Kant.

More schematically, this method of reconstructive interpretation can be broken down into several components: First, when one interprets in this manner, one takes up the question posed by the author, and pursues it with the author over the course of the interpretation (Brandom 2002: 107). Second, one takes up the theoretical machinery offered by the author to answer this question – making use of the various concepts that the author introduces over the course of her inquiry. Third, the interpreter seeks to attribute to the author a plausible answer to the question that she poses, based on the interpreter's own sense of what is plausible (Brandom 2002: 110). Gadamer is a proponent of this method of interpretation, suggesting that when we interpret a text, "we try to understand how what [the author] is saying could be right" (Gadamer 2013 [hereafter TM]: 254).[7] Likewise, Davidson offers a principle of charity instructing the

---

[5] Cristina Lafont provides Gadamer's argument why this method of interpretation is "deeply misconceived": "it is not possible to identify what the author intended to say without identifying first what she was talking about, and the only way the interpreter can identify this is by using his own beliefs about the matter" (2008: 20). Heidegger also makes statements to this effect (see, e.g., BT 152). While I am sympathetic with this concern, I do not dwell on it here, since my aim is to clarify the method of interpretation that Heidegger does endorse.

[6] Brandom calls this more specific form of *de re* interpretation *de traditione* interpretation; the interpreter takes herself to be in the same tradition, occupied with the same issues, as the author.

[7] Here, I follow Cristina Lafont's suggestion, contra Brandom, that Gadamer supports only the more specific form of *de traditione* interpretation (2008: 24ff.).

interpreter to read her own "standards of truth" into the claims that she is interpreting (2001a: 148).

As Cristina Lafont points out, these leading proponents of reconstructive interpretation share a fourth interpretive commitment: they suggest the interpreter ought to *maximize* truth, guided by the interpreter's own beliefs concerning what is true about the subject matter (2008: 21). As Davidson puts this point, an interpretation ought to maximize agreement between the interpreter and speaker: "we want a theory . . . that maximizes agreement, in terms of making [a speaker] right, as far as we can tell, as often as possible" (2001b: 136).[8] This method of interpretation tracks the author's claims, and what can plausibly be claimed about the subject matter (according to the interpreter), so the interpreter can attribute the maximum number of plausible claims to the author. Similarly, Gadamer suggests that we ought not only to "understand how what [the author] is saying could be right," but also to take the text to have a "unified meaning" (TM 256) or "assume its completeness" (TM 255). The task of interpretation is to determine how the text, as a whole, can be right about its subject matter. Indeed, Gadamer suggests that attributing an error to an author represents a failure of interpretation – a failure to determine how the text as a whole is right about its subject matter (TM 256). Gadamer, in his own terms, repeats the imperative to maximize truth when interpreting.

Lafont identifies Gadamer's commitment to maximizing truth as a "methodological disadvantage" of his approach to interpretation, making it difficult to attribute and explain error (Lafont 2008: 22).[9] The

---

[8] As this passage reflects, Davidson first developed his interpretive method in the context of interpreting utterances: when translating a wholly unfamiliar language, the interpreter should translate terms so that as many sentences as possible turn out to be true. However, Davidson himself saw parallels between interpreting utterances and interpreting texts; for example, in a piece on interpreting James Joyce's literary work, Davidson comments that "all reading is interpretation, and all interpretation demands some degree of invention" (see Davidson 1991: 11). Further, other scholars (e.g., Child 2006) have developed the implications of his theory for interpreting texts, both fictional and nonfictional.

[9] Davidson later recognized this shortcoming of his own interpretive method, offering a modified principle of charity as a result: "Charity prompts the interpreter to maximize the intelligibility of the speaker, not sameness of belief . . . interpretation must take into account probable errors due to bad positioning, deficient sensory apparatus, and differences in background knowledge" (Davidson 2001b: xix). Davidson suggests, then, that the interpreter should not simply ascribe her own beliefs to the speaker, but rather imagine "what I *would* have believed if I'd done what he did and been where he was" (282). For example, if one notices a speaker is situated behind a post, one might expect the speaker to have false beliefs about what is happening on the other side. While this provides a good start for attributing error, Davidson offers little guidance concerning how one might attribute error over the course of reading a philosophical work (when the author's visual field, e.g., is not directly apparent). Heidegger offers such guidance – and, as I will explain in Section 3, he does so in reference to errors that are based not on an author's particular position but on the nature of the author's inquiry.

commitment to maximizing truth disinclines the interpreter from recognizing the author's mistakes – from recognizing when the author holds different views from the interpreter. A difference in view is a bad result, to be avoided whenever possible. But authors can and do make mistakes; an interpretive method should be able to identify such mistakes. Further, without a way to mark disagreement between interpreter and author, reconstructive interpreting runs the risk of hermeneutic ventriloquism. I will argue that Heidegger abandons this fourth interpretive commitment; in his interpretation of Kant, he does not attempt to maximize the truth. I suggest that, in doing so, Heidegger's reconstructive interpretation of Kant avoids the risk of hermeneutic ventriloquism.

We can clarify more precisely Heidegger's departure from reconstructive interpreters like Gadamer and Davidson by shifting to the language of agreement. All three interpreters interpret with the aim of establishing agreement – that is, arriving at the author's most compelling take on the subject matter, as judged by the interpreter. However, they depart in their understandings of how to *achieve* that aim. Gadamer endorses reading the text as consistently or coherently providing a compelling account; thus, many localized agreements between author and interpreter achieve large-scale agreement, about the account as a whole. By contrast, Heidegger does not demand consistency from the texts that he interprets. He expects serious philosophers – especially those posing the ontological questions that he and Kant pose – to struggle with their difficult subject matter, making some claims that are promising and others that are less so. Thus, he prescribes the same struggle to interpreters, who must isolate an author's most promising account, differentiating it from those claims that are not quite there yet. Heidegger therefore recognizes the *methodological role of disagreement* in establishing agreement between interpreter and author. In his view, disagreement aids the interpreter in arriving at the author's most compelling account of her subject matter. Thus, disagreement is not a shortcoming or a failure (*pace* Gadamer) of an interpretive method that attempts to establish agreement. Reaching an author's deepest and best answer to her question calls on the interpreter to disagree with those claims that get in the way of her best account.

I will return to Heidegger's departure from Gadamer and Davidson shortly. But first, I would like to introduce some textual evidence showing that Heidegger indeed employs the interpretive method that I have so far attributed to him.

Throughout his interpretation, Heidegger orients himself toward Kant's main question and seeks to locate the most plausible answer to that question. In particular, Heidegger takes up "the real problem of pure reason" stated at the outset of the *Critique*: "How are synthetic judgments a priori possible?" (B19). That is, how can we draw conclusions about the objects we experience independently of our encounters with particular objects? Heidegger claims that "this possibility of ontological understanding, the possibility of a nature in general, the possibility of synthetic knowledge a priori, is the guiding ontological problem overall of the *Critique*" (PIK 276), and commits himself to pursuing this "actual" or "genuine problem" even when Kant seems to stray from it (PIK 209).

Given that Kant attempts to answer his question by inquiring into the various capacities of the human knower and their interrelationships, Heidegger takes it that answering Kant's question requires inquiry into the "constitution" of the human being (PIK 224).[10] After all, this constitution enables the human being to make synthetic judgments a priori. Heidegger is interested in this inquiry, as well. Indeed, he uses the term "fundamental ontology" to describe this type of investigation, both his own task in *Being and Time*, as well as that of Kant in the first *Critique* (BT 13; KPM 1). Both look to the constitution of the human being as a foundation for other ontologies, such as the ontology of natural objects. Pursuing this inquiry with Kant, Heidegger adopts Kant's theoretical machinery; somewhat jarringly for a seasoned reader of Heidegger, Heidegger embraces discussion of the faculties as he pursues Kant's answer to this question.

I have argued that Heidegger takes up Kant's inquiry, interpreting Kant in hopes of answering their shared question. But two objections may occur to the reader at this point. The first objection starts from Heidegger's own stated intentions in the Kant book. In his preface to the first edition, Heidegger says that the book offers a "'historical' [*geschichtliche*] introduction of sorts to clarify the problematic treated in the first half of *Being and Time*" (KPM xix). Is this not a straightforward admission that Heidegger does not deal with Kant's "problematic" but his own? While Heidegger's interpretation of Kant is indeed motivated by his own philosophical project, this does not mean that he got Kant wrong by reading himself into Kant. Heidegger selected Kant as the subject of his historical introduction to *Being and Time* for a reason, and the evidence that I have

---

[10] Heidegger will disagree with Kant about the status of this constitution. For Heidegger, Kant's faculties provide an ontology (namely, the ontology of the human being), whereas for Kant they provide less than that: conditions for experience, that cannot be known themselves as objects. I will treat this disagreement in Chapter 3.

introduced above reveals that reason: Kant is the subject of Heidegger's historical introduction, because Kant is engaged in the same endeavor – a fundamental ontology. Kant offers a good way to introduce *Being and Time*, since Kant *also* attempts a fundamental ontology.

A second objection starts from the term "anthropology." While Heidegger repeatedly denies that his own philosophical project is an anthropology,[11] Kant occasionally adopts this label. As Heidegger recounts, Kant claims in his *Lectures on Logic* that answering the question "What can I know?" (i.e., the question posed in the first *Critique*) is anthropology insofar as it is related to the further question "What is man?" (9:25; PIK 48; KPM 146). If Kant accepts the label of anthropology and Heidegger rejects it, shouldn't Heidegger differentiate their inquiries?

In fact, Heidegger brings up Kant's claim precisely to disagree with Kant's use of this label; Heidegger is adamant that Kant (like Heidegger himself) does not carry out an anthropology. In his 1927–1928 lecture course on Kant, Heidegger suggests that anthropology refers to an "empirical-ontic" inquiry (PIK 48); in the 1929 Kant book, he revises this definition to suggest that anthropology refers to an inquiry that is indeterminate, both in terms of what information it seeks about the human being and in terms of how that information bears on philosophical questions (KPM 147–148). Yet Heidegger takes issue with both senses of the term: anthropology in the former sense does not accurately describe Kant's inquiry, and anthropology in the latter sense is unhelpfully ambiguous. Heidegger suggests that Kant does not seek an empirical account of the human being, as such an account would not explain how we make judgments independently of experience (PIK 50). Rather, Kant seeks (like Heidegger himself) "*the ontological and essential structure of Dasein*, the transcendental constitution of the subject" (PIK 224) – the constitution that enables the subject to make synthetic judgments a priori. For this reason, Kant's inquiry is also quite determinate and can be captured more specifically by another label: fundamental ontology. Heidegger makes these points about anthropology not to disagree with Kant's line of inquiry but to disagree with the label that Kant at one time attaches to it. Heidegger's discussion, then, ultimately serves to erase a superficial difference between Kant's inquiry and Heidegger's own.

Thus, I submit, Heidegger pursues Kant's inquiry, in line with the reconstructive interpretational style of Gadamer and Davidson. It should

---

[11] See, for example, BT 45f., and Heidegger's comments in the Davos debate (KPM 199). See Crowell 2002 for further discussion of Heidegger's opposition to anthropology.

not surprise us that Heidegger takes up a method of interpretation that Gadamer endorses; after all, Gadamer's interpretive method is heavily indebted to Heidegger's work. However, what differentiates Heidegger from Gadamer is that Heidegger disagrees with Kant as he interprets him, attributing errors to Kant. Heidegger identifies and rejects an ongoing strand of argument in the *Critique of Pure Reason*. Indeed, Heidegger claims to find a deep inconsistency in Kant's *Critique of Pure Reason*: two ongoing strands of argument that are in tension with one another. The following passage fills in the players populating his two-strand interpretation:

> the power of imagination and understanding battle with each other for priority as the basic source of cognition. The battle surges back and forth, without a clear outcome. This makes the task of interpretation more difficult. (PIK 198)

This passage paints the first *Critique* as a battle between two faculties for priority; which faculty is the "basic source of cognition"? The first strand of argument suggests that the faculty of imagination, the ability to represent what is not there, has priority; the second strand of argument suggests that the understanding, the ability to organize sensible information with concepts or rules, has priority. In his interpretation, Heidegger opts for the first strand, where the imagination is primary, and rejects the second strand. Heidegger, then, agrees with one strand of argument in the first *Critique*, but disagrees with the other strand.[12]

In contrast to a reconstructive interpretation seeking only agreement between interpreter and author, Heidegger commits himself rather to investigating the tensions in Kant's text. Heidegger claims that "with Kant it is always worth our while actually to pursue even and precisely his labyrinths" (PIK 210). Heidegger not only *acknowledges* the special difficulties and inconsistencies in Kant's thought; they are "precisely" the center of the interpretation. He attends primarily to those moments where Kant "vacillates" and "hesitates," and even where he "unhinges himself and undermines his own foundation" (KPM 39; PIK 219–220, 279, 145–147). As Heidegger clarifies in a discussion of the first edition of the Transcendental Deduction (i.e., the A-Deduction), inconsistencies bring out the central issues with which an author struggles – that which has not yet been "settled" (PIK 220) – providing glimpses of the author's innovative

---

[12] Dahlstrom also recognizes that, according to Heidegger, Kant "wavers" in the first *Critique* (Dahlstrom 1991: 335; Dahlstrom 1994: 307–308). In Chapter 5, though, I'll show how this interpretive commitment helps Heidegger avoid Dahlstrom's objections to the interpretation.

insight into the subject matter under investigation. For example, Heidegger reports that he focuses on interpreting the A-Deduction over the B-Deduction because the former "shows far more unclarity of direction and animation and a far more concrete proximity to phenomena" (PIK 220).[13] When an author vacillates, Heidegger suggests, the author deals directly with the phenomena she is attempting to explain, struggling to bring "the darkness of the phenomena" to light (PIK 220). Pursuing labyrinths will bring out the innovations of the author's account, so long as one isolates her insight into the subject matter, pulling it apart from misstep and error.

Heidegger does not guarantee that every philosophical text will contain labyrinths, but rather suggests that labyrinths are the mark of a "productive thinker" (PIK 220). Aristotle is his only other example of such a thinker. While "second-rate individuals perch comfortably and self-satisfied and conceited in their own opinion," Kant and Aristotle refused to be so easily satisfied (PIK 147). Both thinkers hesitated and vacillated, experiencing "many upsets" in their pursuit of "a fundamental and radical goal" – for Kant, a fundamental ontology.[14] Therefore, Heidegger suggests that inconsistency is "by no means a deficiency of [Kant's] philosophical research." In fact, inconsistencies are what is most "productive and instructive" in Kant's work.[15]

In contradistinction to Gadamer and Davidson, Heidegger suggests that investigating inconsistencies, rather than establishing widespread agreement, serves the aim of reconstructive interpretation: finding a plausible answer to a question pursued by both author and interpreter. Though Heidegger cannot guarantee that we will discover textual inconsistencies as we interpret (as we might be reading a "second-rate" text), he offers a fundamentally different sensibility about how to receive those inconsistencies, when we do encounter them. Rather than viewing them as an indication of failure on the part of the interpreter, Heidegger sees inconsistencies as evidence of the author's struggle to settle some philosophical

---

[13] Kant's productive "unclarity of direction" provides another reason why Heidegger prefers the A-Deduction, beyond his claim that Kant subverts the priority of the imagination in the B-Deduction (KPM 137–139). John Llewelyn challenges the latter claim, suggesting that Heidegger is overly pessimistic about the B-Deduction (Llewelyn 2000: 34).

[14] Other statements suggest that Kant surpasses even Aristotle in his dedication to finding the right answer: "In Kant as in no other thinker one has the immediate certainty that he does not cheat" (PIK 293).

[15] In this way, Heidegger differs from critics like Schopenhauer who see contradictions as grounds for criticism. For example, in *The World of Will and Representation*, Schopenhauer discusses Kant's "fatal confusion of intuitive and abstract cognition" (2010: 467), saying: "Kant was himself obscurely conscious of the contradiction and struggled with it inwardly, but nevertheless would not or could not raise it to clear consciousness; so he cast a veil over it himself and for other people and used all sorts of surreptitious means to evade it" (470). I will return to Heidegger's differences with Schopenhauer's interpretation of Kant in Chapter 4.

issue. Heidegger, then, does not assign to the interpreter the task of eliminating, minimizing, or erasing inconsistencies. Labyrinths are the fertile ground from which philosophical innovation grows; they are a starting point from which an interpreter can begin to piece together the author's most plausible account of the subject matter.

Thus, Heidegger demonstrates that one can interpret reconstructively while holding open the possibility of error, avoiding hermeneutic ventriloquism. Disagreement helps the interpreter locate the author's deepest insights: the parts of the text about which the interpreter is ambivalent (agreeing with some claims, but disagreeing with others) are precisely the places where the author attempts to offer new insight into the subject matter. Further, disagreement helps the interpreter isolate the author's best account, pulling it apart from those claims with which the interpreter disagrees. Disagreement, in sum, allows the interpreter to locate and isolate the account with which she agrees. Because Heidegger substantively disagrees with an ongoing strand of argument in Kant's text, he cannot simply be reading himself into Kant.

2 Attributing Error to Preserve Kant's Insight

Heidegger's interpretation of Kant illustrates how and when it is appropriate to attribute error when interpreting reconstructively. Heidegger's procedure in interpreting Kant suggests that we must privilege the most plausible, insightful answer to the question posed in the text; it is appropriate to attribute error as a *consequence* of pursuing the most promising line of response to Kant's question. Heidegger is willing to sacrifice consistency, then, for the sake of finding the right answer.

In particular, Heidegger argues that Kant's depiction of the imagination contains a deep insight. To preserve this insight, Heidegger must reject a great many *others* of Kant's claims that are at odds with this insight. Heidegger's discussion of each of the major sections of the first *Critique* takes this form. Interpreting the Metaphysical Deduction, the Transcendental Deduction, and the Schematism, Heidegger pulls apart a strand of argumentation prioritizing the imagination, and one prioritizing the understanding. He argues in each case that the strand of argument prioritizing the imagination better meets the ambitions of the section, as well as better serving Kant's overarching goal to explain the possibility of synthetic judgment a priori.

I will illustrate Heidegger's method of interpreting *de traditione* through an example: his treatment of the Metaphysical Deduction, where Kant presents the origin of the categories. The categories are the fundamental, a priori concepts that enable and structure our experience; we must possess such concepts in order to make synthetic judgments a priori (i.e., to judge about objects prior to or independently of experience). Thus, the Metaphysical Deduction is crucial for answering Kant's leading question about the possibility of synthetic judgment a priori.

Heidegger argues that Kant's discussion in the Metaphysical Deduction offers two competing sources of the categories; it is one battlefield between the imagination and the understanding. The more obvious source of the categories is the understanding. After all, the Metaphysical Deduction is a component of the Transcendental Analytic, where Kant has promised "an analysis of the faculty of understanding" (A65/B90). Further, Kant's analysis in this section intends to "research the possibility of a priori concepts by seeking them *only in the understanding as their birthplace*" (A66/B90). According to this strand of argument, the table of categories is derived from a table of judgments offering the logical rules of thought.

Prior to Heidegger, this argument had been called into question. Heidegger cites Hermann Lotze's challenge to Kant's taxonomy of logical judgments, findings that seemed to doom both the table of judgments and the table of categories derived from it (PIK 178). In brief, and as William R. Woodward notes, Lotze proposed several revisions to Kant's table of judgments in his *Logik*, including suggesting that all judgments are affirmative (contra Kant's claim that three different forms of judgment, including negative judgments, fall under the heading "Quality") (Woodward 2015: 161–162). These objections, Heidegger indicates, were widely embraced by the Neo-Kantians, resulting in widespread criticism of the table of judgments (PIK 178). However, rather than rejecting the Metaphysical Deduction with Lotze, Heidegger argues that Kant's discussion suggests another source of the categories: the imagination. In this section of the *Critique* ostensibly devoted to the understanding, Kant suddenly introduces a third faculty – the imagination – just prior to offering his table of categories (A78/B103; PIK 188). If one attends to the discussion "between the table of judgment and the table of categories," Heidegger argues, one can avoid the "all too hurried critique of the table of judgment" and locate a more promising source of the categories (PIK 179). If the source of the categories is the imagination and not the understanding, then Lotze's objections can be avoided.

Heidegger also appeals to Kant's theoretical machinery – Kant's characterization of the faculties, and the characterization of the categories that is developed more fully in the Transcendental Deduction – to argue that the imagination is a more promising source of the categories. In particular,

Heidegger notes that for synthetic judgment a priori to be possible, it is crucial that the categories are *binding*. We can draw a priori conclusions about our experience because a set of fixed, stable rules apply to that experience. Heidegger argues that a spontaneous faculty, as Kant figures the understanding, is not capable of producing binding rules. A completely active faculty can create or produce, but it cannot bind. Only a spontaneous and receptive faculty – the imagination – can both produce a rule and receive it as binding (KPM 108). Elsewhere, Heidegger suggests that this spontaneously receptive imagination is identical with care, the structure of Dasein (PIK 232). Yet at this point in the argument, Heidegger relies on Kant's own depiction of the cognitive faculties to argue that only an origin in the imagination can secure a feature of the categories that is crucial for the possibility of synthetic judgment a priori: their bindingness. To secure this feature, we must reject the strand of argument suggesting that the understanding is the source of the categories.

Heidegger's interpretation of the Metaphysical Deduction offers a paradigm of his method. Heidegger inquires into the source of the categories, which will help explain the possibility of synthetic judgment a priori. He finds two answers – the understanding and the imagination – and he supports the strand of argument putting forth the imagination as philosophically superior, specifically as a response to Kant's own question and in light of Kant's theoretical machinery. From this example, we can see that Heidegger endorses attributing error when a claim or set of claims is in tension with the most compelling line of response to the question posed by a text.

3 Heidegger's Theory of Error

While the leading proponents of reconstructive interpretation seek widespread agreement with the authors whom they interpret, it is debatable to what extent this goal characterizes the practice of contemporary historians of philosophy and scholars of Kant in particular. In contemporary interpretations of Kant, it is common to differentiate between conflicting passages that Kant offers, and opt for one account over the other for philosophical reasons, as Heidegger does.[16] While Heidegger's interpretation of Kant resembles this contemporary approach, I suggest that

---

[16] For example, in her interpretation of Kant's practical philosophy, Christine Korsgaard argues that his so-called contradiction in conception is a practical contradiction, despite her admission that some textual evidence supports other interpretations; she offers "philosophical considerations" to disregard that evidence (1996: 80).

Heidegger offers a more rigorous method of attributing error; in fact, Heidegger offers a novel way to meet Gadamer's demand to treat the whole of the text. While contemporary historians of philosophy often leave aside the implausible account as soon as they motivate the plausible one, Heidegger supports his attributions of error with a theory of error. Heidegger explains *why* Kant errs, rather than simply discarding the strand of argument prioritizing the understanding as philosophically inferior. Heidegger explains how the first *Critique*, as a whole, shows Kant grappling with his insight into the constitution of the human knower, with the promising strand of argument articulating that insight, and the erroneous strand of argument retreating from it out of anxiety. Explaining Kant's errors, Heidegger treats the text as a whole.

While Gadamer considers attributing error to be a failure of interpretation, Gadamer also endorses explaining error when this worst-case scenario cannot be avoided. In particular, Gadamer suggests that when we cannot agree with an author, we ought to explain the author's error by appealing to psychological or historical factors:

> Just as the recipient of a letter understands the news that it contains and first sees things with the eyes of the person who wrote the letter – i.e. considers what he writes as true, and is not trying to understand the writer's peculiar opinions as such – so also do we understand traditionary texts on the basis of expectations of meaning drawn from our own prior relationship to the subject matter.... It is only when the attempt to accept what is said as true fails that we try to "understand" the text, psychologically or historically, as another's opinion. (TM 255–256)

At first, we read the text assuming its truth, interpreting the claims in light of our own familiarity with the subject matter. However, if we are unable to accept some claim or some subset of claims as true, despite our best efforts at charity, we retreat to a third-personal account of the author's "peculiar opinions," taking the error to be the result of psychological or historical barriers. This explanation represents a failure of interpretation, as one is no longer pursuing the goal of interpretation, according to Gadamer – reaching an understanding *with* the author, by "accept[ing] what is said as true." The author's "peculiar opinions" falls outside the whole of meaning (where the complete text is right about its subject matter) that the interpreter attempts to discern.

Like Gadamer, Heidegger seeks to explain an author's errors. However, his method of explanation differs from that of Gadamer in that he does not primarily appeal to psychological or historical barriers. Further, in providing an in-depth and ongoing explanation for Kant's erroneous strand of argument, Heidegger offers a way to account for the whole of the text that departs from Gadamer's method. For Gadamer, accounting for the whole text means taking it to have a single, coherent meaning with which the interpreter can agree. While Heidegger, investigator of inconsistencies, does not demand such coherence, Heidegger accounts for the whole of the text because he does not discard the philosophically inferior argument, or confine his attention to the components of Kant's discussion with which he agrees. Rather, Heidegger explains why Kant's inquiry into the constitution of the human being resulted both in insight and in error. Heidegger provides a way to treat the whole of the text without taking the whole text to be true.

Heidegger suggests that Kant errs, because he inherits a bias common to the philosophical tradition – the predominance of logic and the understanding. The strand of argument prioritizing the imagination breaks with this bias, showing Kant's radical and innovative insight into the subject matter. However, Kant is pulled back into the traditional bias, especially when he attempts to engage with previous thinkers.[17]

Historical bias, however, does not exhaust Heidegger's explanation of Kant's errors.[18] Consider, for example, the following passage:

> Kant retreats [*zurückweichen*] before the consequence of eliminating the priority of transcendental apperception, of understanding, that is, of the traditional, unfounded privileged position of logic. Kant is afraid [*scheut sich*] of sacrificing transcendental apperception to the transcendental power of the imagination. (PIK 279)

According to this passage, Kant did not pursue his own insights into the imagination to their conclusion, because he was *afraid* of eliminating "the traditional, unfounded privileged position of logic." Kant's attachment to the traditional view certainly plays a role explaining Kant's less compelling line of argument, but not why Kant would have *retreated* to that view. I argue rather that anxiety – the core of Heidegger's theory of error – explains this retreat.

Before going any further, however, a note about vocabulary is in order. In *Being and Time*, Heidegger draws a distinction between anxiety (*Angst*) and fear (*Furcht*). One fears concrete, worldly happenings or things, but

---

[17] See Carr (2007) for a fuller account of Heidegger's claim that Kant's arguments are polemical.

[18] Dahlstrom focuses on historical prejudices as the explanation for Kant's wavering (1994: 307), though a footnote points out that Heidegger's language might attribute a psychological failing to Kant: "'*zuruckweichen*' can connote a mere maneuver or a weakness and lack of resolve ... '*schwanken*' can connote a state of honest uncertainty ('wavering') or an impugnable failure of nerve ('vacillating')" (Dahlstrom 1994: 308 n. 27). I aim to explain this sort of language in further detail, explaining why it does not attribute a psychological failing to Kant.

one is anxious about oneself – more precisely, about the kind of being that one is, about the ungrounded character of one's own existence. Since they have distinct objects, the moods themselves are distinct. The reader might worry that Heidegger's language in the passage above points to fear more so than anxiety: when we are *afraid* (as the translation puts it), we feel fear. However, in this and related passages, Heidegger does not use the term "fear" and does not use the verb that he pairs with it, *fürchten* (to fear). Rather, when Heidegger discusses Kant's retreat, he uses the verbs *scheuen* (to be afraid or shy away) and *schrecken* (to frighten or horrify). Heidegger does not use *schrecken* when discussing either mood in *Being and Time*, though he does refer to *Scheu* (shyness) once, listing it as a type of fear (BT 142). However, Heidegger later comes to associate both terms with anxiety, defining anxiety as *Schrecken* (horror), and identifying *Scheu* (shyness) as its accompaniment. For example, in his 1935 lecture course, *Introduction to Metaphysics*, he refers to the uncanny,[19] which "induces panicked horror [*Schrecken*], true anxiety [*wahre Angst*], as well as collected, inwardly reverberating shyness [*Scheu*]" (IM 166, translation modified). Likewise, Heidegger remarks on the proximity between these terms in the 1943 postscript to *What Is Metaphysics?*: "close by essential anxiety [*wesenhaften Angst*] as the horror of the abyss [*Shrecken des Abgrundes*] dwells shyness [*Scheu*]" (PWM 234, translation modified).[20] We will see shortly that in Heidegger's interpretation of Kant, he also suggests that Kant retreats from, being frightened by, the abyss (KPM 117–118). At any rate, given the connection that both verbs come to have to anxiety, a single instance of *Scheu* in *Being and Time* should not decide that Heidegger in the Kant book is discussing fear.

Moreover, Heidegger draws on the verb *zurückweichen* (to retreat or shrink back) repeatedly in his discussions of Kant (BT 23; PIK 279; KPM 118), a term that is explicitly ambivalent between fear and anxiety. Indeed, when Heidegger differentiates between fear and anxiety, he identifies two kinds of "shrinking back" (*Zurückweichen*). First, there is shrinking back in this sense of fleeing; this is grounded in fear, and shrinks back from "a detrimental entity within-the-world" (BT 185). Second, there is shrinking back in the sense of falling: this is grounded in anxiety, and shrinks back from something that "has the same kind of Being as the one who shrinks

---

[19] The sentence in fact refers to the Greek term *deinon*, but elsewhere he renders this term as uncanny (*unheimlich*) (IM 181).
[20] He also explores both as "basic dispositions," assigning them the same fundamental status as anxiety, in his late 1930s work *Contributions (From Enowning)* (14f.).

back" – "Dasein *itself*" (BT 185). Thus, Heidegger's claim that Kant shrinks back is ambiguous between whether he attributes fear or anxiety to Kant. Luckily, Heidegger's distinction between fear and anxiety points to another, more substantive way to decide the issue: we can determine what mood Heidegger attributes to Kant by determining what Kant was afraid of, in Heidegger's view. If he shrinks from some worldly entity or happening, Kant fears; if he shrinks, rather, from the kind of being that we ourselves are, then he is anxious.

At first glance, the passage on Kant's retreat might seem to suggest a worldly event or happening that Kant feared: Kant was afraid of upsetting previous philosophical dogma (perhaps, facing rejection from those peers who subscribe to it). Indeed, this is how Henrich reads Heidegger's claim, and he criticizes Heidegger for charging Kant with a "lack of intellectual courage" (Henrich 1994: 44).[21] If Heidegger offered such an explanation, it would resemble the Gadamerian method of explaining error that I mentioned above, by appeal to psychological or historical factors. Kant offered an erroneous strand of argument, on this reading, due to, say, an idiosyncratic conformism. Such an explanation seems deeply uncharitable (as Henrich rightly points out), as it saddles Kant not only with error but also with a character flaw. Nor is this a convincing explanation; Kant is not a timid conformist, but the thinker who began the *Critique of Pure Reason* with a sharp attack on dogmatism (Aix).

I argue that the above passage on Kant's retreat (PIK 279) gestures rather at another explanation. Kant retreated to the traditional position, prioritizing the understanding, due to anxiety: an anxiety about the very structure of the human being, rather than anxiety about upending traditional philosophical views. I argue, then, that Heidegger's account of anxiety from *Being and Time* figures in his interpretation of Kant as a theory of error. Kant's anxiety is offered as an explanation both for the erroneous strand of argument and for the inconsistency of Kant's account (where an erroneous argument is offered alongside an insightful one). I argue, then, that Heidegger's most controversial comments concerning his interpretive method – that his own approach is violent, that Kant takes certain positions out of being afraid or

---

[21] Schopenhauer, by contrast, does make such charges, for example: "Kant's *fear* of Berkeleyan idealism prevented him from admitting this" (Schopenhauer 2010: 476, emphasis mine). This and similar claims are a part of Schopenhauer's general method of refuting Kant's errors, stated here in regard to the Schematism: "If, as has often been said, an error is only fully refuted when its origin has been established psychologically, I believe that I have accomplished this in the discussion above with respect to Kant's doctrine of the categories and their schemata" (480).

frightened – have far deeper philosophical meaning and greater interpretive merit than one might suspect.

While Heidegger's claim that Kant is afraid might appear initially as a personal attack, Heidegger in fact argues that any ontological inquiry provokes anxiety, as well as the impulse to quell that anxiety (BT 311–312). The source of anxiety, according to Heidegger, is the constitution of the human being. For that reason, inquiring into the ontology of the human being provokes anxiety, as well as the pull to turn away from and cover over the source of that anxiety.[22] Therefore, Heidegger's theory of error does not attribute a psychological idiosyncrasy to Kant, as on the Gadamerian approach. Kant does not experience anxiety because he is an especially timid sort of person, but rather because anyone pursuing this sort of inquiry experiences anxiety.

At this point, Heidegger's approach to interpretation, which inquires into the impulses behind some of Kant's claims, may begin to sound like a hermeneutics of suspicion.[23] A hermeneutics of suspicion approaches the surface-level claims in a text not as truths but as symptoms of a deeper drama; with Nietzsche, one might say that the author's claims are an expression of bodily states or physiological drives; with Freud, the claims might express unconscious desires; with Marx, they might express one's socioeconomic position (Ricoeur 1978). Is Heidegger promoting a suspicious reading of Kant, by suggesting that his claims are expressions of anxiety?

While I will suggest that Heidegger offers Kant's anxiety as a deep motivator of many of Kant's overt claims, Heidegger's commitment to reconstructive interpretation differentiates his method, as significantly more charitable and truth-oriented, from a hermeneutics of suspicion. Centrally, Heidegger is himself pursuing Kant's question about the possibility of synthetic a priori knowledge – and Kant's way of answering that question, by inquiring about the constitution of the human being. Whereas the deep reading of the hermeneut of suspicion is initiated by a question that the interpreter brings to the text (e.g., what physiological state do these overt moral claims reveal?), Heidegger is suspicious *in the service of Kant's question*. Heidegger sees anxiety as a threat to and

---

[22] Heidegger suggests further, in a Kantian vein, that inquiring into any ontology at all (say, an ontology of nature) brings into view the constitution of the human being, who supplies the fundamental concepts making up that ontology (i.e., the human being brings these concepts to the experience of the natural object). For this reason, even an ontological inquiry that does not inquire specifically into the human being encounters the source of anxiety.

[23] Dreyfus (1991) suggests that Heidegger takes up this interpretive method (37).

consequent upon Kant's own line of inquiry – a threat to fundamental ontology – and he appeals to a deep reading when Kant's overt argument fails, in turning away from the most promising line of response to his leading question.

Heidegger's commitment to reconstructing Kant's *best* line of argument also differentiates Heidegger from another nearby interpretive method: Derridean deconstruction. As with Gadamer, we should not be surprised if there are some affinities between Heidegger's interpretive method and that of Derrida, as Heidegger's method influenced Derrida. In particular, we hear echoes of Heidegger in Derrida's insistence that texts "oscillate," offering multiple lines of argument in tension with one another.[24] However, Derrida focuses only on this tension, rather than deciding on one line of argument over another. As Andrew Cutrofello puts it, Derrida thinks texts are "undecidably equivocal" (1990: 158f.) – there is no way of finally deciding the correct strand of argument, so the deconstructive interpreter is tasked with spelling out how and where texts undermine themselves. By contrast, Heidegger finds texts *decidably* equivocal; though there are multiple strands of argument, the best strand of argument can be identified. It can be decided, in particular, by toggling between the author's question and the phenomena it asks about. Some strand of argument offers a better answer to that question, a better account of the phenomena under consideration. Conversely, Heidegger also wants to argue that the other strand of argument is erroneous, and explain why the author fell into this error. Heidegger steps beyond the Derridean deconstruction that notices tensions when he evaluates those strands: opting for one strand of argument, and explaining why the erroneous strand appears nonetheless.

I will now turn to Heidegger's discussions of anxiety to fill out the details of this explanation. In *Being and Time,* Heidegger suggests that human beings experience anxiety due to our fundamental existential structure, whereby we must reveal the world in light of some project but have no overriding reason to pursue that project over another. We are "Being-the-basis of a nullity," responsible for the project we do pursue, as well as those that we do not (BT 285). Due to our fundamental responsibility for the way that we understand the world, we experience anxiety. As Heidegger reviews at the end of *Kant and the Problem of Metaphysics,* there are two possible responses to anxiety. First, we can face that anxiety, "remembering" (KPM 164) – remembering the source of our

---

[24] This language is originally from Derrida (1988: 148), but I discovered it in Cutrofello (1990).

understanding of the world. In so doing, we discover our fundamental responsibility. Second, we can flee from that anxiety, so as not to face our fundamental responsibility – "forgetfulness" (KPM 163), forgetting that and how we are revealing the world around us.

A number of passages indicate that Heidegger thinks that Kant experienced anxiety during the course of his inquiry, and that Kant responded to that anxiety by attempting to flee or forget this anxiety. These passages suggest that Kant retreats to an argument prioritizing the understanding, because he is afraid of his own insight into the imagination – "the dimension of human Dasein, into which Kant in fact looked, only to be scared away from it [*zurückzuschrecken*]" (PIK 189).

In particular, Heidegger suggests that Kant was afraid of assigning the imagination primacy among the faculties for human cognition, because of certain practical commitments that Kant was not willing to relinquish. In particular, Heidegger refers to the moral system that Kant outlined in the *Groundwork of the Metaphysics of Morals* in 1785 (between the first and second editions of the *Critique of Pure Reason*). While the imagination is (by Heidegger's lights) the only faculty capable of binding us to rules, these rules are not inscribed into the imagination; the structure of the imagination is underdetermined with regard to the rules that it takes up. Rather than being governed by determinate rules, the imagination is an "abyss" (KPM 117): "in the radicalism of his questions, Kant brought the 'possibility' of metaphysics to this abyss [*Abgrund*]. He saw the unknown. He has to shrink back [*zurückweichen*]. It was not just that the transcendental power of imagination frightened [*schreckte*] him, but rather in between [the two editions] pure reason drew him increasingly under its spell" (KPM 118).²⁵ This passage suggests not only that Kant shrank back from the imagination out of fright but also that he was drawn under the spell of pure reason. In Heidegger's view, Kant is drawn under this spell because pure reason, as opposed to the underdetermined imagination, could guarantee the stable moral rules to which Kant was committed.

Heidegger's discussion of anxiety at the end of the Kant book identifies the argument that Kant used to quell the anxieties provoked by the abyss

---

²⁵ Heidegger relates the primacy of the understanding to the status of Kant's moral rules too hastily. These rules, after all, stem from a different faculty – reason. Heidegger occasionally appears to conflate the faculties of understanding and reason (see, e.g., PIK 28; KPM 112f.). Because Kant associates both reason and understanding with our spontaneity, Heidegger might be right that the primacy of the (both) receptive and spontaneous faculty of imagination would undermine the universal bindingness of moral laws along with the primacy of the understanding. However, Heidegger must do more to establish this conclusion.

of the imagination. Kant offers the concrete determinations of the categories in place of fully identifying the null structure of human existence: these categories identify the features that Kant took to be the irrefutable constitution of objects. Kant thus suggests that we are bound to a single interpretive framework, rather than recognizing "the constant although mostly concealed trembling of all that exists" (KPM 167, translation modified); on this view, there is no fundamental responsibility for the way one understands the world. Kant then flees from his insight into the imagination, and offers an implausible strand of argument that portrays the categories with which we make sense of the world as the immutable rules of our understanding.[26]

Recognizing the role of anxiety in Heidegger's interpretation of Kant provides us with a better, even transformative understanding of Heidegger's famous admission that his interpretation is "violent" (PIK 247). In his account of anxiety in *Being and Time*, Heidegger claims that "existential analysis ... constantly has the character of *doing violence*, whether to the claims of the everyday interpretation or to its complacency and its tranquillized obliviousness" (BT 311). Heidegger suggests that everyday interpretation flees from anxiety by "closing ... off" interpretation (BT 311), taking its understanding of the world to be the only one possible. Existential analysis does violence to this everyday interpretation by undermining it, revealing that we are bound neither to a single set of categories nor to a definitive list of moral rules. The professed violence of Heidegger's interpretation is not his confession to twisting Kant to his own purposes, as many commentators charge; rather, Heidegger's interpretation is violent in that it undermines the "everyday" explanation that Kant offered in order to quell his anxiety. However, this violence leaves untouched the strand of argument that genuinely pursues the phenomena: the strand of argument prioritizing the imagination.[27]

---

[26] In *Being and Time*, Heidegger maps fleeing from anxiety and facing anxiety onto the terms "inauthenticity" and "authenticity," respectively. Adopting this terminology, Heidegger's claim is that Kant vacillates between authenticity and inauthenticity. Engelland also recognizes that Heidegger "does in effect chastise Kant for inauthenticity" in his late 1920s interpretation of Kant (Engelland 2017: 9), but claims that Heidegger restricts this accusation of inauthenticity to the second edition (see also p. 218). To the contrary, my work here shows that Heidegger thought that Kant vacillated between authenticity and inauthenticity in the first edition.

[27] How often must an interpreter resort to this sort of violence? Presumably, Heidegger would be reluctant to interpret those second-rate thinkers who offer consistent but unilluminating accounts; there is no deeper truth to "wring from [their] words" (KPM 141). The thinkers with whom Heidegger is interested in engaging – thinkers like Aristotle and Kant – experienced upsets in their search for deeper insights, and violence must be used to unearth those insights (clearing away claims

My account of Heidegger's interpretive violence is also consonant with Heidegger's discussion of destruction in *Being and Time*, where he calls for a destruction of the philosophical tradition (with the Kant book being his first extended implementation thereof). In *Being and Time*, Heidegger emphasizes that his interpretive method has a positive component and a negative component. It destroys those philosophical elements that obscure rather than offer genuine insight into the phenomena under discussion; thereby, the interpreter retrieves the genuine insights that past philosophy has to offer (BT 22–23). In the context of the Kant interpretation, Heidegger rejects the strand of argument prioritizing the understanding in order to retrieve genuine insight into the ontological constitution of Dasein, and thus to achieve the goal of fundamental ontology. Echoing Kant's own wording in the *Prolegomena*, Heidegger suggests that a "resolute" reader is required to follow Kant's arguments to their appropriate conclusions, rather than retreat from them with Kant (Ak. 4:274; KPM 170). Heidegger's theory of error offers a general recommendation: when we see an author struggling with the sorts of questions with which Kant struggles, we must seek the tensions and the labyrinths, and be on guard against easy and comforting explanations.

4 Heidegger's Later Retraction of the Kant Book

Heidegger's own critical comments on his late 1920s interpretation of Kant may seem to weigh against my view of Heidegger's interpretive method and its characteristic violence. Indeed, commentators often appeal to these comments in order to support the view that Heidegger is a hermeneutic ventriloquist in his late 1920s interpretation of Kant.[28] Arguably, the most worrying of these comments are offered in his prefaces to the second and fourth editions of *Kant and the Problem of Metaphysics*, published in 1950 and 1973, respectively.[29] Before working through these

---

that are at odds with the deeper insights). Is it possible to offer a philosophical account that is both internally consistent and insightful? Would Heidegger, for example, want to make such a claim about his own fundamental ontology? I think it would be difficult to deny that there are labyrinths within *Being and Time* itself. Indeed, Heidegger's interpretive method would seem to betray a personal familiarity with the tumults of philosophical inquiry.

[28] See, e.g., Gordon (2010: 161) and Engelland (2017: 125).

[29] Heidegger also makes critical comments about KPM in his late 1930s *Contributions to Philosophy* and *The Question Concerning the Thing*, though they are not as sharp as those offered in the later prefaces to KPM. Heidegger's remarks in the *Contributions* are ambiguous, claiming that the violence of KPM is "incorrect historiologically" but "historically essential" (CP 199). In *The Question Concerning the Thing*, Heidegger complains about the style of the book more than the method or findings; "the title of this work is imprecise" (WT 87).

comments, there are two issues to disambiguate: first, the method that Heidegger used in interpreting Kant in the late 1920s, which I have reconstructed and defended in this chapter; second, the way that Heidegger carried out or executed this method. I will suggest that Heidegger's later comments offer very little reason to reject the interpretive method that I have defended in this chapter, and that they offer unpersuasive reasons for thinking that he carried out that method incorrectly.

In the 1950 preface to the second edition, Heidegger seems to criticize his late 1920s method of interpreting Kant, particularly its violence. As I have outlined above, Heidegger initially identifies violence as a feature of his interpretive method: violence is to be used, in textual interpretation (KPM 141) and existential analysis more broadly (BT 311), against those errors that obscure deeper insights. However, in the 1950 preface, Heidegger begins speaking of his violence not as a feature but as a bug of his method. This discussion is worth quoting at length:

> Readers have taken constant offense to the violence of my interpretations. Their allegation of violence can indeed be supported by this text.
>
> Philosophicohistorical research is always correctly subject to this charge whenever it is directed against attempts to set in motion a thoughtful dialogue between thinkers. In contrast to the methods of historical philology, which has its own agenda, a thoughtful dialogue is bound by other laws – laws which are more easily violated. In a dialogue the possibility of going astray is more threatening, the shortcomings more frequent. (xx)

In 1950, Heidegger portrays violence as a sort of mistake into which an interpreter can easily fall when interpreting a text, a mistake that becomes possible when that interpretation attempts a thoughtful dialogue instead of a philological or scholarly interpretation. This violence amounts to a tendency to go overboard, which works "against" having a thoughtful dialogue with another thinker. Heidegger's later depiction of his interpretive violence seems to capitulate to his critics, rather than capturing the actual role of violence in the interpretation; he depicts his violence as a shortcoming, rather than an interpretive tool used to clear away error. These later comments do not do justice to his interpretive method in the late 1920s. Because Heidegger equivocates on the term "violence," his comments provide little reason to reject the violence that he initially builds into his interpretive method – the violence that clears away unconvincing, anxiety-driven arguments, so that one can get to the truth about the subject matter.

The precise mistake to which Heidegger admits in this passage speaks to the second issue – his success in carrying out his interpretive method.

Which "law" of interpretation did Heidegger "violate," in his later estimation; in what way did he "go astray"? Heidegger's comments in the preface to the fourth edition shed light on this issue: Heidegger suggests that he "overinterpret[ed]" Kant by interpreting "the *Critique of Pure Reason* from within the horizon of the manner of questioning set forth in *Being and Time*" though "in truth ... Kant's question is foreign to it" (KPM xviii). The problem, in short, is that he got Kant's question wrong, taking it to be similar to the one posed in *Being and Time*. Heidegger suggests that his later interpretations of Kant attempt to correct this error – "to retract the overinterpretation" (KPM xviii).

In the 1935–1936 reinterpretation of the *Critique of Pure Reason*, he attributes a different question to Kant, marking the space between Kant's question and his own. I would argue that the reinterpretation is in fact weaker than the late 1920s interpretation of Kant. The new question that Heidegger attributes to Kant – namely, what is a thing? (WT 37) – fails to do justice to Kant's Copernican revolution, where Kant turns his attention from "the objects" to "the cognition" that makes them possible (Bxvi). Kant asks not only about things but also about the human knower who experiences these things, as recognized in the late 1920s characterization of Kant's project as a fundamental ontology.[30]

While I think there are reasons to object to Heidegger's later criticism of his own interpretation of Kant, it is important to recognize that the issue at hand – whether Heidegger accurately identified Kant's question – does not undermine the interpretive method that I have defended in this chapter. In fact, Heidegger's later concerns with the interpretation show a continued commitment to this interpretive method. Specifically, Heidegger expresses his continued commitment to a central tenet of his late 1920s interpretive method: the interpreter must pursue the question posed by the author. And it is through adhering to the tenets of this interpretive method – pursuing the question posed by the author, taking up the concepts offered

---

[30] Heidegger might also reevaluate his late 1920s interpretation of Kant due to Heidegger's later reformulation of his own philosophical project. While Heidegger perceived a close connection between his own philosophy and that of Kant in the late 1920s, later developments of his project may have provoked him to rethink the closeness of this connection (Herman Philipse also entertains this explanation for Heidegger's critical comments in the fourth preface; see Philipse 1998: 427). Indeed, Heidegger endorses an article that explains the evolution of his Kant-interpretation in just this manner. In the piece, Hansgeorg Hoppe suggests that Heidegger's interpretations of Kant reveal a "shift in emphasis from the subjectivity of the subject to the objectivity of the object," which correlates with "the overall development of Heidegger's thinking from the analysis of Dasein ... to thinking about Being itself as the ground of the there" (Hoppe 1970: 286, translation my own). For the classic treatment of the "turn" in Heidegger's thinking over the course of his career, see Richardson 1993.

to answer that question, identifying the most plausible line of response, and identifying and explaining the errors that obscure that plausible line of response – that an interpreter avoids hermeneutic ventriloquism.

5 Conclusion

While many see Heidegger as reading himself into Kant, I have argued that Heidegger's distinct approach to reconstructive interpretation avoids this mistake. Heidegger keeps fixed the leading question of Kant's analysis, takes on Kant's theoretical machinery, and identifies the most plausible line of response. However, unlike some proponents of reconstructive interpretation, he also attributes error; he identifies and rejects an implausible line of argument appearing in Kant's text. Heidegger's theory of error, further, explains why Kant went astray. Heidegger thereby demonstrates how one can interpret reconstructively while avoiding the risk of hermeneutic ventriloquism.

In interpreting Kant as he does, Heidegger attributes to Kant a compelling, innovative insight into the imagination: the categories of thought originate in the imagination rather than the understanding. While this interpretive method may not read a work as offering a consistent, and consistently convincing, line of argument, it offers its own kind of charity: it seeks out and attempts to foster the growth of the best, most exciting ideas that one encounters in what one reads.

CHAPTER 2

The Receptivity and Spontaneity of Cognition

In Chapter 1, I argued that the following passage enumerates the two competing strands of argument that Heidegger finds in Kant's *Critique of Pure Reason*:

> the power of imagination and understanding battle with each other for priority as the basic source of cognition. The battle surges back and forth, without a clear outcome. This makes the task of interpretation more difficult. (PIK 198)

In this chapter, I argue, further, that this passage provides a road map for situating Heidegger's interpretation of Kant against that of the Marburg Neo-Kantians. Heidegger supports the strand of argument that gives priority to the power of imagination as the basic source of cognition. By contrast, the Neo-Kantians support the strand prioritizing the understanding. Viewed from the perspective of Heidegger's two-strand interpretation, which finds competing arguments in Kant's text,[1] both schools of thought pick up a strand of argument on offer in Kant's text; that is, there is textual support for both interpretations. However, they disagree about which strand of argument is the most promising.

Though both interpretations have evidence on their side, in this chapter I will highlight one benefit of Heidegger's interpretation over that of the Neo-Kantians. When the Neo-Kantians prioritize the understanding, they deny what Henry Allison calls Kant's "discursivity thesis."[2] Kant insists that two qualitatively different faculties are required for human cognition: the receptive faculty of sensibility that receives intuitions from without, and the spontaneous faculty of understanding that organizes that sensible

---

[1] The Marburg Neo-Kantians, for their part, were also sympathetic to this idea. For example, Paul Natorp, discussing the work of Hermann Cohen, remarks that "Cohen was not denying (and it is in fact not deniable) that there is more than one tendency at work in Kant, and that no straightforward equilibrium between the various motifs has been established" (2015: 180).
[2] See Allison 2004: 13.

content with concepts. Departing from Kant, the Neo-Kantians deny that we possess a separate faculty of sensibility, insisting that human cognition is understanding through and through.

Heidegger, however, reinstates the discursivity thesis (or so I will argue). This is, at first, not obvious from the mere fact that he prioritizes imagination; indeed, the fact that he prioritizes a single faculty, the imagination, might seem to suggest that Heidegger too surrenders Kantian discursivity. However, we will see that Heidegger's argument that the imagination is the source of cognition rests crucially on the claim that the imagination is both receptive *and* spontaneous. Indeed, it is this polyvalence that enables the imagination to be the source of the various elements that are required for human cognition. Where the Neo-Kantians deny Kantian discursivity, Heidegger affirms it.

The narrative that I will tell in this chapter is in tension with a standard narrative about Heidegger's interpretation of Kant: that it prioritizes the passive aspects of human cognition where the Neo-Kantians prioritize spontaneity. This standard narrative has taken a few different forms. Some readers emphasize *receptivity*, Kant's word for the broad capacity to receive "representations" or "impressions" (A50/B74). For example, Peter Gordon, in his account of Heidegger's debate with the Neo-Kantian Ernst Cassirer, reports that "the disagreement between Cassirer and Heidegger turns upon this fundamental distinction between spontaneity and receptivity" (Gordon 2010: 6–7), their respective interpretations of Kant dividing along these lines.[3] Other readers focus on the specific form of our (human) receptivity, *sensibility*, which "receives representations insofar as it is affected in some way" (A51/B75). For example, Daniel Dahlstrom reports that "in direct contrast to the neo-Kantianism of Cohen and Natorp, Heidegger shifts the center of gravity of the positive part of the critical philosophy from the understanding to sentience [i.e., sensibility]" (1991: 340).[4] Others, finally, focus on *intuitions*, those "immediate"

---

[3] Sebastian Luft endorses this general framing, though remarks that it is "somewhat too coarse to do justice to their mutual differences and commonalities" (2011: 508). Jeffrey Andrew Barash qualifies that Heidegger "restricted the terms 'receptivity' and 'spontaneity' to his interpretation of Kant's philosophy" (2012: 444); Heidegger does not equate receptivity with "thrownness," as Gordon seems to do, and would not take thrownness to be primary in the equiprimordial structure of care.

[4] Dahlstrom clarifies that he translates *Sinnlichkeit* as "sentience" (1991: 349). Though, closer to the account that I will defend here, Dahlstrom elsewhere draws the contrast as follows: "Heidegger thus takes his cues from the Marburg Neo-Kantians' attempt to uncover the unity of the Doctrine of Elements.... However, this unity is to be achieved, not at the cost of the Transcendental Aesthetic, as the Marburg Neo-Kantians propose, but only by showing 'how both [Aesthetic and Logic] rest upon a common and original foundation'" (Dahlstrom 1994: 302).

representations that our sensibility enables us to receive (A19/B33). Such readers emphasize that, in the early pages of Heidegger's Kant book, Heidegger argues that "cognizing is primarily intuiting" (KPM 15),[5] and maintain that intuition retains this primacy throughout the book.[6] While these readings largely acknowledge the discursivity of Heidegger's reading of Kant,[7] they frame Heidegger's response to the Neo-Kantians in terms of the weight he places on our cognitive passivity – whether receptivity, sensibility, or intuition.[8]

I argue that this standard narrative underemphasizes the real payoff of Heidegger's Kant interpretation, as well as its precise benefit over Neo-Kantian readings: by arguing that the source of cognition is the multifaceted imagination, Heidegger unifies Kant's cognitive faculties without giving up Kant's discursivity thesis.

To make my case, I'll begin by discussing Heidegger's convergence with the Neo-Kantians: he agrees that Kant's cognitive psychology requires a deeper unity. However, he disagrees with their way of unifying cognition – not only because they suggest that cognition is understanding, but also because they suggest cognition is univocal, or nondiscursive. I then turn to the opening discussion of intuition, where Heidegger does insist that intuition is primary for cognition, as many readers have emphasized. However, I will argue this is only the starting point of Heidegger's argument. The opening discussion argues that the discursivity of cognition is in fact a consequence of the primacy of intuition; intuition requires a qualitatively different element in order to yield cognition. Thus, this discussion ultimately presses the question: How are two qualitatively different faculties unified? Heidegger's answer, as we will see, appeals to the faculty of imagination: a faculty that is not receptive, or even primarily receptive, but rather a faculty that unifies receptivity and spontaneity.[9]

---

[5] In a 2010 article, Dahlstrom also appeals to these passages to argue that Heidegger offers a realist interpretation of Kant. I challenge this argument in Chapter 6.
[6] See Truwant 2022: 102–104; de Boer and Howard 2019: 363; and Piché 2000: 102.
[7] For example, Claude Piché remarks that "Heidegger's position is not the symmetrical opposite of Cohen's. There is no one-sided reliance on intuition here" (2000: 201). See also Truwant 2022: 103–104; de Boer and Howard 2019: 373; Dahlstrom 1991: 344–345; and Gordon 2010: 146.
[8] There is some overlap between these accounts. For example, while de Boer and Howard gloss the position of the Kant book in terms of the primacy of intuition, they also endorse Dahlstrom's claim that sensibility is the "center of gravity" (de Boer and Howard 2019: 363).
[9] In Chapter 6, I will return to and complete my argument for this claim, since Heidegger's interpretation of the Transcendental Deduction reveals which element of the imagination is primary.

1 Heidegger Contra the Neo-Kantians

As Cassirer indicated in his 1929 debate with Heidegger, Heidegger is prone to sweeping claims about Neo-Kantianism. Indeed, when Cassirer presses Heidegger to identify the Neo-Kantians against whom his interpretation is directed, Heidegger replies: "if I should name names, then I say: Cohen, Windelband, Rickert, Erdmann, Riehl" (KPM 193). This list includes a wide swath of Neo-Kantians, representing both the Marburg and Southwestern schools of Neo-Kantian thought.[10] Heidegger's interpretive works on Kant do not engage with each of these thinkers in detail. Yet Heidegger's scholarly engagement with two Neo-Kantians of the Marburg School, Hermann Cohen and Paul Natorp, reveals the intervention that he attempts into a tradition that privileges human spontaneity.

Some commentators see ideological or political undertones in Heidegger's engagement with the Neo-Kantians, particularly in his debate with Cassirer. In 1929, when Heidegger debated Cassirer in Davos, the Neo-Kantian movement had already become a target of anti-Semitism, directed at both Cassirer and Cassirer's teacher Hermann Cohen.[11] However, others have argued that "no social or political differences interfered with the equally obvious admiration and respect with which [Heidegger and Cassirer] regarded one another" during this period before Heidegger joined the Nazi Party in 1933 (Friedman 2000: 6–7).[12] In line with the latter view, my work in this chapter will highlight that Heidegger's engagement with the Neo-Kantians is characterized not only by disagreement but also by agreement; he explicitly endorses and builds on parts of the Neo-Kantian reading of Kant. Further, even as Heidegger disagrees with these thinkers, he engages them deeply and seriously, philosophically motivating his departures from them. In the passages

---

[10] Hermann Cohen headed the Marburg School (eventually succeeded by Natorp and then Cassirer) and Wilhelm Windelband and Heinrich Rickert (Heidegger's own teacher) headed the Southwestern School (see Gordon 2010: 56–57 for an overview of the two schools). Alois Riehl is known for advancing a realist reading of Kant (see Heidelberger 2006).

[11] In particular, John Michael Krois cites the "Bruno Bauch affair" of 1916, in which Bauch "claimed in a *völkisch* political periodical that because Cohen was Jewish, he was not really a German and not able to understand Kant" (Krois 2004: 246–247). Moreover, Krois refers to a public lecture given in 1929, just before the Davos debate, in which Othmar Spann – to an audience that included Hitler – "began with an attack on 'neo-Kantianism'" and referred to both Cohen and Cassirer as "foreigners" (Krois 2004: 247).

[12] I am indebted to Simon Truwant's study of the Davos debate both for discussion of this background and for the reference to Friedman (Truwant 2022: 5–6).

I will review below, Heidegger shows, as Friedman put it, "admiration and respect" for Neo-Kantian readings.

While Heidegger is largely critical of the Neo-Kantian reading of Kant, his engagement with the Marburg School hinges on a point of agreement, as Karin de Boer and Stephen Howard have argued (2019: 363–364). Heidegger attributes a "penetrating" and "significant" insight to Cohen and Natorp (PIK 53):

> Cohen and Natorp noticed as clearly as no one else before that the *Critique* lacks an ultimate encompassing unity, in the sense namely that this unity and *the ground of this unity of the transcendental aesthetic and logic was not explicitly brought to light by Kant*. (PIK 54)

The Marburg Neo-Kantians recognized that Kant failed to bring together adequately the analyses offered in the Transcendental Aesthetic and the Transcendental Logic. The Transcendental Aesthetic treats sensibility, whereas the Transcendental Logic treats understanding. The aim of Kant's Transcendental Deduction is to show that sensibility and understanding are in the right kind of contact, coming together to yield cognitions, which conceptually process intuitive content. However, the Marburg Neo-Kantians (and Heidegger with them) hold that Kant failed to unify the faculties of sensibility and understanding: Kant does not adequately show how they are unified and what enables them to be unified – that is, "the ground of this unity."[13]

The Neo-Kantian question about the unification of sensibility and understanding – "the problem of the unity of intuition and thinking," as Heidegger dubs it in 1926 (Logic 226) – primarily concerns how to unify the a priori elements that each faculty relies on in its respective contribution to cognition. Kant, after all, inquires into the possibility of synthetic judgment a priori, the robust understanding that we have of objects independently of experience. The faculty of sensibility relies on the a priori forms of intuition, space and time; since these intuitive forms enable us to have intuitions, everything we intuit is spatiotemporal. By contrast, the faculty of understanding relies on a priori concepts, or categories; these enable and constrain our conceptualization of objects, such that we appreciate objects as substantial, causal, and so forth. There is a stark contrast between the a priori forms of intuition and the a priori concepts. Intuitions provide an immediate representation – relating directly to some particular – with the a priori forms of intuition enabling this kind of representation. By

---

[13] I will discuss Heidegger's reason for holding this view in Chapter 5. In brief, he believes that Kant creates a chasm between sensibility and understanding when he claims that intuition is structured by time, but indicates that understanding is atemporal, or removed from the condition of time.

contrast, concepts provide a mediate representation, representing by way of a universal – some mark that applies not just to one but to many. This stark contrast between intuition and concept brings out the difficult task that Kant faces in the Transcendental Deduction: given the diversity of their formats (intuitions, on the one hand, versus concepts, on the other), how can sensibility and understanding be unified?

Heidegger suggests that the Marburg Neo-Kantians solve this problem by attempting to "dissolve the twofoldness of sensibility and understanding" (Logic 225). In particular, they subordinate sensibility to understanding, arguing that sensibility is merely a branch of understanding. This solution eliminates the diversity of formats that makes understanding and sensibility seem difficult to unify, construing the forms of space and time not as a priori intuitions but as a priori concepts. Evidently, the Marburg Neo-Kantians disagreed about where exactly the forms of sensibility would fit into Kant's table of categories, with Cohen and Natorp offering conflicting answers. As de Boer and Howard point out, Cohen "describes Kant's Transcendental Aesthetic as a 'weakness' in Kant's grounding of mathematical natural science" and treats the forms of space and time in relation to the categories of quantity (de Boer and Howard 2019: 362; Cohen 1902: 11).[14] By contrast, as Heidegger quotes in the 1927–1928 lecture series, Natorp claims that if Kant's system were "more rigorously built," the forms of space and time "would have doubtlessly had to find their place in modality" in Kant's table of categories (PIK 53; Natorp 1923: 277).[15] Leaving aside the question of *where* to locate space and time among Kant's categories, however, the Marburg Neo-Kantians agree: identifying sensibility as its own distinct faculty was a mistake on Kant's part. Sensibility is reduced to understanding; the discursivity thesis, denied.

Though Heidegger often criticizes the overemphasis that Western philosophy has placed on logic and understanding (see, e.g., KPM 170–171), he suggests surprisingly that "precisely this radical onesidedness of the Marburg School has advanced Kant-interpretation more than all attempts at mediation" (PIK 54). Heidegger endorses the strategy of grounding Kant's elements of a priori cognition in one faculty, rather than attempting to mediate between two distinct faculties; indeed, he himself will adopt this strategy. Heidegger agrees that sensibility and understanding must be

---

[14] As Poma notes, however, this position is only a development of Cohen's later thought: earlier work does "not yet reduce intuition to thought" (1997: 51; for this reference I am indebted to de Boer and Howard 2019: 362).
[15] See also Natorp 2015: 185–186.

unified by a common origin, and inquires with the Neo-Kantians after the origin that unifies their a priori units, that is, the pure intuitions and categories. However, Heidegger suggests that the Marburg School "looked for the solution in the wrong direction" (PIK 54). Namely, they attempted to unify the faculties by identifying the spontaneous faculty of understanding as the source of the a priori units of cognition.

Given Kant's distinction between the faculties of sensibility and understanding, and Heidegger's claim that the faculty of understanding is the "wrong direction" in which to seek their unity, it is tempting to think that Heidegger seeks unity in the faculty of sensibility instead. To be sure, there are passages, for example, in Heidegger's opening discussion of intuition, that lend credence to the view that Heidegger attempts something of a reversal to the Neo-Kantian tradition: while the Neo-Kantians subordinate sensibility to the understanding, Heidegger insists on "the essentially subordinate place of 'all thinking'" (KPM 17).[16] Heidegger claims:

> In order to understand the *Critique of Pure Reason* this point must be hammered in, so to speak: cognizing is primarily intuiting. From this it at once becomes clear that the new interpretation of cognition as judging (thinking) violates the decisive sense of the Kantian problem. All thinking is merely in the service of intuition. (KPM 15)

Here, Heidegger rejects the Neo-Kantian view privileging understanding, where cognition is viewed as thinking.[17] Heidegger's response seems to be that we should prioritize the passive elements of cognition instead, insofar as it is the receptive faculty of sensibility that receives intuitions, and, for Heidegger, "cognizing is primarily intuiting." Where the Neo-Kantians privilege spontaneity, it would seem, Heidegger privileges receptivity.

However, if this is Heidegger's answer to the Neo-Kantian question, it is puzzling that Heidegger continues his passage thus:

> Thinking is not simply alongside intuition, "also" at hand; but rather, according to its own inherent structure, it serves that to which intuition is primarily and constantly directed. If thinking is to be essentially relative to intuition, then both intuition and thinking must have a certain inherent relationship that allows their unification. (KPM 15–16)

---

[16] "All thinking" is in scare quotes because Heidegger is interpreting this passage in Kant: "In whatever way and by whatever means a cognition may relate to objects, that through which it relates immediately to them, and at which all thought as a means is directed as an end, is intuition" (A19/B33). I return to Heidegger's reading of this passage on p. 54 below.

[17] Though Heidegger does not explicitly refer to the Neo-Kantians in this passage, it is clear that Heidegger's comment targets "the Kant-interpretation of the Marburg School" when he says that, for them, "cognition here means primarily thinking, excluding intuition" (PIK 146).

After Heidegger asserts the primacy of intuition, he asks how thinking and intuition are unified; if thinking is in service to intuition, then they must have some "inherent relationship that allows for their unification." What is striking about this passage is that Heidegger raises the precise question that he takes up from the Neo-Kantians – how are intuition and thinking, sensibility and understanding, unified? – but he does so *after* asserting that cognizing is primarily intuiting. This suggests that whatever primacy the passive aspects of cognition have over the active aspects of it, this does not answer the question of how they are unified.

I argue therefore that Heidegger does not assert the primacy of intuition to *answer* the Neo-Kantian question, but rather to *raise* that question anew: if sensibility is in fact its own separate, even primary, faculty – if the Neo-Kantian solution will not work because sensibility is *not* a component of understanding – then how *is* sensibility unified with understanding? This passage, taken as a whole, does not suggest that sensibility plays a similar role for Heidegger as the understanding does for the Neo-Kantians. Heidegger does not dissolve the twofoldness of cognition by subordinating understanding to sensibility, posing it as a branch of sensibility. Rather, there are two qualitatively different elements of cognition – elements that must have some "inherent relationship" – and he asks after that relationship.

Further, it is too quick to assume that sensibility would be (by Heidegger's lights) the right direction for answering the Neo-Kantian question, simply because understanding is the "wrong direction." For Heidegger rejects the idea that there are only two fundamental faculties for Kant. Rather, Heidegger highlights those passages where Kant refers to a "triad of faculties" (KPM 96): sensibility, understanding, and the imagination, which Kant defines as "the faculty for representing an object even *without its presence* in intuition" (B151). Heidegger denies Kant's occasional claims that the imagination is subordinated, either to understanding or sensibility, suggesting instead that the strongest version of Kant's argument recognizes the imagination to be a distinct faculty (KPM 94–96).[18] If there are three faculties and not two, then it is not obvious that sensibility is the right direction in which to seek unity.

Which faculty, then, is the origin unifying sensibility and understanding, the source of Kant's a priori units of cognition? As we have seen, Heidegger suggests that the first edition of the *Critique of Pure Reason* offers two distinct and in fact contradictory answers, where "the power of

---

[18] I will discuss this argument further in Chapter 3.

imagination and understanding battle with each other for priority as the basic source of cognition" (PIK 198). Where the Neo-Kantians pick up (and expand on) the strand of argument privileging the spontaneous understanding,[19] Heidegger endorses the strand of argument privileging the imagination. The imagination is precisely the faculty that comes to the fore in Heidegger's own reading of the Transcendental Deduction (the argument at the center of the Neo-Kantian's "significant" and "penetrating" question for Kant): "the Transcendental Deduction ... shows that the power of imagination represents not just one faculty among others, but rather their mediating center" (KPM 124). While Heidegger acknowledges that Kant vacillates between prioritizing the understanding and the imagination, Heidegger thinks that we should opt for his interpretation, because it takes up (and expands on) the philosophically superior strand of argument.[20]

It must be underscored that sensibility is not even in the running to be the "basic source of cognition" for Heidegger. Rather than the receptive faculty of sensibility, Heidegger privileges the receptive and spontaneous imagination in precisely the way that the Neo-Kantians privilege the spontaneous understanding: it is the source of the a priori elements that enable and structure our experience of the world around us. Heidegger does not privilege receptivity in place of the Neo-Kantian privileging of spontaneity.

Yet Heidegger's opening discussion of intuition does assert some sort of primacy of sensibility over understanding. I must therefore explain how it fits with my interpretation, where imagination, rather than sensibility, is the source of cognition. I'll do this in Section 2, before turning in Section 3 to Heidegger's claim that imagination is the source of cognition, as that which unifies the a priori units of cognition.

---

[19] In so doing, the Neo-Kantians follow in the footsteps of the German Idealists, who themselves follow in the footsteps of Kant's second edition of the *Critique of Pure Reason*. In the second edition, Heidegger suggests, Kant no longer vacillates, but rather decides the battle in favor of the faculty of understanding (KPM 171). While Heidegger acknowledges that the Neo-Kantians offer an epistemological reading of Kant in contrast to the metaphysical reading offered by the German Idealists, in particular Fichte (PIK 50), Heidegger charges both movements with overemphasizing spontaneity. He thus positions himself against a long post-Kantian tradition that preceded him. For more on the Neo-Kantians' epistemological reading, see Crowell 2001. I will turn to Heidegger's relationship to the German Idealists in Chapter 3.

[20] This brings out a methodological point of agreement between Heidegger and the Neo-Kantians, which Dahlstrom identifies: "like his Marburg predecessors [Heidegger] reads the KrV not primarily for its internal consistency or its author's intentions, but rather for its adequacy" (Dahlstrom 1991: 332; see also Piché 2000: 186).

2 Heidegger's Opening Discussion of Intuition

In this section, I examine Heidegger's claim that "cognizing is primarily intuiting" (KPM 15; see also PIK 61). We will see that Heidegger argues for this priority because, on his reading of Kant, intuition determines "the fundamental character of cognition" (KPM 24). However, in my view, this claim does not compromise Kant's discursivity thesis, which Heidegger affirms: thought is "in the service of" intuition, but intuition also requires the determination of thought. Therefore, Heidegger does not eliminate the role of spontaneity in cognition as the Neo-Kantians do for receptivity. Further, Heidegger's claim that intuition is primary for cognition is not the end of the story. Heidegger's ensuing discussion transitions from discussing the character of cognition to discussing the *source* of cognition, the kind of being (i.e., us human beings) who makes this experience possible – that source being Heidegger's overriding concern. And this source, Heidegger insists, is both receptive and spontaneous.

According to Kant's discursivity thesis, the faculties of sensibility and understanding are both required for cognition. When one cognizes, one experiences something determinate; one makes sense of a being that is given, appreciating it as a being of some kind (B137). The discursivity thesis maintains that in order to have a cognition – in order to appreciate the being before oneself – one cannot rely solely on sensibility nor on understanding. Sensibility on its own would provide a conceptually undifferentiated perceptual jumble; one would not appreciate the sort of object that stands before oneself. Likewise, understanding on its own would lose all contact with the empirical world; there would be nothing given that subsequently could be determined conceptually. Rather, we need both sensibility and understanding to cognize. In Kant's well-known formulation connecting our actively organizing concepts and passively receiving intuitions, "thoughts without content are empty, and intuitions without concepts are blind" (A51/B75).[21] The discursivity thesis, then, can be broken down into two parts: First, without the receptive faculty of sensibility, understanding has no content to think. Second, without the spontaneous faculty of understanding, there is no way to make sense of what we intuit.

I argue that Heidegger reinstates the discursivity thesis; thus, where the Neo-Kantians overemphasize spontaneity, Heidegger restores balance, affirming with Kant the discursive nature of human cognition. This gives Heidegger's interpretation one advantage over that of the Neo-Kantians.

---

[21] Heidegger also cites and analyzes this passage, at PIK 61.

However, before I make my case, I must address one way in which Heidegger's account of intuition might seem to read Heidegger's own views into Kant, rather than engaging seriously with Kant's thought. Namely, in claiming that, for Kant, intuition is primary for cognition, Heidegger attributes to him a position that defined the phenomenological tradition. Indeed, Heidegger acknowledges that Husserl holds this thesis, as well, identifying it as a commonality between Husserl and Kant: "at the present time and independently of Kant, Husserl, the founder of phenomenological research, rediscovered this fundamental thrust of cognition in general and of philosophical cognition in particular" (PIK 57).[22] However, attributing this thesis to Kant is something resisted not only by the Neo-Kantians but by Husserl himself. After all, it was beside this opening discussion of intuition where Husserl penned the question "is this Kant?" in his own copy of Heidegger's Kant book (Husserl 1997: 442). While this attribution might seem like a prime example of hermeneutic ventriloquism – attributing a philosophical thesis to Kant that defined the philosophical school to which Heidegger himself ascribed, and that few of his contemporaries recognized as Kantian – Heidegger aims in this opening discussion to pull this view out of Kant's words (rather than, say, introducing his own external premises).

However, Heidegger's engagement with phenomenology in the Kant interpretation goes beyond this single thesis, that cognition is primarily intuiting. This thesis, rather, points to a larger claim – one that will be crucial to understanding Heidegger's interpretation of intuition, as well as the subsequent parts of his interpretation. As I already argued in my account of Heidegger's interpretive method in Chapter 1, Heidegger endorses the strand of argument in Kant that he thinks is phenomenologically compelling, doing justice to the phenomena that it attempts to explain. That is, Heidegger does phenomenology while he interprets Kant, considering the phenomena for himself as he interprets and evaluates Kant's claims about them.[23] Moreover, as other commentators have also noted,[24] Heidegger sees Kant as himself proceeding phenomenologically: "in its basic posture the *method* of the first *Critique* is what we, since

---

[22] Thanks to Colin McQuillan for pointing this passage out to me.
[23] Dahlstrom also comments on the phenomenological component of Heidegger's interpretive method, discussing it in relation to the Transcendental Deduction: "Heidegger's interpretation, here as elsewhere, is unmistakably phenomenological. He labors to retrieve the lived but overlooked senses of Kant's nomenclature, insofar as they are essential to cognition" (Dahlstrom 2010: 290).
[24] Engelland 2017: 67–119; Truwant 2022: 69–78; Han-Pile 2005: 86–87.

Husserl, understand, carry out, and learn to ground more radically as *phenomenological method*" (PIK 49).

The precise method that Heidegger attributes to Kant can be clarified in reference to Heidegger's discussion of the phenomenological method in his 1927 lecture course, the *Basic Problems of Phenomenology*. Here, Heidegger claims that "phenomenology is the method of ontology" (BPP 20). It is the method, that is, for the sort of investigation that both Heidegger and Kant undertake, which inquires into the basic makeup of beings, the criteria that qualify them as beings – what Heidegger will call their Being, and what for Kant is captured by the synthetic a priori judgments of metaphysics. Heidegger borrows a term from Husserl, "phenomenological reduction," to spell out how phenomenology proceeds:

> Being is to be laid hold of and made our theme. Being is always Being of beings and accordingly it becomes accessible at first only by starting with some being. Here the phenomenological vision which does the apprehending must indeed direct itself toward a being, but it has to do so in such a way that the Being of this being is thereby brought out so that it may be possible to thematize it. Apprehension of Being, ontological investigation, always turns, at first and necessarily, to some being; but then, *in a precise way, it is led away from that being and led back to its Being*. We call this basic component of phenomenological method – the leading back or reduction of investigative vision from a naively apprehended being to Being – *phenomenological reduction*. (BPP 21)

In this passage, Heidegger claims that we must draw our account of *ontology* – of what fundamentally characterizes beings, that is, their Being – from our experience of particular beings. The "apprehension of Being" (i.e., of the basic constitution of a being), must start from the apprehension of a being. The rationale for this procedure, as covered in the passage, is that the ontology into which we are inquiring is the ontology of particular beings; as Heidegger puts this point, "Being is always the Being of beings." To capture, then, what we would like to capture in our ontology, we have to begin with the beings who have that Being – who have that fundamental constitution. Ontological (synthetic a priori) conclusions about Being must be evidenced and drawn from particular (as Heidegger will say, *ontic*) beings.

If attributing a phenomenological method to Kant seems like a stretch, its upshot is just this: Kant's ontology is not constructed from out of thin air, but is rather tethered to those beings that it attempts to characterize. Heidegger's attribution of this method to Kant has the ring of a compliment: Kant is a true philosopher, who does not merely play with words but rather looks into the phenomena themselves. And on Heidegger's reading, it is the Transcendental Aesthetic, with its analysis of intuition, in which beings are given, that secures this connection. Thus, he repaints what for the Neo-Kantians was a weak part of Kant's system, lacking rigor, as a great strength – precisely what tethers Kant's investigation to those beings that it attempts to characterize.

Heidegger maintains that Kant's investigation in the Transcendental Aesthetic starts from empirical cognition, the observation of some particular being,[25] using this as a basis for his ontological investigation:

> Kant begins the thematic examination of the doctrine of the elements as such (that is to say the introduction to the transcendental aesthetic) with a general discussion of that which belongs to cognition [*Erkenntnis*] in general. And he carries out this discussion in terms of cognizing [*Erkennen*] as it is initially and mostly familiar to us, namely in terms of ontic cognizing or experience, because pre-ontological cognizing is at first hidden from us. (PIK 56).

That is, the Transcendental Aesthetic, at first, examines a familiar experience of a being. From here, we can begin to appreciate its ontological features – the pre-ontological understanding that this experience contains, though it is usually hidden from us. This pre-ontological understanding will point to the synthetic judgments a priori that can be made about beings. But Kant will go even further, asking after what makes this ontology possible – thus proceeding to the constitution of the human being, the human capacities that allow for ontology (again, as covered in Chapter 1, Heidegger sees Kant as engaging in fundamental ontology). But for now, what is important to recognize is that Heidegger's opening discussion of intuition follows the procedure that he claims to find in Kant – it begins from a familiar experience of a being.

To be clear, in my reading, I avoid one common conclusion about the opening discussion of intuition: that Heidegger begins from a realist standpoint, where we are among beings that exist independently from the human perspective, possessing certain metaphysical properties in themselves (minimally, existence, but also, e.g., their own spatial and temporal natures, causal properties, etc.). I will return to this dimension

---

[25] Heidegger makes it clear that Kant does not consider just any kind of being, but a particular one that reduces the scope of his investigation: "For what Kant calls existence, using either *Dasein* or *Existenz* ... we employ the terms '*Vorhandensein*,' 'being-extant,' 'being-at-hand,' or '*Vorhandenheit*,' extantness.' These are all names for the way of being of natural things in the broadest sense" (BPP 28). I will discuss this scope in Chapter 3.

of my reading and discuss it in detail in Chapter 6. But notice that I avoid the realist reading here by maintaining that Heidegger's opening discussion of intuition treats a kind of experience that we have of beings, rather than how they are inherently or in themselves. On my reading, Heidegger does not attribute any independent metaphysical properties to beings. Rather, he describes an experience, where we see beings *as* having a certain metaphysical constitution, and he inquires into the conditions for that experience (along with Kant). And this inquiry, as we will see in the current and ensuing chapters, leads back to the human perspective rather than to how things are in themselves. One upshot of my reading is that Heidegger's Kant interpretation is less radical, at least on this score;[26] he does not force Kant into a realist mold.[27]

So, according to me, Heidegger sees Kant's Transcendental Aesthetic as starting from and examining a sort of experience; his opening discussion of intuition, which interprets the first lines of the Aesthetic, mirrors this approach. In this experience, broadly, we are "existing in the midst of beings that already are, beings to which [we] have been delivered over" (KPM 19). More specifically, when we cognize a being, we encounter a "concrete thing" (PIK 58) – something immediately before us, a bodily presence rather than something dreamed up or remembered. We experience these concrete beings as being independent from us, having existed prior to our contact with them. As Heidegger puts this point, "finite intuition sees that it is dependent upon a being which exists in its own right" (KPM 18); "this intuition presupposes the being to be encountered via intuition as already being" (PIK 59). (Notice that Heidegger in these passages makes it clear that we are "seeing" beings in a certain way, "as" something. We will see that he is not always this careful.) When we cognize, we experience "a being already at hand" (PIK 17).

On Heidegger's reading, the first sentence of the Transcendental Aesthetic (which in his view is "usually appraised too lightly" [KPM 15]) singles out the cognitive capacities that allow for this familiar experience, as well as identifying a hierarchy between those capacities. In this sentence, Kant says:

---

[26] Realist readings of Kant have been offered, including by Heidegger's contemporary Alois Riehl, and, more recently, by Lucy Allais. I briefly discuss Riehl's interpretation in Chapter 6, and address Allais' interpretation in the conclusion.

[27] I thank an anonymous referee for asking how my reading of this section avoids a realist reading.

> In whatever way and through whatever means a cognition may relate to objects, that through which it relates immediately to them, and at which all thought as a means is directed as an end, is intuition. (A19/B33)

According to Heidegger's reading of this passage, cognition involves both thought and intuition, but intuition has priority: "all thinking is merely in service to intuition" (KPM 15) – or, more carefully, "it serves that to which intuition is primarily and constantly directed" (KPM 15–16). Assigning priority to intuition out of the two cognitive faculties, Heidegger nevertheless (in his more careful formulation) gives intuition the status of a middle manager: if thought is to think an object, it will have to go through intuition, which secures a relation to the object.[28]

While finding a hierarchical relationship between intuition and thinking, Heidegger nevertheless recognizes that both are required for cognition. Indeed, Heidegger offers a revision to a standard gloss of Kant's discursivity thesis, where sensibility and understanding are on equal footing, in a "reciprocal and fully balanced relationship" (KPM 16). In the lecture series, Heidegger explores this hierarchy in terms of the relationship between the two faculties: "we must note that, not only is intuition a basis for thinking, but also that thinking only has the function of determining intuition" (PIK 61). Intuition is primary because it provides thinking with its content, as well as delimiting its contribution to cognition: thinking "serves only the interpretation and determination of what is rendered accessible in intuition" (PIK 57). In the Kant book, Heidegger emphasizes further that intuition is primary precisely due to its impact, more broadly, on cognition: "cognizing is primarily intuiting" (KPM 15). Specifically, intuition is primary for cognition because it explains the essential features of human cognition:

> The finitude of human cognition must first of all be sought in the finitude of its own intuition. That a finite, thinking creature must "also" think is an essential consequence of the finitude of its own intuiting. Only in this way can the essentially subordinate place of "all thinking" be seen in the correct light. (KPM 17)

Human intuition, on its own, secures two features essential to cognition: intuition explains why human cognition is finite, and it explains why human cognition requires a faculty of understanding. Because intuition is finite – requiring for its content to be given from elsewhere – cognition

---

[28] Thanks to Karin de Boer (2022: 1–2), Anja Jauernig, and other North American Kant Society participants for a helpful discussion of Kant's passage, and Heidegger's interpretation of it.

as a whole is finite. Intuition infuses cognition as a whole with finitude because it is the "initial representing" that gets any cognition up and running (KPM 25); therefore, subsequent cognitive processes remain dependent for content to be given from without. Further, because intuition is finite, human cognition requires thinking; finite intuition must be determined by thinking in order to become general and communicable. Cognition therefore must be a "synthesis" of two elements, intuition and thinking (KPM 20). This second feature means that even if cognizing is *primarily* intuiting, it is not *only* intuiting.

Therefore, the primacy Heidegger attributes to intuition *implies* the "twofoldness" of cognition; it implies, that is, that cognition is composed of two elements that cannot be reduced to one another. This is not the Neo-Kantian move that asserts the primacy of one faculty in order to reduce cognition to one element. For Heidegger, the primary faculty, primary though it is, requires a faculty of a character different from itself.

Let's unpack the two ways in which intuition determines the character of cognition, according to Heidegger. Sensibility depends for its content to be provided from without, which it receptively "takes up" (KPM 18). Heidegger borrows a Kantian term in order to capture this dependency: in order for us to have an intuition, we must be "affected" (A10/B33/KPM 18). Sensibility makes its contribution to cognition, giving a being, only insofar as it is affected. As Heidegger puts this point, "finite intuition of the being cannot give the object from out of itself. It must allow the object to be given" (KPM 18). Thinking, in turn, relies on the content supplied by intuitions; without intuition, thinking would have nothing to think. Through intuition, thinking is also dependent on affection, the source of intuitive content. Because intuition initiates any act of cognition, and is dependent for its content to be given from without, cognition as a whole (both sensibility *and* understanding) is dependent for its content to be so given. Cognition, as a whole, is dependent on affection.

One might worry that the language of "affection" pushes again toward a realist reading of Heidegger's opening discussion of intuition. After all, Heidegger considers here not the *experience* of an independent being, but the deeper *conditions* for that experience. His reference to affection seems to point not only to a deeper human capacity (to receive affection) but to a being's (independent, metaphysical) capacity to affect. The language of "affection," indeed, created classic problems for Kant (pressed, famously, by F. H. Jacobi), insofar as he sought to hold back from making claims about what things are like, absent the human perspective.[29] While Heidegger does not treat these problems directly, his use of this term immediately invites a metaphysically indeterminate reading of it, steering away from efficient causality. In the lecture series, Heidegger glosses the "affect" of the "intuitable being" (*anschaubare Seiende*) on the "cognizing being" (*erkennende Wesen*) as follows: "this intuitable being must announce itself by itself [*von sich aus melden*],[30] i.e., this being must concern [*betreffen*] the cognizing being, must touch [*rühren*] the cognizing being, must do something [*etwas an-tun*] to it, as it were, and must make itself noticeable [*sich bemerkbar machen*]" (PIK 59). How this being announces itself, touches us, or makes itself noticeable remains wholly indeterminate; it "must do something." When he introduces the term in the Kant book, Heidegger even more carefully (if more tortuously) refrains from discussing an affecting "being" at all: "Finite intuition, however, cannot take something up unless that which is to be taken up announces itself [*sich meldet*]. According to its essence, finite intuition must be solicited or affected [*angegangen, affiziert werden*][31] by that which is intuitable in it" (KPM 18). This passage encourages us to see the "intuitable" as a participant in our cognition of it – one that "allows for" (KPM 19) and even solicits it – but not one with determinate metaphysical properties (e.g., spatiotemporal features possessed independently from our perspective). If *something* must be given to us in order for us to have experience, it remains indeterminate *what*, precisely – what affects us (and even *how* it affects us) independently of our human ways of experiencing it.[32] Heidegger's ensuing discussion will not dig further into this "something" that affects us. Affection interests him here insofar as it is informative about us – about the sort of (finite) cognition that we have.

Indeed, Heidegger argues that our intuition, which relies on affection, explains why human cognition as a whole is *finite* and not *infinite* (PIK 59). It might be tempting to draw the distinction between infinite cognition and finite cognition, Heidegger suggests, on the basis of the faculties that each form of cognition uses: according to Kant's account, infinite

---

[29] See, e.g., Allison's discussion of Jacobi's dilemma (2004: 64–73). Allison's treatment of this issue aligns with the approach I find in Heidegger: Kant's term does not provide a "metaphysical explanation" (2004: 70).

[30] Compare with Heidegger's language at BT 72.

[31] Compare, e.g., with BT 106. Macquarrie and Robinson translate *angehen* as "to matter."

[32] Heidegger must offer this metaphysically indeterminate reading of affection for another reason, which we cannot quite appreciate yet. We will see in Chapter 6 that Heidegger provides an account of self-affection, where we affect ourselves; further, we will see in Chapter 3 that Heidegger does not extend the category of causality to the sort of beings that we are.

cognition has only an intuitive faculty, whereas finite cognition has a faculty for intuiting and a faculty for thinking. However, Heidegger argues that one can already distinguish between infinite and finite cognition by comparing their intuitive faculties. Infinite intuition is creative; it creates the beings that it represents (indeed, *by* representing those beings), in each case bringing into existence "the unique, singular being as a whole" (KPM 17). Here, Heidegger recalls Kant's discussion of the *intuitus originarius*, the intuition that is original in that it is "one through which the existence of the object of intuition is given" (B72). By contrast, for finite intuition, "what is intuited must be given to the intuition from somewhere else – what is intuited is not produced by intuition" (PIK 59). This recalls Kant's *intuitus derivativus*, which as Kant says is "dependent on the existence of the object ... possible only insofar as the representational capacity of the subject is affected through that" (B72).[33] Infinite and finite cognition are already distinct, then, based on their intuitive faculties, where the one creates its own content, and the other depends for its content to be provided from without.

The character of infinite and finite intuition, Heidegger suggests further, determines their respective relationships to thinking. Infinite intuition does not require thinking, because it already cognizes the being completely; after all, its representations create individual beings. Again, this follows Kant's characterization of infinite cognition, where "all of its cognition must be intuition and not *thinking*, which is always proof of limitations" (B72). By contrast, finite intuition requires thinking. Because finite intuition is limited, it requires something beyond itself to rise to the level of cognition (hence, Kant's claim that this additional thing, thinking, is "always proof of limitations"). Finite intuition, affected immediately, "always remains bound to the specifically intuited particulars" (KPM 19). However, Heidegger asserts, "the intuited is only a cognized being if everyone can make it understandable to oneself and others and can thereby communicate it" (KPM 19). Because intuition, as particular, cannot determine what is general and communicable, cognition requires something else: thinking. Therefore, because human cognition is finite, it must also be discursive; because human cognition depends for its content from

---

[33] This passage is difficult in the same way that Kant's references to affection are; namely, it seems to attribute an independent "existence" to the being that affects us. Heidegger's own phrasings in the Kant interpretation sometimes inherit this difficulty. However, I think that we can understand such locutions as follows: these passages point to a dependence on a metaphysically indeterminate "something" (as Heidegger puts it); but we understand that something in relation to what, from our perspective and in our experience, exists.

without, it requires the determination of understanding. Discursivity is a downstream consequence of finitude.

While Heidegger's account of why finite intuition requires understanding is fragmentary,[34] we can get a sense of what finite intuition lacks (and requires to rise to the level of cognition) if we start from Heidegger's suggestion that infinite cognition immediately cognizes a whole being. Minimally, then, infinite cognition "discloses a being" (KPM 22) – though here, presumably, in a direct, complete, and very individual sort of way (i.e., it is not appreciated as a being of some kind, but as the very individual that it is). Finite intuitions, however, do not provide this minimal thing; what they provide does not rise to the level of a being. Finite intuitions give particular angles, slices, or fragments. But concluding that these are angles, slices, or fragments *of a being* requires something more – some guidance on what to make of intuited particulars, an interpretation of what is given in intuition. Finite intuition, Heidegger says, is "something in need of determination" (KPM 20). General, communicable concepts provide this kind of guidance, because a concept "grasps many under one" (KPM 19–20). Concepts apply not only to this particular intuition but to several, providing direction on how to relate multiple particular intuitions (e.g., this intuition is a front view of some being, and that intuition a back view of it). Even if not achieving the comprehensive wholeness that is immediately cognized by infinite cognition, concepts do give access to a being (e.g., "chalk" or even "body") with some stable identity across multiple intuitions; they provide "a determination of the intuited as this or that" (19).

This task brings out how even the spontaneity of thinking is finite. Thinking "brings something forth" (KPM 21), but not in the sense that it is creative; it does not create beings as infinite intuition does. Further, thinking does not even create the universal that it employs to represent beings; "in terms of its content, the universal is derived from the intuitable" (KPM 21).[35] Rather, thinking is spontaneous in that it determines how intuitive content is to be unified with other intuitive content. By determining how to relate intuitive content, thinking produces the form of the concept. While thinking does not itself create the content of its

---

[34] I'll return to this claim in Chapter 6. What will help us make sense of it, there, is the idea that cognition is driven by a sort of historically contingent project, with standards of success that intuition does not meet on its own.

[35] This claim appears to be restricted to empirical concepts, which the understanding must derive from what is intuited. However, Heidegger denies elsewhere that the understanding can create the a priori concepts, i.e., the categories.

concepts, its activity "helps to set forth the content of the object" – say, attending to some component of that intuitive content over others. Thinking is "productive" or spontaneous, because it determines how and what to generalize, creating relationships between sensible intuitions (KPM 21).

Heidegger's ensuing discussion transitions from the familiar experience of a (particular, ontic, or empirical) being to the deeper, a priori conditions that make this experience possible: an ontological understanding that we bring to our experiences of beings, which is itself made possible by the kind of beings that we are. In the lecture series, Heidegger indicates that intuition – "*the building site of all cognizing*" (PIK 58) – will continue to have priority at these deeper levels: "If cognizing as such is intuition and if all other possible ways of relating to objects stand in service to intuition, then synthetic cognition a priori, too, is primarily intuition. And then ontological, i.e. philosophical, cognition is also originally and ultimately intuition – but intuition in a sense which is precisely the central problem of the *Critique*" (PIK 57). This passage seems to suggest that, just as intuition is primary when we encounter some particular being, it will continue to be primary when it comes to the ontological understanding that we bring to beings. However, the end of this passage is telling, for Heidegger indicates that he may be working now with a different "sense" of intuition. And, indeed, even as Heidegger in this discussion more explicitly identifies what "underlies ontological cognizing" – namely, time, which is for Kant a form of intuition – Heidegger raises doubts about "to what extent time is supposed to be an intuition" (PIK 58).

My ensuing sections will help us see why Heidegger worried in the 1927–1928 lecture series about equivocating on the meaning of the term "intuition" – and why he in the 1929 Kant book declared instead that to inquire into the source of cognition, it "appears sufficient to hold on to the simple and reflexive duality of its [cognition's] elements" (KPM 25). Namely, intuition for Kant is allied with receptivity; we have intuitions due to our mere receptivity, receiving content from without. However, as Heidegger inquires more deeply into the forms of intuition and the categories, he discovers that both of these a priori elements require a source that is both receptive and spontaneous. Thus, the model of time that is to ground them cannot be Kant's form of time, allied squarely with the receptive faculty of sensibility; this model of time must unify receptivity and spontaneity.

In affirming that our cognition – whether empirical or a priori, ontic or ontological – is both receptive and spontaneous, Heidegger's account faces a challenge different from the Neo-Kantians for answering their question: How are sensibility and understanding unified; in particular, what is the origin that unifies their a priori units? Unlike the Neo-Kantians, Heidegger need not demonstrate that one faculty *reduces* to the other, unifying Kant's cognitive picture by dissolving its characteristic discursivity. The challenge that Heidegger faces, then, is finding a source that can unify receptivity and spontaneity, allowing each one expression as "elements" of that source (KPM 25). We now turn to Heidegger's argument that the imagination is that source.

3 The Spontaneity and Receptivity of the Imagination

The imagination, the faculty for representing what is not there, is Heidegger's answer to the Neo-Kantian question: it is the faculty that unifies Kant's cognitive psychology. In this section, I outline four places where Heidegger insists that the imagination is both receptive and spontaneous: (1) his discussion of the empirical capacities of the imagination (what Kant calls the "reproductive imagination"), (2) his discussion of the a priori or transcendental capacity of the imagination (what Kant calls the "productive" imagination), (3) his argument that the imagination (and no other faculty) is the source of the forms of space and time, and (4) his argument that the imagination (and no other faculty) is the source of the categories of the understanding. The third and fourth arguments reveal Heidegger's answer to the Neo-Kantian question: the imagination is the "common root" or "condition of the possibility" unifying sensibility and understanding (KPM 103), as the cognitive source of the a priori units that each faculty uses to cognize objects.

The empirical capacities that Kant assigns to the imagination already demonstrate that it is both receptive and spontaneous, according to Heidegger. These empirical capacities include recalling a memory and fantasizing – capacities that, in general, represent "an object even *without its presence* in intuition" (B151). In these cases, the imagination is spontaneous in that it creates an image. However, it is also receptive because it reproduces content that was previously experienced. For example, when we remember, the imagination is "restricted merely to bringing back via the visualizing of what was perceived earlier" (KPM 92). Further, when we imagine fantastic images, we combine empirical contents that were previously experienced, even if they were not experienced in this exact combination (e.g., adding a horn to the body of a horse when imagining a unicorn). As Kant explains in the *Anthropology* (Ak.7: 168–169), and

The Spontaneity and Receptivity of the Imagination 61

Heidegger paraphrases, the imagination even in fantasizing cannot form "the content of the image simply from out of the nothing, i.e. from out of that which has never before and nowhere been experienced" (KPM 92). Thus, both empirical functions show that the imagination, at least in its empirical capacity, is receptive and spontaneous: its "'formative power' is simultaneously[36] a 'forming' that takes things up (is receptive) and one which creates (is spontaneous)" (KPM 91).[37]

Heidegger argues that the a priori function or "transcendental power" of the imagination is likewise receptive and spontaneous. However, rather than forming an image of some empirical particular (whether previously intuited or fancifully composed), the transcendental power of the imagination produces the a priori forms of intuition and the a priori categories – "forming the look of the horizon of objectivity as such" (KPM 92). We will see in a moment why Heidegger thinks that the imagination *must* be the faculty that produces these a priori units. However, I will first sketch what this production looks like, according to Heidegger.[38] I will focus on what is most crucial for my argument: Heidegger's idea that the a priori function of the imagination – the production of a priori elements – is both receptive and spontaneous. Further, following the confines of Heidegger's own discussion, I will focus solely on the form of time, leaving aside the comparatively less universal form of space (which structures only external, physical experience, and not also internal, mental experience).

Heidegger argues that the transcendental power of the imagination forms "the pure image of time" prior to the intuition of any particular object, providing the ontological properties that any encountered object will have (KPM 92). In particular, Heidegger describes the image of time as comprising a "sequence of nows"; on the persisting timeline, one moment follows another (KPM 93, 135). With this image, the imagination represents "the totality of possibilities" for intuited objects (KPM

---

[36] Here and elsewhere, when I speak of "simultaneous" features of the imagination, I mean that they are equiprimordial. They are equally fundamental for the structure of the imagination, and they are unified, referring to and requiring one another.

[37] This argument offers a potential line of response to an objection raised by Taylor Carman. Carman suggests that Heidegger's "anti-Neo-Kantianism" is ungrounded; Heidegger's interpretation privileging the imagination "poses no threat to Cassirer's project" in particular, because the imagination, as a maker of images, is essentially spontaneous (Carman 2010: 137; see also Grene 1957: 67 and Weatherston 2002: 147, who likewise portray the imagination as spontaneous). Heidegger's discussion here shows that Heidegger does recognize the spontaneity of the imagination but suggests that its spontaneity is always constrained by a receptivity – restoring balance where the Neo-Kantians see only spontaneity.

[38] This sketch will be developed further in Chapter 4, where I discuss Heidegger's interpretation of the Schematism.

108), creating expectations for the empirical objects that we will encounter. Therefore, rather than being one image among others, this pure image of time is a horizon: a perspective or orientation that guides our uptake of empirical particulars.

Gordon also recognizes that Heidegger traces Kant's cognitive picture back to an initial "orientation," but Gordon aligns this orientation with receptivity. Outlining Heidegger's position in contrast to the neo-Kantians, Gordon says that "Heidegger's more explicit complaint ... was that the Marburg neo-Kantians had erased from their portrait of human knowledge its most crucial feature: *receptivity*. Knowledge is always born of an orientation toward the world and a dependency upon the world via intuitions" (2010, 128). However, the idea that this orientation is a facet of our receptivity sits uneasily with Heidegger's repeated insistence that the imagination – what forms this orientation in forming an image of time – is receptive and spontaneous. Further, Heidegger is explicit that the *transcendental* capacity of the imagination is both receptive and spontaneous – saying, for example, that Kant's discussion of that capacity in the *Critique of Pure Reason* "shows both the intuitive character and the spontaneity [of the imagination] in a much more original sense" than the discussion of the empirical capacities outlined in Kant's *Anthropology* (KPM 93).

Why does forming the image of time require both receptivity and spontaneity? To spell this out, it is instructive to consider Heidegger's comments that the transcendental activity of the imagination is a *self-forming* (KPM 62) or a *self-affection* (KPM 132).[39] This language points to two reciprocal capacities: First, the *capacity to form or affect* – to contour or articulate time, say, as a sequence of moments following one another. But second, the *capacity to be formed or be affected* – to take up these determinations, sustaining them in an image. These capacities are comparable to the spontaneity and receptivity of empirical cognition outlined above. Spontaneity determines, acting on intuitions; receptivity takes up, receiving affection. For something like a perspective, orientation, or horizon to be formed – for the image of time to be something that guides our uptake of empirical particulars – both capacities are needed. To provide specific guidance regarding that uptake, the image of time must be determined.[40] But for these determinations to provide ongoing guidance – something

---

[39] I return to Heidegger's account of self-affection in Chapter 6.
[40] Heidegger gets at this point in the following passage: "In advance, then, there must be ... something which regulates by giving a standard. It must open up in advance the horizon of the standing-against, and as such it must be distinct" (KPM 83).

The Spontaneity and Receptivity of the Imagination 63

like a perspective rather than a flash in the dark – they must be taken up. The transcendental activity of the imagination, therefore, requires both spontaneity and receptivity.

Heidegger suggests that the pure image produced by the imagination is the source of both the forms of intuition and the categories of the understanding: the single horizon that it forms contains both elements. The categories are "artificially isolated" aspects of the pure image of time (KPM 104), isolating different determinations of that image (e.g., the persistence of time is isolated by the category of substance). By contrast, the form of intuition, time, is the "unified whole" that is so determined (KPM 100). I'll review here Heidegger's negative argument that the imagination performs this a priori function: that no other faculty – especially the Neo-Kantian answer, the understanding – is capable of producing the a priori units of cognition.[41] This argument relies centrally on the claim that the imagination is both receptive and spontaneous.

We begin with the forms of space and time. Heidegger eliminates several potential sources for the forms of space and time, beginning with the usual source of our intuitions: our experience. While empirical intuitions "receiv[e] something at hand or present" (KPM 122), pure intuitions precede contact with the outside world, and in fact enable this contact to take place. Armed with the pure intuitions of space and time, sensibility is then in a position to receive information about objects that are spatially and temporally ordered (KPM 99). Because space and time *enable* contact with empirical particulars (i.e., concrete beings), the intuitions of space and time cannot be given from without; space and time are not intuited "in the manner of a thematic, apprehending, taking-up of something at hand" (KPM 101). Space and time must have a cognitive source, rather than coming from experience.

Heidegger considers, therefore, the cognitive faculties that might be the source of the pure intuitions in lieu of the external world, settling on the imagination (specifically in its transcendental capacity). Heidegger does not entertain the idea that sensibility might produce the forms of space and time itself, though we can surmise his reasoning. Namely, since sensibility is merely receptive, it could not *create* the forms of intuition; the (merely) receptive sensibility gains its content only from without. The fact that the pure intuitions are pure (i.e., not from experience) means that they must

---

[41] As I argue in Lambeth (2019), Heidegger's argumentative style – an argument from elimination – resembles both Kant's and Hume's treatments of the imagination. My reconstruction in this section expands on the argument from elimination that I outline in section 2 of that piece.

come from a spontaneous faculty, that is, a faculty that can create: "on the grounds of its purity pure intuition possesses the character of spontaneity" (KPM 107). However, Heidegger contends that the faculty that creates the pure intuitions of space and time must be spontaneous and receptive – and, therefore, "as pure, spontaneous receptivity, [pure intuition] has its essence in the transcendental power of the imagination" (KPM 107).

Though the spontaneity of the understanding might seem to make it a contender for creating the forms of intuition, Heidegger argues in opposition to the Marburg School that the understanding could not be the source of space and time (KPM 102). He emphasizes that the intuitions of space and time are *images*, suggesting their source in the "image-giving imagining" (KPM 100) that "gives looks (images) from out of itself" (KPM 99), rather than the faculty of understanding, which deals in concepts and not images. Images are distinct from concepts in that "what is intuited in pure intuition does not have the unity which characterizes the universality of a concept" (KPM 100). In opposition to the unity of concepts, space and time are "unified wholes."

This distinction can be clarified by returning to Kant's basic characterizations of concepts versus forms of intuition. Concepts provide rules, such that an object falls under a concept if it fulfills certain criteria; for example, the concept of a dog provides the criteria that the object must be a "four-footed animal" (A141/B180). Such concepts unify objects with others of their kind. However, space and time are not criteria that some (or even all) objects must fulfill in order to be classified as objects of a certain kind. They do not provide criteria that might capture an individual object, such that the object falls under a rule; we do not take the object to qualify as "space" (i.e., as a token of space) in the way that we might take it to be a dog. Rather, space and time are the wholes within which objects appear (A24/B39f.). The pure intuitions, then, would not originate in a faculty that unifies with rules. Rather, the imagination must be the source of the forms of space and time. The imagination, after all, is the spontaneous cognitive faculty with the same format as our receptive faculty; it is the faculty that can create an image, giving a unified whole.

Heidegger argues that the categories, like the pure intuitions, require a spontaneous and receptive source, stating his aim as follows: "if pure thinking is to be of the same essence [as pure intuiting], then as spontaneity it must at the same time exhibit the character of a pure receptivity" (KPM 107). Heidegger does not consider sensibility as a possible contender for producing the categories, just as he did not consider it as a contender for forming the pure intuitions. Rather, he treats understanding and imagination as the only real contenders for being the source of the categories. Thus, his argument focuses on eliminating the possibility "that the understanding is something that stands on its own" (KPM 104), with the categories being "the apparent achievement of the understanding" (KPM 106).

Though Heidegger's treatment of the forms of intuition implicitly relies on the idea that concepts are rules (in contradistinction to the forms of intuition), Heidegger's treatment of the categories explicitly appeals to Kant's claim that concepts are rules. According to Heidegger, and as I reviewed briefly in Chapter 1, the fact that categories are "binding" rules demonstrates why understanding could not be their source. Concepts, in general, provide criteria uniting the objects that meet those criteria. But categories, further, are rules that apply to *all* objects: as Kant says, they "necessarily pertain to the cognition of objects" (A126), being criteria that *any* object must meet to be an object at all. We hold *these* rules fixed in our cognition of the world around us. At this basic level, the way we conceptualize the world around us is not "random"; "only this Being-in-opposition and no other is taken up" (KPM 108). As a rule that constitutes our fundamental understanding of an object, and constrains the way we conceptualize the world around us, a category is "binding" (KPM 108).

Heidegger argues that the establishment of the categories as *binding* rules requires receptivity; thus, since the understanding is spontaneous alone, it cannot be their source. If understanding has the capacity to create a rule, it does not have the further capacity to *receive* that rule as binding. But the categories, according to Heidegger, are "only there in the letting-be-ruled which takes things up" (KPM 108). The categories must be received, "clutch[ed]," or taken up to be fixed as a binding rule (KPM 132). To establish the categories as categories, the receptivity that lets something be given is required.

To take Heidegger's point, consider again the spontaneity of understanding. According to Heidegger's interpretation of Kant, understanding is spontaneous in that it determines how to relate intuitive content. Determining how to generalize from particulars, understanding grasps the many under one. Because understanding is supposed to be spontaneous, and spontaneous alone, Heidegger finds nothing in the faculty that could constrain its activity to a single set of rules. If organization is purely spontaneous, why not relate intuitive content using a modified table of categories, or by way of a new table of categories entirely?[42] To constrain cognition to a single set of rules – rather than generating new rules for

[42] I thank Elise Frketich for discussion of this point.

every encounter with an object – receptivity is required. The categories, then, are dependent on a source that is both spontaneous and receptive: the imagination, which can both create rules and receive them as binding.[43]

Heidegger draws, then, on the spontaneous and receptive character of the imagination to support his claim that the imagination is the origin of the a priori units of cognition. In this crucial argument in his 1929 Kant book, Heidegger does not privilege receptivity; rather, he highlights the unified receptivity and spontaneity that is required for producing the a priori units of cognition.

4 The Imagination and Time

I now turn to the claims that Heidegger makes in the final pages of his Kant book, that the imagination is "root[ed] in time" – that is, that time "makes possible the transcendental power of the imagination" (KPM 137) – or even that the imagination *is* time (KPM 123). I'll focus on the latter claim, that the imagination is time, and return to the former theses later in the section. This claim poses a problem for my interpretation, because when Kant discusses time as a form of intuition, he discusses something that is squarely a feature of sensibility over understanding.[44] Heidegger's claim that the imagination is time, then, might make it seem like the imagination is equivalent to sensibility. Indeed, this claim is at the heart of many of the accounts that suggest Heidegger privileges sensibility – for "the ultimate ground of our preliminary understanding of the being of

---

[43] Heidegger is aware that his argument has implications for Kant's practical philosophy, which suggests that we are bound to certain a priori moral rules. Indeed, Heidegger follows this argument with a consideration of practical reason, suggesting that here, too, "the self-submitting, immediate, surrender-to ... is pure receptivity; the free, self-affecting of the law, however, is pure spontaneity" (KPM 112, original ellipses); thus, practical reason, too, has its "origin" in the transcendental power of the imagination. Henri Declève's 1970 monograph, *Heidegger et Kant*, explores the practical dimension of Heidegger's late 1920s interpretation of Kant. Heidegger further develops his reading of Kant's practical philosophy in the 1930 lecture course, *The Essence of Human Freedom*.

[44] To be clear, Kant also discusses time as a *formal intuition*. Here, time is "more than the mere form of intuition": "the form of intuition merely gives the manifold, but the formal intuition gives unity of the representation" (B160–161). The formal intuition is not only the form of our receptivity, then, but also the active synthesis of that form (such that it is a unified representation). Therefore, even if Heidegger was using the word "time" in a Kantian sense when he claims that the imagination is rooted in time, it would be ambiguous whether this claim commits him to the receptivity of the imagination. However, I'll argue in what follows that Heidegger no longer uses time in a Kantian sense when he claims the imagination is rooted in time. For a treatment of Heidegger on the distinction between forms of intuition and formal intuitions, see Blattner 2006.

beings is not transcendental imagination, but time ... qua form of inner intuition" (de Boer and Howard 2019: 373).[45]

I argue that when Heidegger claims that the imagination is time, he is no longer referring to time as a form of intuition. Rather, he is discussing what he names "temporality" in *Being and Time*. Time in this sense is the structure that holds together receptivity and spontaneity; it is no longer aligned with sensibility alone. I argue, then, that Heidegger's claim that imagination is time confirms my interpretation where imagination, contra sensibility, is both receptive and spontaneous.

In addition to confirming my interpretation, my argument has broader implications. Commentators on Heidegger's Kant interpretation are often reluctant to connect Heidegger's interpretation of the imagination with his own positive characterization of Dasein, particularly Dasein's temporality (i.e., Dasein's fundamental, temporal structure). Sacha Golob, for example, suggests that Heidegger does not endorse the account of the imagination that he reconstructs in his Kant book – for "'*Einbildungskraft*' does not even appear in SZ [*Being and Time*]" (2014: 121). William Blattner, further, brackets Heidegger's interpretive works in his reconstruction of Heidegger's early theory of time, suggesting that it is unclear when Heidegger speaks in his own voice in these works (1999: xvi). However, if I am right that the imagination is temporality, there is a much tighter connection between Heidegger's own characterization of Dasein and the account of the imagination offered in the Kant book: the "imagination" here is the "temporality" that appears elsewhere. This means that the Kant interpretation *can* tell us about Heidegger's own position – in particular, his account of temporality.[46] As I will develop in Chapter 6, I think that Heidegger's discussion of imagination in his interpretive works on Kant further develops the claim that Heidegger hastily defends at the end of *Being and Time*: that temporality is the source of our understanding of time as a sequence of nows.

Let us turn, then, to Heidegger's claim that the imagination is time, which he makes after arguing that the imagination is the common root of sensibility and understanding. As a form of sensibility, time is a feature of human receptivity for Kant. If (1) the imagination is the fundamental

---

[45] See also Lynch 1990: 363–364.
[46] Golob does recognize that we can find some of Heidegger's ideas in his interpretive works, but thinks Heidegger's claims about the imagination are one specific place where we cannot do this, since Heidegger does not emphasize imagination elsewhere. However, I contend that Heidegger's claims about the imagination are relevant to his views because for him the imagination is temporality.

faculty, (2) the imagination is time, and (3) time is a feature of receptivity, does Heidegger offer a philosophy of receptivity after all?

The key to interpreting Heidegger's claim that the imagination is time, I suggest, is to notice that Heidegger is now operating with a definition of time that departs from that of Kant. In this discussion, Heidegger explicitly transitions from the "nonoriginal essence of time," toward which Kant was oriented, to "original time" (KPM 136–137). That is, rather than discussing the "sequence of nows" that is a form of intuition for Kant, Heidegger is now discussing "pure self-affection" (KPM 140): "the original, threefold-unifying forming of future, past, and present in general" (KPM 137). Heidegger suggests, further, that there is a grounding relationship between these two models of time: the sequence of nows is "nonoriginal" and self-affection "original" precisely because time in the latter sense is the source of time in the former sense: "time as pure self-affection allows the pure succession of the sequence of nows to spring forth for the first time" (KPM 135).

The distinction that Heidegger makes between nonoriginal time and original time recalls the distinction he makes between the ordinary understanding of time and temporality (*Zeitlichkeit*) in *Being and Time*. The ordinary understanding of time is defined in precisely the same terms – a "pure sequence of 'nows'" (BT 239) – and Heidegger again associates this model of time with Kant, who "remained oriented towards the traditional way in which time has been ordinarily understood" (BT 24). Further, Heidegger explicitly identifies temporality with "original time." He says that if he can show that the ordinary understanding of time "arises" from temporality, then "we are justified in designating as 'original time' the temporality which we have now laid bare" (BT 329)[47] – and argues, in the final chapter, that temporality *is* the "source" of the ordinary understanding of time (BT 405). Moreover, temporality is similarly characterized as unifying the three temporal modes of past, present, and future: "this phenomenon has the unity of a future which makes present in the process of having been" (BT 326). Heidegger's overlapping terminology in the Kant interpretation and *Being and Time* provides strong evidence that the "original time" to which Heidegger's discussion transitions at the end of his Kant book refers just to the temporality of *Being and Time*.

---

[47] Translation modified. Macquarrie and Robinson translate *ursprüngliche Zeit* as "primordial time," but I use "original time" to match Taft's translation of KPM; on this score, BT and KPM use identical vocabulary.

Heidegger is explicit that the transcendental imagination is *original* time, as the source of time as a sequence of nows (i.e., Kant's model of time): "The sequence of nows, however, is in no way time in its originality. On the contrary the transcendental power of imagination allows time as a sequence of nows to spring forth, and as this letting-spring-forth it is therefore original time" (KPM 123). Like *Being and Time*, the Kant book puts forth a model of time that is purported to be the source of Kant's model of time. And it is the former sort of time, original time, that he identifies with the imagination, rather than the form of intuition that Kant identifies as time.

Heidegger does not identify the imagination with the Kantian model of time – that is, the sequence of nows aligned with human receptivity. Rather, Heidegger returns to themes that he visited in *Being and Time*, identifying the imagination with temporality, which is supposed to be the source of Kantian now-time. Therefore, Heidegger's claim that the imagination is time does not identify the imagination with the receptive faculty of sensibility by referring to Kant's model of time. However, could temporality be receptive in the way that Kantian time is? If this were the case, it would explain why some theorists recognize that Heidegger relates the imagination to temporality rather than the pure intuition of time, but ally imagination with sensibility nevertheless.[48]

According to Heidegger's discussion in *Being and Time*, temporality is the fundamental structure of the human being, or Dasein. While this discussion does not employ the language of receptivity and spontaneity, Heidegger argues that temporality is supposed to unify the various characteristics that are fundamental to Dasein but not reducible to one another; it unifies, that is, the "equiprimordial" features of Dasein. In particular, temporality holds the *facticity* of Dasein together with its *existence* (BT 327–328). Temporality, in *Being and Time*, is defined not by one feature, but as what holds together a plurality of irreducible features. We should expect that the original time of the Kant book, therefore, is not characterized by one feature – namely, receptivity – but rather holds together a plurality of features. Those features, in the language of the Kant interpretation, are sensibility and understanding. And, indeed, if temporality did hold together sensibility and understanding, it would provide an answer to the Neo-Kantian question that Heidegger takes up – what unifies Kant's cognitive faculties? – and an answer consistent with his

---

[48] See, e.g., Dahlstrom 1991 and 2010, and Gordon 2010: 130.

argument contra the Neo-Kantians that sensibility and understanding are two necessary faculties for human cognition.

I suggest, therefore, that Heidegger's claim that the imagination is original time does not commit him to a philosophy of receptivity. This claim is consistent with his claim that the imagination is not only receptive; it is receptive and spontaneous. Indeed, Heidegger is explicit that original time is not allied with receptivity: "temporality [*Zeitlichkeit*] ... is now no longer on the side of sensibility and receptivity" (PIK 270). Further, and more positively, Heidegger is explicit that his association of the imagination with original time supports its receptive *and* spontaneous character: "Original time makes possible the transcendental power of imagination, which in itself is essentially spontaneous receptivity and receptive spontaneity. Only in this unity can pure sensibility as spontaneous receptivity and pure apperception as receptive spontaneity belong together and form the unified essence of a finite, pure, sensible reason" (KPM 137). *How* original time unifies these features is, I believe, the major question with which Heidegger is grappling in the Kant interpretation[49] – and, indeed, this would make sense given the sketchy account that he provides at the end of *Being and Time*, and given that the Kant book is supposed to "introduce" and "supplement" that work (KPM xix).[50] However, *that* the imagination, as original time, is supposed to unify these features should at this point be clear.

Further, the material from *Being and Time* can shed light on Heidegger's odd proliferation of theses concerning the relationship between time and imagination in the Kant book – theses that at first seem inconsistent. How can time be the condition of the possibility of the imagination, and also be identical with it? *Being and Time* contains the same proliferation of claims concerning the relationship between temporality and Dasein's care structure – the structure that in the first division is supposed to hold together the equiprimordial characteristics of Dasein. On the one hand, temporality is "the primordial condition of the possibility of care" (BT 372).[51] On the other hand, temporality is "the meaning of care"

---

[49] Heidegger's answer will be provided in the interpretation of the Transcendental Deduction, which I reconstruct in Chapter 5.
[50] In particular, as I mentioned in Chapter 1, Heidegger suggests that the Kant book provides a "'historical' introduction" to the first part of the book, and a "supplement" to the second part (KPM xix). This second part was to treat Kant's theory of time, with a focus on the Schematism, but that part never appeared.
[51] See also BT 353, 360.

(BT 323). Once again, the lines between condition and identity seem to blur.

Blattner offers the following interpretation for these passages connecting temporality and care: "In identifying originary temporality, Heidegger is not applying a template to an independent phenomenon; he is drawing out and bringing into view the structural heart of care ... he is showing how care's internal structure is inherently unified because originarily temporal" (Blattner 1999: 124). The same solution can work to explain Heidegger's claims about the imagination and temporality. Temporality explains how the imagination – in particular, its characteristic receptivity and spontaneity – is unified. However, temporality is not something independent, that unifies the imagination from without. Temporality is the structure of the imagination, that structure which makes the imagination possible as the unity of spontaneity and receptivity.

Even when characterizing the time at the "root" of the imagination, then, Heidegger insists on the "twofoldness" of Kant's theory, contra the Marburg Neo-Kantians. Heidegger's interpretation therefore puts him closer to Kant's position than the standard account recognizes, though the position does go beyond Kant. As in Kant's discursivity thesis, spontaneity and receptivity are two nonequivalent components of human cognition (indeed, human *being*) that cannot be reduced to one another.

As I will explore in more detail in Chapter 3, Heidegger also goes beyond Kant by abandoning Kant's idea that there is not much we can say to ontologically characterize the human knower. For Kant, we are not justified in applying categories like causality and substantiality to the "I"; its content is quite empty. While Heidegger suggests that "Kant is wholly right when he declares the categories, as fundamental concepts of nature, unsuitable for determining the ego," he complains that Kant "has not shown that the 'I act' cannot be interpreted in the way in which it gives itself, in this self-manifesting ontological constitution" (BPP 145). Heidegger argues that we have access to ontologies beyond the ontology captured by the categories, and that Kant was wrong for recognizing only the latter ontology. Spelling out how sensibility and understanding are unified (but not reduced to one another) in the same structure, held together in their irreducibility, characterizes the fundamental constitution of the human being even if not by way of traditional categories like substantiality and causality. However, even as Heidegger goes beyond Kant in putting forward a robust, ontological characterization of the human being, his work at this level iterates Kant's discursivity thesis: not only is human *cognition* both spontaneous and receptive; the human *being* is both spontaneous and receptive.

5 Conclusion

The Marburg Neo-Kantians privilege spontaneity, eliminating the contribution of receptivity to human cognition. In response, Heidegger reasserts (with Kant) the necessary role of the receptive faculty of sensibility in forming cognitions, and suggests further that sensibility is primary in that it determines the character of cognition. However, this primacy of sensibility does not compromise the necessary contribution of understanding to cognition. Heidegger recognizes that both receptivity and spontaneity are necessary for cognition, in opposition to the Neo-Kantian elimination of receptivity.

However, Heidegger joins the Neo-Kantians in attempting to find a source that can unify Kant's discussion of intuitions and concepts. Instead of turning to the understanding, with the Neo-Kantians, Heidegger turns to the imagination, arguing that the source of the forms of intuition and categories must be both spontaneous and receptive. Heidegger's Kant interpretation does not offer a philosophy of receptivity; if we are to accept or reject it as a viable interpretation of Kant, it cannot be on this basis. Rather, what is most pressing for evaluating this interpretation is testing Heidegger's claim that the imagination can unify receptivity and spontaneity – only if this claim holds do we have a successful answer to the Neo-Kantian question with which Heidegger begins.

CHAPTER 3

A Common Root
Heidegger's Foundationalism

At the end of the introduction to the *Critique of Pure Reason*, Kant says that

> there are two stems of human cognition, which may perhaps arise from a common but to us unknown root, namely sensibility and understanding, through the first of which objects are given to us, but through the second of which they are thought. (A15/B29)

These preliminary remarks set up the ensuing sections of Kant's book: the Transcendental Aesthetic treats sensibility, through "which objects are given to us," and the Transcendental Analytic treats understanding, through "which they are thought." However, it is Kant's passing reference to a "common but to us unknown root" that captivates Heidegger, becoming something of a running theme in *Kant and the Problem of Metaphysics*.

It is unsurprising that Kant's reference to a common root would grab Heidegger's attention. After all, as I reviewed in Chapter 2, Heidegger concurs with the Neo-Kantians that Kant did not say enough to explain how sensibility and understanding come together to form human cognition. This passage, however, identifies a point of contact between sensibility and understanding: a common root. Therefore, developing Kant's passing remark provides an avenue for supplementing Kant's account just where it needs supplementing – spelling out the unity between sensibility and understanding.

Further, given Heidegger's fondness for everyday terminology over traditional philosophical terms, it is unsurprising that he would pounce on a term with rich everyday connotations. Indeed, his discussion often plays up these connotations, bringing out meanings that other interpreters may have neglected (perhaps by confining themselves to an abstract, philosophical understanding of the term rather than considering its everyday uses).[1] The common root is not a hard floor or a solid base, Heidegger insists; rather, it "lets the stems grow out from itself, lending them support

---

[1] For more discussion of these linguistic practices, see Lambeth (2021a).

73

and stability" (KPM 97). Further, the root "is not just an external bond which fastens together two ends. It is originally unifying ... it forms the unity of both of the others" (KPM 96). The common root is not a latch connecting two things that had already been formed; rather, the common root forms the separate stems of sensibility and understanding, and provides stability and sustenance to them even after they have grown.

However, Heidegger's attempt to inquire further into Kant's common root has earned him criticism. Commentators such as Dieter Henrich are quick to point out that the root in Kant's passage is not only common, but also "to us unknown."[2] Heidegger's inquiry, such commentators suggest, goes beyond the bounds of Kant's philosophical system, attempting to know something that is in principle unknowable. Kant's explanations end at a diversity of cognitive faculties and can go no further; by attempting to press on to a common root, Heidegger joins a long line of Post-Kantian interpreters who surpass the bounds of what we can know.[3] On Henrich's reading, therefore, Heidegger's interpretation cannot be motivated by Kant's philosophical system; it can be motivated only by Heidegger's own work in *Being and Time*.[4] Thus, Heidegger's transgression beyond the bounds of what we can know, according to Kant's philosophy, is supposed to provide specific evidence that Heidegger reads himself into Kant.

In this chapter, I will respond to these objections on Heidegger's behalf. I will highlight that, unlike other Post-Kantian interpreters, Heidegger does not ground the faculties in a homogeneous root that collapses the differences between sensibility and understanding – a line of interpretation

---

[2] Heidegger also cites a later passage that references the common root without this qualification; here, "the 'common root' is reputed to exist" (KPM 26). In particular, Kant says in the architectonic that he will "begin only at the point where the general root of our cognitive power divides and branches out into two stems, one of which is **reason**" (A835/B863). In line with Heidegger's two-strand interpretive method, this is a place where Kant is ambiguous, waffling between two different accounts of the common root – one where it is unknown whether the common root exists, and the other where its existence is affirmed. As ever, Heidegger encourages us to opt for the more promising strand of argument.

[3] I thank Colin McQuillan for pressing me on this objection, and highlighting the continuity between this tradition of interpretation and Christian Wolff's pre-critical metaphysics, in his comments on my presentation at the 2021 Central Division meeting of the American Philosophical Association. My work in this chapter initially began as a response to his concerns.

[4] In his book on Heidegger's Kant interpretation, Martin Weatherston echoes the objection that Heidegger's search for a common root is motivated by Heidegger's own philosophical preoccupations, though he appeals not to the scope of Kant's critical system, but rather to the task of the Transcendental Deduction (Weatherston 2002: 35). Though I focus on Henrich's version of the objection, my work in this chapter answers Weatherston's charge by showing the precedents for Heidegger's search for the common root in German Idealist interpretations, and examining the impetus for this search in Kant's own thinking.

that posits a deeper cause for Kant's cognitive faculties, beyond the bounds of what we can know. Thus, I argue, Heidegger offers a foundationalism that delves into the foundations of Kant's faculty psychology without giving up its diversity. In so doing, I argue, Heidegger does not seek a foundation that is beyond the bounds of what Kant thinks we can know, a deeper cause that overextends the category of causality; rather, he seeks to explain more fully the structural interrelationships between the cognitive capacities that Kant already identifies. We'll see, therefore, that Heidegger's discussion of the common root is less of a departure from Kant than many suspect.

With Chapter 2, this chapter will continue to build our understanding of the role of the imagination in Heidegger's preferred strand of argument, and why Heidegger sees this strand of argument as particularly promising. We will see that Heidegger continues to seek a line of argument that can better navigate the challenges that other interpreters of Kant have encountered. Even if Heidegger does not cite his sources rigorously, his interpretation is informed by the successes and failures of previous interpretive efforts. However, while this chapter will help us better to appreciate Heidegger's preferred strand of argument, it does not fully develop that strand of argument. I focus here on clarifying the role that imagination is to play in Heidegger's interpretation, in reference to the main metaphors that Heidegger adopts from Kant to express that role. The arguments explaining how and why the imagination plays this role are still to come, in subsequent chapters.

1 Heidegger's Insistence on Human Finitude

Henrich argues that Heidegger's search for a common root takes him beyond the bounds of what we can know ("appearances") and into the realm of what we cannot ("things in themselves"). Thus, on Henrich's view, Heidegger joins other Post-Kantian interpreters – principally, the German Idealists – who undermine Kant's distinction between appearances and things in themselves. More sympathetic interpreters, such as Karin de Boer and Stephen Howard, worry that Heidegger's Kant interpretation underemphasizes this distinction, even if it does not violate it; Heidegger lays undue emphasis on how to build up our metaphysical knowledge, rather than paying heed to Kant's limitations on that knowledge (de Boer and Howard, 2019: 368).

To start, I will review Heidegger's own treatment of the distinction between appearances and things in themselves. This textual evidence will show that, while German Idealists like Hegel explicitly attempt to surpass Kant's distinction, Heidegger makes no such attempt. In this way, Heidegger's interpretation upholds a pillar of Kant's transcendental idealism: the idea that human cognition is limited, rather than absolute. As evidence, I will review a discussion of Kant's distinction that occurs early in the Kant book, where Heidegger offers a standard, two-aspect reading of the distinction. Next, I will highlight Heidegger's ongoing emphasis on human finitude, an emphasis that insists on the limitations of human cognition.

Early in the Kant book, Heidegger reviews Kant's distinction between appearances and things in themselves. He invokes this distinction precisely to elaborate the finitude, or limitations, of human cognition, which he sees as a theme of "fundamental significance" in Kant's first *Critique*.[5] Prior to introducing Kant's distinction, Heidegger has already explained why the faculties themselves – the "structure of cognizing" – are finite. As we saw in Chapter 2, human knowers are confined to cognizing only those beings that are given to us (in sensibility), and by way of mediate concepts (in understanding). To further explore human finitude, Heidegger turns to the finitude of the cognition that can be obtained by these finite faculties.

In particular, human knowers cognize *appearances* and not *things in themselves*. Heidegger's interpretation of this distinction is aligned with what contemporary interpreters of Kant call a "two-aspect view."[6] That is, the appearance and the thing in itself do not refer to two different beings, in two different worlds (the so-called two-world view), but rather refer to two different perspectives on one and the same being.[7] Heidegger identifies these perspectives as follows: "The double characterization of the being as 'thing in itself' and as 'appearance' corresponds to the twofold manner according to which it can stand in relationship to infinite and finite cognizing: the being in standing-forth [*Entstand*] and the same being as object [*Gegenstand*]" (KPM 22). The God's-eye view of the infinite knower cognizes beings exactly as they are in themselves, and not by way of more general concepts that range over

---

[5] Here is the quote in full: "By virtue of the fundamental significance which finitude has for the problematic of the laying of the ground for metaphysics, the essence of finite cognition should come to be illuminated from still another side, namely, with a view toward what is cognizable in such cognition" (KPM 21).

[6] Beatrice Han-Pile also recognizes that Heidegger endorses a two-aspect, and rejects a two-world, reading of this distinction (2005: 85). As she notes (n.6), Graham Bird and Henry Allison also endorse this reading of Kant.

[7] Heidegger implies that the Marburg Neo-Kantians fail to grasp this point, apparently taking the thing in itself and the appearance to be two separate beings. Thus, Heidegger suggests that "the denial of things in themselves in the conception of Kant by the Marburg School comes from a misunderstanding of what Kant meant by the thing in itself" (PIK 69).

many beings (such as "table" and "chair"). By contrast, the finite knower cognizes those same beings in a different way: only through the sensible content that it is given, and by way of mediate concepts that conform to that content. For us, the being "reveals itself in accordance with the manner and scope of the ability that finite cognition has at its disposal to take things up and to determine them" (22). The finite knower cognizes beings as they appear to us, relative to our finite ways of cognizing.

On Heidegger's construal, these two perspectives are mutually exclusive: God cannot cognize the appearance any more than we can cognize the thing in itself. For God to cognize an appearance, God would have to be dependent on that being for content, receiving sensible information about that being in the way that we human beings do. In other words, to access appearances, God would have to be finite and limited in a way that we ourselves are – which is fundamentally at odds with God being an *infinite* knower. Likewise, we finite knowers do not know how the being is in itself, independent of our ways of relating to it. As Heidegger puts this point, "finite cognition as finite necessarily conceals at the same time, and it conceals in advance so that the 'thing in itself' is not only imperfectly accessible, but is absolutely inaccessible to such cognition by its very essence" (KPM 23). Those faculties that secure our access to appearances simultaneously bar us from cognizing things in themselves; our cognition is only through those faculties, restricted to their ways of taking up and conceiving the being. The access that they provide is a sort of filtered access, relative to our ways of cognizing; however, to cognize the thing in itself we would have to cognize what that being is like, unfiltered. We finite knowers are in principle incapable of cognizing things in themselves. The thing in itself indicates human finitude, because it is a place where our cognition cannot reach.

Though this discussion in the Kant book provides no indication that Heidegger wishes to abandon Kant's distinction between appearances and things in themselves, Heidegger does show hesitancy about things in themselves in the 1927–1928 lecture series. However, the concerns that he raises there do not suggest that he wishes to deny the finitude of human cognition or to expand the reach of our categories beyond where Kant thought they could go. Principally, Heidegger criticizes the vision of God to which the idea of the thing in itself seems to commit us: a "representing God" who possesses an infinite intuition, cognizing beings in the act of producing them (PIK 68–69).[8] Further, he criticizes the assumption that beings are essentially

---

[8] As Han-Pile points out, Heidegger arguably endorses a more restricted or "negative" view of the thing in itself, where the thing in itself is not the object of God's knowledge, but rather what a being is like "*bracketing of the conditions under which transcendental determination operate*" (2005: 94). Han-

"produced" (PIK 68), that is, creations of a *deus faber*. As I understand him, Heidegger suggests here that we should otherwise cash out human finitude, rather than cashing it out in comparison to an infinite knower, as this comparison relies on questionable assumptions.[9] This is not to deny human finitude but to ask for an alternate way to set that finitude into relief.[10]

At any rate, Heidegger does not introduce these concerns into the Kant book, indicating that his argument uncovering the common root does not rely on critiquing Kant's concept of the thing in itself – and, certainly, not encroaching on its territory, as this territory is not in dispute even when he criticizes the concept. Indeed, Heidegger concludes his account of Kant's distinction by affirming that "these concepts of appearance and thing-in-itself . . . are fundamental for the *Critique*" (KPM 24). Further, Heidegger continues to trumpet the finitude of the human being over the course of his monograph. Heidegger both translates this finitude into his own philosophical vocabulary and raises concerns when his interpretation of Kant seems to undermine the finitude of the human knower.

Heidegger first explores human finitude by enumerating the limitations of the human cognitive faculties that Kant identifies and by probing Kant's distinction between appearances and things in themselves. However, a later discussion (provided after Heidegger gives a preliminary interpretation of the major sections informing his interpretation) introduces Heidegger's own term, horizon, to discuss finitude. In the Kant interpretation, this horizon is supposed to unify the a priori elements that Kant thinks we bring to experience: the form of time and the categories of the understanding (specifically, the horizon is the form of time as it is determined by those categories). Yet Heidegger also introduces this term on the

---

Pile notes that Henry Allison (2004) presents this latter conception of thing in itself as Kant's own view. I will not adjudicate here whether Heidegger's endorsement of this more restricted notion commits Heidegger to a version of transcendental idealism (a topic that has been debated at length, e.g., by Blattner [1994, 1999, 2004] and Carman [2000, 2003]), though I will turn to his temporal idealism in Chapter 6. My response to Henrich in this section is not that Heidegger is a transcendental idealist, but rather that Heidegger takes there to be limits on human cognition and does not aim to surpass those limits.

[9] Heidegger also refers to the "absurd" problems that the concept has introduced into the Post-Kantian tradition, suggesting that "denying things in themselves" would avoid these confusions (PIK 69). Though in the same breath he himself rejects some of these critiques – as mentioned in footnote 7 above, the Marburg Neo-Kantians are supposed to misunderstand the thing in itself – he evidently finds a concept that would accrue such misunderstandings to be more trouble than it's worth. See Truwant (2022: 114) for a summary of the absurdity that Paul Natorp finds in the concept.

[10] Heidegger's philosophy suggests two alternate avenues. First, in *Being and Time*, Heidegger briefly considers what things would be like absent the human standpoint (discussed in footnote 8 above). Second, Heidegger's later philosophy inquiring into the "history of Being" explores alternate ontological frameworks offered up by human history itself.

very first page of his own magnum opus, *Being and Time*, clarifying much later that the horizon "determines that *whereupon* factically existing entities are essentially *disclosed*" (BT 365).[11] We can understand the horizon as a particular framework or perspective that guides how beings (i.e., particular, "factically existing entities") show up for us. The horizon lays out what sort of beings we might encounter over the course of our experience, providing a basic sense of what it means for something to be – the form that any and all beings must take. In so doing, as Heidegger puts it in the Kant book, the horizon provides "ontological knowledge" where "the Being of the being becomes discernible in a preliminary way" (KPM 87). Our access to beings is enabled by this horizon, which "must be unthematic, but must nevertheless be regularly in view" (87). As something that shapes any encounter we have with particular beings, the horizon is formed (in Kantian terms) a priori. And, Heidegger emphasizes, this is a horizon that *we create* a priori (e.g., by determining the form of time by way of the categories).

In the Kant book, the horizon continues to suggest a particular view – a determinate, limited perspective on beings rather than a view from nowhere. Nevertheless, Heidegger raises the concern that his account of the horizon undermines the human finitude of "fundamental importance" to Kant's account. Specifically, Heidegger worries that our ability to create a horizon conflicts with human finitude. We are, after all, supposed to rely on the givenness of beings for us to cognize them, but here we seem to generate cognition ourselves:

> Is it not the case, then, that even ontological cognition which occurs in the transcendental power of imagination is "creative"? And if ontological cognizing forms transcendence, which in turn constitutes the essence of finitude, then is not the finitude of transcendence burst asunder because of its "creative" character? Does not the finite creature become infinite through this "creative" behavior? (KPM 85)

Though Heidegger leaves these questions hanging, his raising them alone reflects a concern with upholding the finitude of the human being. But further, he is unequivocal that our creation of a horizon – if it in any way threatens our finitude – does not amount to the creativity of the "*intuitus*

---

[11] On the first page, the term "horizon" is used to frame Heidegger's philosophical project: "Our provisional aim is the Interpretation of time as the possible horizon for any understanding whatsoever of Being" (BT 1). The quote from BT 365 also refers to time, or the "horizon of temporality," as what discloses beings.

originarius" of the infinite knower (KPM 85). Thus, as I will elaborate, our creation of a horizon does not give us access to things in themselves.

In particular, Heidegger clarifies that our creation of a horizon is an ontological creativity, and not an ontic creativity. When we create a horizon, we create a framework that allows us to encounter beings (KPM 87). That is, we come to appreciate the basic criteria that allow something to count as a being at all, an appreciation that then informs our encounter with any particular being. When we create a horizon, we do not create a being itself, thereby exercising the kind of cognition possessed by the infinite knower who creates beings and in so doing cognizes them fully: "Do beings come to be known then in this 'creative' ontological knowledge – i.e. are they created as such? Absolutely not" (KPM 85). As opposed to undermining the idea that we possess finite rather than infinite cognition, Heidegger's account of the ontological horizon, rather, unearths a condition for our kind of finite cognition: in creating a horizon, we create only what gives us access to beings, such that we can come to know them in particular empirical instances.

Indeed, Heidegger eventually suggests that our reliance on an ontology affirms our finitude; our "transcendental neediness" is in fact "the innermost finitude that sustains Dasein" (KPM 165). Or again, as Heidegger comments in his debate with Ernst Cassirer, "ontology is an index of finitude" (KPM 197). Creative as it is, our creation of an ontological horizon limits us to a certain way of seeing beings; otherwise put, it constrains us to a particular perspective on beings. The fact that we need such a perspective to access such beings – that the human being "requires 'Ontology,' i.e. understanding of Being" (172) – means, further, that our cognition of beings will always be limited. Thus, where the infinite knower's creativity provides full access to the being, our human creativity limits that access.

Heidegger's commitment to the finitude of the human being is confirmed in the final pages of his Kant interpretation in a direct criticism of German Idealist interpretations: "What does the struggle against the 'thing in itself,' which started with German Idealism, mean, other than the growing forgetting of what Kant struggled for: that the inner possibility and necessity of metaphysics, i.e., its essence, are at bottom brought forth and preserved through the more original working-out and increased preservation of the problem of finitude?" (KPM 171). In struggling against the thing in itself, the German Idealists miss an essential component of Kant's philosophical project: the finitude of the human being. Heidegger offers his interpretation as an alternative to the German Idealists. Unlike the German Idealists, Heidegger recognizes the human being is finite, offering a limited perspective on beings and lacking access to things in themselves.

Heidegger's discussion of Kant's distinction between appearances and things in themselves, and his ensuing discussion of human finitude, underscore our limited perspective on the beings that we encounter; we cognize these beings by way of a particular interpretive framework, which reveals "and conceals at the same time." However, Heidegger's account does not acknowledge that certain kinds of beings are altogether inaccessible to us, according to Kant's transcendental idealism. These are the beings that cannot show up within our interpretive framework at all; in more Kantian terms, they violate the conditions of our experience. For example, according to our a priori understanding of causality, we are constrained to conceive of changes as following from previous states, according to certain causal laws. We are therefore not capable of experiencing a change as spontaneously caused; we always take new states to follow from previous ones necessarily. Thus, we are incapable of experiencing beings that are defined by their spontaneous causality, such as God (who is purported to be the first cause) and the human soul (which is purported to act freely). Such beings cannot appear to us, even partially or in a limited way; we are barred from cognizing them altogether.

Heidegger's omission of this point might fuel de Boer and Howard's objection that Heidegger does not adequately address Kant's limitations on our metaphysical knowledge. Even more concerningly, one might worry, with Henrich, that Heidegger's own inquiry into the common root of the faculties of sensibility and understanding attempts to access the human soul – access that is precluded by Kant account. That is, one might worry that even if Heidegger does not *intentionally* undermine Kant's transcendental idealism, his interpretation *effectively* undermines that transcendental idealism. Indeed, Henrich suggests that an inquiry into the common root – regardless of whether it explicitly challenges Kant's transcendental idealism – surpasses the realm of appearances and seeks to access a thing in itself. As Henrich puts this point, "the task of revealing the common root reaches beyond the limits of human knowledge" (1994: 19). Moving forward, I will turn to German Idealist interpretations of Kant – interpretations that also inquire into the common root of sensibility and understanding – and explain why such accounts surpass the bounds of what we can know. Then, I will turn to Heidegger's own account of the common root, arguing that his account responds to challenges with and improves upon German Idealist interpretations of Kant.

2 The Promise of a Homogeneous Root

The German Idealists are well known for attempting to overcome Kant's dualism between the faculties of sensibility and understanding. Paul Franks, for example, suggests that the German Idealists, from Reinhold forward, are committed to "Derivation Monism," which he defines as "the view that, in an adequate philosophical system, the a priori conditions of experience must somehow be derived from a single, absolute first principle" (Franks 2005: 17). More specifically, several German Idealists take on the task of identifying a fundamental power or faculty from which the faculties of sensibility and understanding can be derived. Heidegger identifies several who, like he himself, assign to the imagination a central role in this derivation, though they, unlike Heidegger, see the imagination as essentially spontaneous (aligned with the activity of thinking). This group includes "Fichte and Schelling, and in his own way Jacobi as well" (KPM 97). Heidegger later names Hegel as a German Idealist who also overemphasizes spontaneity, though he does not directly acknowledge the likewise central role of imagination in Hegel's interpretation of Kant.[12] Nevertheless, one can appeal to Hegel to summarize this line of thinking: "The productive imagination must rather be recognized as what is primary and original.... And the imagination is nothing but reason itself" (Hegel 1977: 73).

Likewise seeking a fundamental faculty, Heidegger acknowledges his resemblance to German Idealist interpretations of Kant. He also sees the influence of German Idealism in Neo-Kantian interpretations of Kant, like those offered by Cohen and Natorp. Heidegger and the Neo-Kantians in fact offer a divided inheritance of German Idealism. Heidegger takes the imagination to be fundamental, but does not take the faculty to be purely spontaneous. By contrast, and as we saw in Chapter 2, the Neo-Kantians adopt the idea that spontaneity is fundamental, but do not attribute that spontaneity to the imagination.[13] Nevertheless, both veins

---

[12] Heidegger's discussion might implicitly acknowledge this point. Heidegger reports that the German Idealists see "the pure power of imagination as a function of pure thinking" (138), and suggests that this interpretation of the imagination aligns with Kant's revisions to the second edition of the first *Critique*. Later, he criticizes Hegel, a German Idealist, for following the second edition and prioritizing thinking, though Heidegger does not explicitly invoke Hegel's views on the imagination: "And yet, in the second edition of the *Critique of Pure Reason*, did Kant not give mastery back to the understanding? And is it not a consequence of this that with Hegel metaphysics became 'Logic' more radically than ever before?" (KPM 171). Heidegger might not have bothered to be explicit about Hegel's treatment of the imagination here, as he may have assumed the reader's familiarity with it.

[13] At least, the Marburg Neo-Kantians who are Heidegger's frequent targets: Cohen and Natorp. Ernst Cassirer, however, pegs the imagination as the fundamental faculty, and construes it as an

of interpretation follow the German Idealists in attempting to identify a fundamental faculty.

Despite its ambitions of unifying Kant's philosophical system, the German Idealist interpretations of Kant face criticism. However, before expanding on these interpretations and the objections that they face, I would like to explain why so many Post-Kantians from the German Idealists forward have been tempted to overcome Kant's faculty dualism. Indeed, a motivation for overcoming dualism is contained in Kant's own philosophical project. In providing this account, I disagree with Henrich's objections that Heidegger's Kant book "presupposed the unity of the faculties as a demand that needed no explanation" and that we can only turn to the ambitions of *Being and Time* to "justify this presupposition" (1994: 48). In my view, Kant's own project explains why his interpreters seek to unify the faculties. Nevertheless, turning to another of Heidegger's borrowed metaphors can help to fill out this explanation.

Recall that Kant's larger aim in the *Critique of Pure Reason* is to determine how synthetic a priori judgments are possible. Heidegger prefers to think of this task in terms of another metaphor that he borrows from Kant: that of a foundation, or a laying of the ground (*Grundlegung*). In particular, Kant warns against erecting "an edifice with cognitions that one possesses without knowing whence, and on the credit of principles whose origin one does not know, without having first assured oneself of its foundation [*Grundlegung*] through careful investigation" (A3/B7). True to form, Heidegger suggests that, when interpreting Kant's discussion of laying a foundation, "the expression's meaning is best illustrated if we consider the building trade" (KPM 1).

In particular, Heidegger reconstructs, Kant is attempting to provide a foundation for metaphysics: a knowledge of beings that is necessary and universal (KPM 6). Metaphysical principles are, indeed, synthetic a priori judgments. As principles that are about beings, they are synthetic. These principles are, as Kant would say, "ampliative" (A10/B23) because they tell us something about beings ("every event has a cause"), rather than offering the analytic truths that follow from conceptual analysis ("all bachelors are unmarried"). Further these principles are a priori, as an a priori origin is the only thing that can secure their necessity and universality. The knowledge we gather a posteriori from experience is particular and incidental (yes, this rock is warm, but we needn't conclude that all rocks are warm).

---

active faculty (see Truwant 2022, esp. part I). In this way, he follows those ideas of the German Idealist interpretation with no split heritage.

Only the forms of knowledge that we bring to our experience can be necessary and universal.

Kant seeks the foundation that can support such judgments. However, as with a real building, Heidegger argues, we should not think of laying the ground as slipping a foundation under some prefabricated structure, an "already-constructed building" (KPM 2). Rather, the ground is first laid, providing guidance for the structure that can then be built atop it. Applied to metaphysics, this means that Kant is not slipping a foundation under the metaphysical principles handed down to him through tradition. Rather, laying the ground for metaphysics must provide guidance for what can be built upon it – "a projecting of the building plan itself so that it agrees with the direction concerning on what and how the building will be grounded" (2). The foundation will determine which metaphysical principles can be supported (and those which cannot).[14]

To provide a foundation for these metaphysical principles, Kant must do two things. First, he must identify the a priori structures that we bring to experience: for him, these will end up being the a priori concepts and the a priori forms of space and time. These elements alone can supply the universal and necessary features of our experience, as they promise to structure each and every one of our experiences. But, second, Kant must explain how these a priori structures come together to form a metaphysics: knowledge, not of the implications of this or that concept but of beings; knowledge, not of what is contained in the isolated concept of cause but of how this concept shapes our spatiotemporal experience (such that "every event has a cause"). That is, Kant must explain how the categories of the understanding combine with the forms of space and time, such that they yield synthetic a priori principles. To answer his main question, Kant must explain the a priori contact between sensibility and understanding.

From here, we can see why Post-Kantians from Reinhold to Heidegger have sought a common root for Kant's dual faculties: such a root seems to promise the contact between sensibility and understanding that forms a basis for metaphysical principles. To mix Kant's metaphors, the common root supports an edifice of metaphysical principles that enumerate the fundamental makeup of the world around us: a treehouse of knowledge.

---

[14] This moment in Heidegger's analysis provides one way to respond to de Boer and Howard, who worry specifically that Heidegger's adoption of the foundation metaphor pushes him to focus on *building up* metaphysical knowledge, rather than *limiting* it. However, in this passage, Heidegger indicates that laying a foundation for metaphysics requires determining which metaphysical principles can be built upon it – this implies, I think, that some traditional metaphysical claims might have to be discarded.

Thus, Kant's own philosophical ambitions help to explain why many Post-Kantians were tempted to overcome his faculty dualism.

Nevertheless, in identifying a common root, the German Idealists are charged with returning to a precritical, rationalist position that Kant explicitly rejects – for example, when he rejects the rationalist Christian Wolff's notion of a fundamental power of representation. As we will see in more detail in the next section, Wolff identifies his basic power by abstracting to a general commonality shared by both faculties. He thereby identifies a *homogeneous root*, a single kind of capacity or faculty that can unite our cognitive psychology, a root that unites the stems and that in so doing collapses the differences between them. The German Idealists likewise identify a homogeneous root, but offer a somewhat more complicated story explaining why it counts as a common root. Namely, they argue that a single faculty – engaging in a single kind of activity – generates the various cognitive faculties that Kant identifies.

Often enough (and like Heidegger's own account of the common root), the German Idealists find their basic faculty on the pages of Kant's text, though Kant himself does not explicitly identify that faculty as the common root. For example, as Henrich reconstructs, Fichte argues that self-consciousness is the basic faculty: an "I" that actively thinks itself, comparable to the faculty of apperception identified by Kant. However, in thinking itself, this "I" discovers a moment of receptivity in its activity, for it is not only thinking, but also something thought – not only the subject but also the object of knowledge. These distinct moments generate imagination, which holds together or synthesizes those moments; intuition, which is generated in the movement between those moments; and understanding, which reflects on and conceptually determines intuition (Henrich 1994: 41–43). On this account, the imagination is prior to sensibility and understanding, in line with Heidegger's claim that Fichte, like other German Idealists, "attributed an essential role to the power of imagination" (KPM 97).

Hegel, by contrast, finds a basic power in a different faculty named in the pages of Kant's treatise: the faculty of intellectual intuition (Guyer 2000: 49–50). This is the single faculty possessed by the infinite knower mentioned above, whereby the infinite knower completely cognizes a being simply by representing it. Hegel argues that this intuitive intellectual activity can generate the separate moments of intuiting and thinking, producing the dual capacities that Kant introduces. After all, intellectual intuition immediately intuits beings, like sensibility, but it knows or thinks those beings, like understanding. As de Boer reconstructs, this account squares with the primacy of the imagination, because the intuitive intellect "brings about the primordial synthesis of the imagination" (2000: 215). Thus, for both Fichte and Hegel, imagination plays a primary role generating understanding and sensibility, but this role is still subordinate to active thinking – performed by the "I" of apperception or by the intuitive intellect.

Paul Guyer identifies two kinds of dualism rejected by Hegel's account (Guyer 2000: 37–39): in addition to rejecting the dualism between the faculties of sensibility and understanding, Hegel's interpretation rejects Kant's dualism between appearances and things in themselves. Since the intuitive intellect cognizes beings immediately and completely, its cognition is not routed through our forms of sensing (i.e., piecemeal and through the forms of space and time) and thinking (i.e., through mediate, more general concepts). Thus, it does not know individuals as they appear to us, according to our ways of cognizing. Intellectual intuition knows individuals as just the individuals that they are – that is, as things in themselves. In arguing that our faculties descend from a capacity for infinite knowledge, Hegel radically challenges the limitations that Kant places on human knowledge.

More broadly, the German Idealists offer a variety of critical stances on the thing in itself, with Hegel offering perhaps the most brazen perspective. Without digging into these nuances, I will in the next section outline one way in which the German Idealist quest to overcome faculty dualism likewise violates the dualism between appearances and things in themselves: their positing of a common root relies on metaphysical claims that transgress the boundaries of what we can know, on Kant's view.

3 The Perils of a Homogeneous Root

While a fundamental, homogeneous faculty might lend a deeper unity to Kant's cognitive psychology, Kant himself rejected the idea of such a faculty. Corey Dyck (2014) argues that this rejection, appearing in the Appendix to the Transcendental Dialectic, is an implicit response to Christian Wolff, who identified representing as the fundamental faculty.[15] Insofar as the German Idealists make the Wolffian move of identifying a

---

[15] More generally, Dyck argues, Kant's arguments in the Dialectic are directed at the rationalists who are his more recent predecessors, more so than classic rationalists like Descartes and Leibniz. My ensuing discussion is indebted to Dyck's account, especially the textual evidence that he identifies to spell out Kant's argument.

fundamental faculty, they find themselves at odds with Kant's claims in the Appendix.

The Appendix follows and builds off claims from the Paralogisms, which inquire into what we can know about the soul – figured here as the self-consciousness, or apperception, that necessarily accompanies each of our representations. In the First Paralogism (A348), for example, Kant wonders if we can infer that a causally efficacious substance is responsible for the moments of self-consciousness in our experience – moments, that is, where we not only have an experience, but are aware of ourselves as having that experience. Kant argues that we cannot; such an inference would exceed the bounds of our experience. The running theme of Kant's Dialectic is that we are permitted to apply the concepts of the understanding to what we intuit, but we are not permitted to apply them further. We can know only the beings that can appear to us sensibly; cognition, after all, requires intuition and thought. For example, I can draw conclusions about the causal properties of what I sense (e.g., the current pushing a ship downstream). However, I cannot reason my way to conclusions about beings that I am in principle incapable of sensing; for example, I cannot know the causal properties of God. Kant argues that the "I" of apperception is more like the infinite being than like the current pushing the ship. The "I" is a structure of consciousness, constantly accompanying our representations, but it does not appear sensibly; it is something like the frame of our experience, rather than the content of that experience. As Kant puts this point, "For the I is, to be sure, in all thoughts; but not the least intuition is bound up with this representation" (A350). Since the "I" of self-consciousness does not appear sensibly, we are barred from applying the categories to it and, thus, from knowing it as an object. We cannot know that this "I" is causally attached to a particular substance (or, by contrast, immaterially traveling from body to body) – much less that our consciousness is caused, for example, by an immortal, freely acting substance, as some traditional accounts of the soul would have it.

The Paralogisms warn against applying the categories to the particular faculty of apperception to build metaphysical knowledge of that faculty. Apperception figures into Kant's account as a condition of experience, but we cannot know it as an object of that experience. As Henrich points out, this move can be generalized to our other cognitive faculties (1994: 29). Like apperception, these faculties are the conditions of our experience, but do not appear sensibly in that experience. Just as we cannot access the deeper material conditions for apperception, we cannot access the deeper material conditions for sensibility or imagination, either. Hence, the faculties in general have a peculiar status in the first *Critique*: they figure into the account as conditions of our experience, but we cannot know them by way of the categories – that is, by applying concepts like substance and cause to them. The categories, Kant insists, are reserved for the beings that sensibly show up in our experience.

The argument of the Appendix is built upon these more generalized concerns, explaining why we also cannot know a basic power underlying our dual faculties of sensibility and understanding. The Paralogisms show that we cannot claim to know the faculties as causally efficacious substances. To suggest further that these faculties are the effects of a common cause (i.e., a basic power) is even more metaphysically dubious. For not only would such a move illicitly treat the faculties as causally interacting substances; it would also trade on the assumption that these faculties must be united by a common cause, an assumption to which Kant denies we can help ourselves. Thus, arguing for a basic power goes well beyond the evidence provided by our senses.

Let's review Kant's argument in the Appendix precluding knowledge of a basic power. In this section, Kant supplies his method for identifying faculties. On Kant's view, our own cognitive activities – our ways of representing – give evidence of certain faculties as conditions of our experience. We would not be able to engage in these cognitive activities, were it not for the capacity to do so; we reason, then, from these "effects" to the "powers" that they express (A648–649/B676–677). So, remembering something gives evidence of memory, or a capacity to remember; daydreaming gives evidence of a capacity to fantasize; coming up with a good joke gives evidence of wit. Kant notes that this procedure for identifying capacities at first leaves us with a great variety: "one must assume almost as many powers as there are effects" (A648–649/B676–677). Yet we need not remain at this level of great variety, and indeed would be unsatisfied to do so.

Kant explains that we are not satisfied with such diversity, because human reason demands that we systematize our knowledge, simplifying and unifying what we know about appearances. Just as we are not satisfied knowing that there are various animals – sheep, dogs, pigs – but rather try to unify that knowledge under more general concepts like "mammal," so are we unsatisfied ending our inquiries at a mess of human cognitive faculties. He also identifies the procedure for systematizing our faculty psychology: if our cognitive activities could be explained by various combinations of more general capacities, then we can simplify our faculty psychology, whittling down the number of faculties. Kant writes: "Initially a logical maxim bids us to reduce this apparent variety as far as possible by discovering hidden identity through comparison and seeing if imagination combined with consciousness may not be memory, wit, the power to distinguish, or perhaps even understanding and reason" (A649/B677). One can indeed read the *Anthropology* as spelling out some of the combinations by which more general capacities explain particular cognitive activities.[16] For example, both memory and fantasy are attributed to the faculty of imagination (Ak.7:175, 7:182): as the capacity to represent what is not there, our possession of imagination explains why we can represent the past (as in memory) or fantastical scenarios (as in fantasy). But further, both make use of the content provided by sensibility (Ak.7:168), though memory recalls entire intuitions, while fantasy draws on only parts of them (recombining them fantastically). By explaining these activities by a combination of still more general capacities, we can whittle down our list of faculties, arriving at a smaller number of capacities explaining our various cognitive activities.

However, Kant explains that this procedure can take us only so far: we can simplify no further than the faculties of sensibility, imagination, and understanding. This stopping point is indicated, as Dyck remarks (2014: 206), as early as the Transcendental Deduction: "There are however three original sources (capacities or faculties of the soul), which contain the conditions of the possibility of all experience, and cannot themselves be derived from any other faculty of the mind, namely *sense, imagination,* and *understanding*" (A94/B127). We can simplify no further than these faculties, because the cognitive activities that we used as evidence for our faculties can take us no further. With a narrower repertoire of faculties, we can no longer explain the activities with which we started.

Take, for example, the capacity to represent – that is, the very capacity that Wolff identified (and Reinhold later reinstated) as the basic power from which all other capacities descend. Can the "hidden identity" of sensibility and understanding be discovered through their mutual reliance on this more general capacity? This move would work if the power to represent enabled both sensibility and understanding, similar to how the power to represent what is not there, along with some content from sensibility, enabled remembering and fantasizing. However, the power to represent offers only a partial explanation for these capacities. Sensibility

---

[16] See Kraus 2019 for further discussion of how the *Anthropology* relates to Kant's account in the Appendix.

not only represents, but represents content we receive from without; understanding not only represents, but represents in conceptual form. The power to represent on its own does not enable the capacity to sense nor to understand; further, if the power to represent is to be a basic power, then there is no other power with which it could combine to fill in the explanation. We cannot get to a basic power of representation by Kant's means of simplifying our faculty psychology.

This example suggests that the prospects are dim for identifying any basic power at all. In the *Anthropology*, Kant appeals to the dissimilarity between sensibility and understanding to explain why we cannot access their common root: "Despite their dissimilarity, understanding and sensibility by themselves form a close union for bringing about our cognition, as if one had its origin in the other, or both originated from a common origin; but this cannot be, or at least we cannot conceive how dissimilar things could sprout forth from one and the same root" (Ak.7:178). While Kant often emphasizes the stark contrast between sensibility and understanding (one faculty receptive, the other spontaneous), the contrast need not be a stark one to get his meaning here. If the common root is a single, basic power, with no other powers to combine with it, it remains a mystery how it could yield two (or more) dissimilar capacities. Our inability to access a basic power is a numbers game, more so than a conclusion derived from the particular characters of sensibility and understanding: we cannot explain multiple dissimilar capacities by way of only one simple power.[17]

We would, for the sake of systematicity, prefer to unify our knowledge of the faculties by identifying a single fundamental faculty, rather than ending with three. However, on Kant's view, we lack justification for identifying such a faculty. The evidence from our cognitive activities takes us only as far as three faculties. Further, a logical argument, to the effect that we *must* possess a single, fundamental faculty, cannot fill in this gap. Kant asks:

> For by what warrant can reason in its logical use claim to treat the manifoldness of the powers which nature gives to our cognition merely as a concealed unity, and to derive them as far as it is able from some fundamental power, when reason is free to admit that it is just as possible that all powers are different in kind . . .? (A651/B679)

Based on logic alone, there is little reason to conclude that our faculties are derived from a fundamental power, since it remains possible that there are

---

[17] Thanks to Jacqueline Mariña for a helpful discussion of this point.

several fundamental faculties, different in kind and thereby lacking a common, fundamental power between them. If the analysis of our cognitive activities does not lead to a fundamental power, then our explanation must end at irreducibly diverse sources.[18]

If we do not simplify our faculty psychology on Kant's explanatory basis, then we simplify it by some other means. Indeed, Kant suggests that this simplification relies on illicit metaphysical moves. Identifying a common root requires taking our "subjective necessity" for a simplified faculty psychology as "objectively necessary" (A648/B676), so that "this idea of a fundamental power in general does not function merely as a problem for hypothetical use, but pretends to objective reality" (A650/B678). Since we cannot reach the basic power in virtue of its explaining our cognitive activities, we reach that power rather by assuming that our diverse faculties *must* have a common cause. Based on the Paralogisms, we should already be unwilling to treat a faculty (like apperception) as an effect from which we can reason to a cause. Kant's discussion in the Appendix upholds the illegitimacy of this move, even in the face of reason's demand to simplify our faculty psychology: we cannot assume our faculties have a common cause just for the sake of an elegant theory. There is no reason (evidential or logical) to assume that our faculty psychology bottoms out in a single basic power, however satisfying such a simplification might be.

From here, Wolff's mistake becomes clear. Wolff's basic power of representation cannot be put forth as an explanation for our cognitive activities; though the power identifies a commonality between the faculties of sensibility and understanding, this commonality fails to explain fully the activities enabled by those faculties.[19] Further, his identification of the basic power of representation is not supported by a logical argument, for it is logically possible that we possess multiple fundamental faculties, rather than a single basic power. Thus, Wolff's argument must rely on the illicit metaphysical assumption that there must be a basic power, treating the faculties as effects that must share a common cause. However, this move goes beyond the bounds of our experience, specifically by extending the category of causality further than it can go. We do not sense our cognitive capacities, and thus cannot apply categories like causality to them. Wolff's

---

[18] As Henrich summarizes, "the thought which today one is hardly willing to explicitly carry through, viz., that subjectivity is constituted of several mutually independent factors, contingent in their reciprocal relations, is here indeed assumed by Kant as a possibility that remains where all insight ends" (Henrich 1994: 21).

[19] As Henrich reconstructs, it was Crusius, before Kant, who worried about the "arbitrarily abstracted general power" offered by Wolff (Henrich 1994: 23).

simplification of our faculty psychology relies on extending our concepts beyond their reach.

The German Idealists make a different, but related mistake. The German Idealists also simplify our cognitive psychology, but now by way of a generational story, where one faculty serves to generate the rest through its activity. Consider how this simplification also differs from Kant's method for simplifying our cognitive psychology: the fundamental faculty is not offered up as the capacity enabling some particular cognitive activity, like remembering or sensing. More capacities must be on the table besides, for example, self-consciousness to explain these particular activities. Rather, the fundamental faculty is supposed to generate the faculties enabling such activities. The method departs from explaining the conditions of our cognitive activities, to explaining the generation of faculties themselves. Insofar as this is a causal story, where the activities of one faculty causes another faculty to come into being, the German Idealists also extend the concept of cause beyond where it can go.[20] We are not permitted to treat faculties as causal entities in their own right, even if the benefits include unifying the faculties that need unifying in order to explain the possibility of synthetic a priori judgment.

This looks like bad news for Heidegger's interpretation, which also seeks a common root for sensibility and understanding. But in what follows, I will show that though Heidegger identifies a common root, he does not attempt to overcome Kant's dualism, in contrast to the other Post-Kantian interpreters. Rather than attempting to identify a more fundamental, homogeneous faculty beyond or behind Kant's analyses, Heidegger examines the fit between the heterogeneous faculties that Kant already ascribes to the human being. By embracing of the heterogeneity of the faculties, I will argue, Heidegger's quest for a common root does not surpass the bounds of what we can know.

4 A Heterogeneous Root

It's easy to think that Heidegger, like the German Idealists, similarly attempts to simplify the faculties by rooting them in a single,

---

[20] There are avenues for the German Idealists (and their interpreters) to avoid this problem. For example, James D. Reid argues in response to Henrich that Fichte does not take there to be *causal* relationships between the faculties (2003: 276); further, Reid suggests that for Fichte the faculties are "equiprimordial" and that Heidegger borrows this language from Fichte (2003: 268 n. 86). What is important for my argument is that Heidegger has an interpretation that avoids this objection, thus avoiding a potential pitfall for an interpretation seeking a common root.

homogeneous power. Indeed, the Neo-Kantian Ernst Cassirer attributes to Heidegger a "monism of imagination" that denies the "dualism of the sensuous and intelligible world" (Cassirer 1967: 148).[21] Like the German Idealists, Heidegger asks after what unifies sensibility and understanding, and answers that the imagination is the "unifying root" (PIK 283). However, Heidegger also denies that his common root is a basic power: "the transcendental power of imagination ... is not something that could be thought of as a 'basic power' of the soul" (KPM 98). He insists, further, that he does not offer some "monistic-empirical explanation of the remaining faculties of the soul based on the power of imagination" (KPM 98).[22] Rather than finding some deeper, homogeneous faculty behind Kant's dual faculties, Heidegger speaks rather of an "essential structure" (KPM 98) or an "original unity" (KPM 99) that brings them together. That is, Heidegger attempts a unification that maintains the heterogeneity of the unified elements, rather than dissolving it: "the original, rich wholeness of one which is composed of many members," rather than "the empty simplicity of an ultimate principle" (KPM 45). Such a unification relies on explaining how the faculties fit together, rather than arguing that they derive from some homogeneous capacity.

Though Henrich claims that Hegel's interpretation is "probably ... the model" for Heidegger's interpretation (Henrich 1994: 43), Henrich does recognize where Heidegger departs from the German Idealists: "according to Heidegger, each of those speculative interpretations, from Wolff to Hegel, but also Kant's skepticism regarding the possibility of such an enterprise, presupposes that the unity in question, insofar as it is original and indestructible, must consist in a simple structural element" (48). Rather than unifying the faculties in a "simple structural element," Heidegger insists that the common root is a pluralistic structure of "equiprimordial moments" (49). However, Henrich does not recognize that this position is a development of Kant rather than something externally motivated, by Heidegger's own work in *Being and Time*. My analyses in this section will show, however, the Kantian passages to which Heidegger responds: in particular, Heidegger picks up on Kant's insistence on the

---

[21] I am indebted to Truwant (2022) for bringing this passage to my attention.
[22] Indeed, Heidegger in *Being and Time* offers critical comments on this move: "The phenomenon of the equiprimordiality of constitutive items has often been disregarded in ontology, because of a methodologically unrestrained tendency to derive everything and anything from some simple 'primal ground'" (BT 131). The unrestrained search for a basic power misses what Heidegger calls "equiprimordiality": when multiple structures are equally basic, jointly serving to constitute something.

diversity of the faculties, while also trying to build on Kant's claims that they are complementary and even "inseparably combined" (A102). In so doing, I will argue, Heidegger avoids Kant's objections to Wolff and, by extension, the German Idealists. Thus, Heidegger's interpretation of the common root can be motivated by Kant's thought and the shortcomings of previous Kant interpretations, rather than Heidegger's own *Being and Time*.

Just where Heidegger puts forth the imagination as Kant's common root, he adds a footnote distinguishing himself from earlier interpreters who sought a common root in the imagination:

> The explicit characterization of the power of imagination as a basic faculty must have driven home the meaning of this faculty to Kant's contemporaries. Thus Fichte and Schelling, and in his own way Jacobi as well, have attributed an essential role to the power of imagination. Whether in this way the essence of the power of imagination as seen by Kant was recognized, adhered to, or even interpreted in a more original way, cannot be discussed here. The following interpretation of the transcendental power of imagination grows out of another way of questioning and moves, so to speak, in the opposite direction from that of German Idealism. (KPM 97–98 n. 196)

Though this footnote refrains from evaluating the German Idealist interpretation of the imagination, it seems to imply that such interpretations misunderstand Kant's faculty of imagination; Heidegger, at any rate, will take his own interpretation in the opposite direction. Heidegger explicitly comments on the viability of these interpretations on later pages: "All reinterpretation of the pure power of imagination as a function of pure thinking – a re-interpretation which 'German Idealism' even accentuated subsequent to the second edition of the *Critique of Pure Reason* – misunderstands its specific essence" (KPM 138). It might be tempting to think that Heidegger objects to the German Idealist interpretation simply because it construes imagination as *thinking*, and Heidegger rejects the idea that thinking could be the fundamental faculty. Heidegger does repeatedly lambast the philosophical tradition for its prioritization of thinking. Yet the surrounding discussion makes it clear that Heidegger's own interpretation also departs from the homogeneity of the German idealist interpretation, where imagination is *only* thinking.

Heidegger sees German Idealist interpretations as following in the tradition of the second edition of the *Critique of Pure Reason*, to the detriment of their interpretations. According to Heidegger, the second edition revises the status of the imagination, portraying it (or, at least, its transcendental or productive capacity) as "an effect of the understanding on sensibility" – "spontaneity" (B152). This edit effaces the heterogeneity of the imagination, apparently blocking the most promising path to unifying the Transcendental Aesthetic and Analytic. From here, we can appreciate where Heidegger thinks he differs from the German Idealists, who likewise attribute a fundamental role to the imagination in unifying sensibility and understanding:

> If, however, as occurs in the second edition, the transcendental power of imagination is deleted as a particular grounding faculty and if its function is taken over by the understanding as mere spontaneity, then the possibility of grasping pure sensibility and pure thinking with regard to their unity in a finite, human reason diminishes, as does even the possibility of making it into a problem. (KPM 137)

The German Idealists make the mistake not only of prioritizing thinking, in keeping with the broader philosophical tradition, but also of eliminating the heterogeneity of the imagination. When one begins to see the imagination as a "function of the understanding,"[23] rather than something that shares in both sensibility and understanding, one loses the question of how those two faculties come together, as well as the most promising avenue for answering that question.

Beyond his comments on the German Idealists, Heidegger's discussion of Kant's dualistic faculty psychology – his "duality of stems" (KPM 96) – indicates that Heidegger's search for a common root does not seek to reduce the diversity of Kant's faculty psychology. Heidegger in fact embraces this diversity by insisting on not a *duality* of basic faculties but rather a *triad* of basic faculties. In line with his two-strand interpretation of Kant, Heidegger argues that Kant equivocates on the number of basic faculties: sometimes the basic faculties are two, but other times they are three. There is conflicting textual evidence, going in both directions. Thus, Heidegger entreats us to favor the better argument, which on his view is the triad thesis. The three basic faculties, as Heidegger interprets them, lead us to the unity of the faculties in a threefold temporal structure.

Kant's larger framing of the book points to a duality of faculties. The structure of the first *Critique* makes room for sensibility (in the Aesthetic) and understanding (in the Analytic), leaving the imagination "homeless" within this structure (KPM 95). Kant's framing comments often reinforce this duality, such as in the first sentence of the Analytic: "Our cognition arises from two fundamental sources in the mind, the first of which is the reception of representations (the receptivity of impressions), the second the faculty for

---

[23] Kant added this phrase to his own copy of the first edition, replacing "function of the soul" (A178).

cognizing an object by means of these representations (spontaneity of concepts)" (A50/B74). Further, the introduction to the Dialectic proclaims that there are "no other sources of cognition besides these two" (A294/B350).

In support of the triad thesis, though, Heidegger refers to the very passage where Kant explains that we can simplify our cognitive psychology no further than "three original sources ... *sense, imagination,* and *understanding*" (A94/B127). Moreover, just before enumerating the "supreme principle of all synthetic judgments," Kant points to three sources of our "a priori representations" (A155/B194). This comment itself refers back to the strategy of the A-Deduction, which seeks to link three syntheses: one in intuition, one in imagination, and one in concept (see especially A98f., A115). While such passages might not provide the considered judgment of framing remarks, they are crucial parts of the first *Critique* that are likely to find Kant wrestling with the phenomena themselves; here, Kant deals directly with central philosophical issues rather than taking a removed, summarizing perspective.

In such passages, Heidegger suggests, one can begin to see how Kant's faculties are unified. In particular, Heidegger offers a temporal interpretation of the three syntheses that Kant distributes among the three basic faculties in the A-Deduction. That is, each synthesis is linked to a different temporal capacity: the capacity for reaching back into the past (imagination), the capacity for taking up what is present (intuition), and the capacity for reaching ahead into the future (understanding). While the details of this interpretation will be laid out in Chapter 5, we can appreciate here both the violence of Heidegger's strategy and how it differs from Wolff's search for a basic power. Like Wolff, Heidegger tries to identify what sensibility and understanding have in common; he finds that Kant overstates their differences, for both faculties are related to time. Applied to the understanding, this claim is violent, for it denies several passages in the first *Critique* that portray the understanding as atemporal (in line with traditional portrayals of the understanding). Be that as it may, Heidegger departs from Wolff in that this commonality does not help him arrive at a single power from which understanding and sensibility are supposed to be derived.[24] Rather, our temporal capacities form a complex whole. Complex, because reaching back, seizing, and reaching ahead are different

---

[24] Heidegger's endorsement of the Marburg Neo-Kantians becomes visible here. Instead of finding homogeneity among sensibility and understanding by backtracking to a more general faculty, the Marburg Neo-Kantians suggest that the dual faculties are not so diverse as initially thought – for both are forms of thinking. For example, Natorp contrasts object-thinking with lawful-thinking (as reported by Truwant [2022: 114 n. 15]). Heidegger's approach also surpasses "all attempts at mediation" (PIK 54) because Heidegger suggests that the two faculties are time-related.

capacities that cannot be reduced to one another. Whole, because each of these capacities refers to the other two, depending on the others to perform its own characteristic activity. The ambition of Heidegger's Kant interpretation is to show how understanding and sensibility are unified in this complex, threefold structure.

Why call this heterogeneous structure a root? For Heidegger, the imagination is root-like not in that it collapses the differences between the two stems of cognition, but rather in that it "lets the stems grow from out of itself, lending them support and stability" (KPM 97). Like a root sustains and stabilizes its stems, the imagination sustains and stabilizes sensibility and understanding. The threefold, transcendental structure of the imagination sustains sensibility and understanding by producing the a priori elements used by each faculty. In Chapter 2, I explained why the imagination is supposed to be the source of these a priori elements, as the a priori forms of intuition and the a priori concepts each require both spontaneity and receptivity for their production. Rather than rehearsing those arguments, I will here consider how this productive work of the imagination sustains and stabilizes the empirical work of sensibility and understanding.

The a priori intuitions of space and time are, on Kant's view, quite determinate. For example, time is a singular whole. There is only *one* form of time (simplistically, everything is on a single timeline, such that everything can be temporally related, e.g., three hours apart). Specific stretches of time are only limitations, or parts, of this larger whole; t_1 and t_2 carve out different segments of the same timeline. This form conditions every specific, empirical intuition that we might have. That is, all the sensible information that we take up is experienced as occupying a specific time. As the imagination, on Heidegger's view, creates this a priori form, it sustains and stabilizes the empirical work of sensibility: the a priori form of time enables empirical intuiting, and stabilizes that activity by holding fixed a determinate picture of time. Despite the vast variety of what we sense, time remains a single whole.

Transitioning to the understanding, the a priori concepts, or categories, commit us to a determinate view of what the contents of the world are like. For example, we understand the concept of cause as necessary following – that is, one state follows another necessarily, according to a rule. This concept enables our experience of particular events, such that we can experience some state as following necessarily from an earlier state. If the imagination produces such concepts, then it sustains the empirical work of the understanding, where different events (for example) are identified. It also provides the stability of a single version of causality, fixed over the course of our many and various experiences. Our understanding of causality does not waver, for example, between efficient and spontaneous causality. Rather, the conceptual acts of the understanding are consistent and comparable.

Importantly, and as will become evident when we turn to Heidegger's interpretation of the Schematism, the imagination does not produce these a priori forms separately; rather, they are produced in a complex but unified process. In this process, time is affected or formed, and the categories affect or form it. It is this process that produces the determinate senses of space and time, as well as the categories, preparing them for their empirical roles. On Heidegger's view, neither the pure intuiting of time nor the pure thinking of the categories is possible outside this process, as isolated a priori elements. The receptivity of the form of time is required to fix the categories, sustaining them as rules (KPM 108); the spontaneity of concepts is required to determine the form of time so that, for example, it takes the particular form of a sequence of moments on a timeline.[25]

From these considerations, we can begin to see why for Heidegger the heterogeneous root of imagination is not only a *sustaining* root but also a *unifying* root: the imagination is "a making-possible of the original unity of both and with it the essential unity of transcendence as a whole" (KPM 95). The imagination allows each faculty, individually, to have unified activity ("making-possible the original unity of both"). In sensibility, everything is taken up into one whole, and in understanding, a consistent set of concepts is applied. But, further, the complex structure of the imagination unifies sensibility and understanding, where they play qualitatively different but reciprocal roles in that structure.

Heidegger's common root lacks the metaphysical baggage of his predecessors. His root is not a basic power, comprising a single simple capacity. It is a unification of the capacities that Kant already identified (using, presumably, his approved procedure of reasoning from activities to capacities). Thus, Heidegger need not rely on the illicit metaphysical move, that reasons from the faculties as effects to their common cause. The root is already there, in the interconnections between Kant's faculties of sensibility, imagination, and understanding. Heidegger does not,

---

[25] For example, the following is one passage where the heterogeneous components of this process are described: "But this unified whole must allow itself to be discerned in advance regarding this togetherness of its manifoldness which is for the most part indistinct. Pure intuition – originally unifying, i.e., giving unity – must *catch* sight of this unity" (KPM 100).

further, establish an order of causal precedence between Kant's faculties, a narrative that turns from the evidence of our cognitive activities to the faculties themselves as potential causes and effects of one another. Heidegger does not identify a single faculty as generational, or causally prior, to the other two, but rather emphasizes that three qualitatively different capacities are unified in a complex structure. Heidegger, in brief, is not tracing a causal story from a Kantian faculty to a deeper cause.

One might worry, though, that Heidegger relies on an illicit metaphysical move of a different variety. Even if Heidegger does not identify a deeper, common cause for the faculties, perhaps he takes there to be causal community among them; perhaps they are united, on Heidegger's view, because they causally interact with one another. Such a view would likewise make an illicit metaphysical move, because it would extend the category of causality to the faculties even though we cannot sense them. According to Kant's critical philosophy, this would extend the category of causality beyond its bounds. However, I see Heidegger as making a more radical (and more promising) suggestion. For Wolff, Kant, and the Post-Kantian tradition, to find a common root is to establish causal relations between the faculties; establishing the unity of the human perspective relies on telling a certain kind of causal story (where all faculties lead back to a common cause). Heidegger, in my view, thinks that we can unite the faculties – arriving at the common root – by spelling out *relations of a different kind* between them.

Such relations are hinted at by Kant's own passages, where Kant suggests a complementarity between the faculties. We saw the *Anthropology*, for example, refer to the "close union" between sensibility and understanding (Ak.7:178). Likewise, the first *Critique* gestures at their reciprocal cognitive roles: while understanding "works on the raw material of sensible sensations" (A1), "all thought ... must ultimately be related to intuitions, thus, in our case, to sensibility, since there is no other way in which objects are given to us" (A19/B33). Finally, and very importantly for Heidegger's reading of the Transcendental Deduction, Kant claims that the syntheses he ascribes to each of the faculties are "inseparably combined," enumerating the mutual dependency that indicates their inseparable combination (A102). Heidegger wants to deepen and make good on these relational claims, which should not, if Kant is making them, refer to causal relations (on pain of overextending the concept of cause).

Spelling out these claims would set up some sort of a priori contact between those faculties that need to relate to one another for us to make synthetic a priori judgments: the faculty of understanding and the faculty of sensibility. In so doing, it would establish a point of contact between the a priori forms of intuition and the a priori categories, the very elements that need to combine for us to have synthetic a priori principles. Indeed, and as we have seen, Heidegger has even more specific things to say about this combination: the categories affect or form time, articulating its determinate structure.

However, I must provide evidence that this is in fact Heidegger's radical move. Some of this evidence will come in Chapter 5: in my treatment of the Transcendental Deduction, we will see how Heidegger cashes out Kant's claim that the respective syntheses attributed to sensibility, imagination, and understanding are inseparably combined. Here, I propose to motivate my reading by turning to Heidegger's comments on Kant in *Being and Time*. These will show that Heidegger endorses Kant's conclusion in the Paralogisms, that categories like causality and substantiality ought not be extended to the human being. They will show, further, that Heidegger wishes that Kant had said more about the human being by some other means, if not by way of the categories themselves. Doing so will introduce a new sort of metaphysical baggage, however: a sort of being who is not captured by Kant's categories.

In *Being and Time*, Heidegger approves of Kant's conclusion in the Paralogisms, that we are not to develop our knowledge of human beings by applying the categories to them (BT 318).[26] The ideas of physical endurance over time (i.e., substantiality) and lawlike interactions between particulars (i.e., causality) do not do justice to the distinct kind of beings that we are. However, Heidegger still holds that "an *ontological* Interpretation of Selfhood is possible" (BT 318); accordingly, Heidegger complains that Kant "failed to provide an ontology with Dasein as its theme or (to put this in Kantian language) to give a preliminary ontological analytic of the subjectivity of the subject" (BT 24, 318). Where Kant suggests that the human subject must remain unknown, Heidegger insists that we can press on, and say more about the structure of the human being. His idea is that Kant's own system betrays a familiarity with a sort of being different from those beings that Kant makes the sole object of our knowledge – a *human*

---

[26] Heidegger also endorses the outcome of the Paralogisms in passing in the Kant book: "Should Kant, who worked out the paralogism of substantiality based on the particular laying of the ground for ontology, have meant by the 'fixed and perduring' I something like a mental substance?" (KPM 135). Heidegger implies that the answer is no. Further, Heidegger elsewhere criticizes those moments in Kant where Kant himself seems to go back on his findings in the Paralogisms, conceiving the existence of the human being like the existence of an object. For example, in the 1927 lecture series, Heidegger says: "One thing remains striking. Kant speaks of the *existence* [*Dasein*] *of the person* as he does of *the existence of a thing* [*Ding*]. He says the person exists as an end in itself. He uses 'exist' in the sense of presence-at-hand" (BPP 147, translation modified; see also EHF 168, 203).

being quite different in structure from the objects that appear to us. Heidegger agrees with Kant that one cannot know this being by way of Kant's theoretical categories, but disagrees with Kant's further conclusion that if we cannot know the human being by way of the categories, we cannot know the human being at all.

According to Heidegger, Kant's account is hampered by the fact that he recognizes only one kind of being: the substantial, causally related beings that populate the realm of appearances. In *Being and Time*, Heidegger dubs these sorts of beings "present-at-hand" and suggests that metaphysicians, Kant included, have myopically focused on this kind of being; this charge is repeated in his 1927–1928 lecture series, when he says that "beginning in antiquity and up to and beyond Kant, a being is understood primarily as a being that belongs to 'nature,' that is, a being understood as present-at-hand" (PIK 30). Kant's critical system nonetheless challenges this one-note conception of a being, insofar as the human knower lies at the basis of the system and yet eludes these categories – by Kant's own arguments in the Paralogisms, and by Kant's depictions of our cognitive architecture, which hint at noncausal relations of complementarity and combination. However, since Kant was confined to a limited conception of what counts as a being – the present-at-hand alone – he did not recognize that his analyses of the human cognitive faculties were on the verge of identifying an entirely different kind of being. As a result, Kant failed to provide a fuller analysis of the kind of beings that we are; he does not spell out the noncausal relationships that hold between our cognitive faculties. Heidegger's account of the imagination, however, is supposed to fill in this lacuna, examining the faculties themselves for the key to their fit, such that they are unified to characterize one kind of being.

However, admitting a being of this kind has an interesting result: the definiteness with which we know appearances is not possible for our kind of being (i.e., our *human* being). Consider an appearance – say, the ship that moves downstream in Kant's Second Analogy. Determinate predicates can be applied to this sort of being: it's made of a certain kind of material, has a determinate length, and moves at a quantifiable speed. Or, more basically, it is a substance in causal community with other beings, such as the wind and river current pushing it downstream. The human knower, for Heidegger and Kant both, cannot be captured by these concepts – neither a priori categories (e.g., substance) nor the empirical concepts built upon those categories (e.g., wooden). While we can describe the sort of structures that we human beings bring to experience, there is something that is and must remain open-ended about this description. Certainly, we are given over to what we intuit in space and time, which we struggle to understand. However, in Heidegger's view, we are not unequivocally bound to these depictions of space and time, nor to the conceptual resources that we use to make sense of our experience. Rather, they make up an interpretive scheme to which we commit ourselves. If we are always knowers, it remains open whether we must be *this* kind of knower.

Thus, there is a sense in which the root *does* remain unknown for Heidegger: we human beings are not some enduring, determinate thing that can finally be pinned down and defined once and for all. We are not a present-at-hand floor or base. Indeed, Heidegger appreciates the way in which Kant's passing reference to a common root unsettles his ensuing inquiry. Kant's inquiry, from the first naming of the "common but to us unknown" root, evades a complete and settled answer: "it leads not to the crystal clear, absolute evidence of a first maxim and principle, but rather goes into and points consciously toward the unknown" (KPM 26). The common root remains unknown in the way we remain unknown to ourselves: the basic way that we understand the world, and ourselves in relation to that world, could be challenged, revised, and even upended. In this partial way, Heidegger does justice to Kant's claim that the root is "to us unknown." While the kind of beings we are, captured by the threefold structure of the transcendental imagination, is known, the content informing that structure remains open-ended, as determinate rules for cognizing the world around us are not inscribed into the structure itself.

Heidegger's open-ended reading of the common root also bears on the other metaphor that he uses to frame his interpretation: providing a foundation for metaphysics. Partway through his interpretation, Heidegger predicts that

> The further unveiling of the originality of the ground-laying will be even less likely to lead to an absolute explanatory basis than did the stages of the setting-free of the ground covered by Kant that have already been presented. The strangeness of the previously laid ground which must have forced itself upon Kant cannot disappear. Rather, it will increase with the growing originality, if indeed man's metaphysical nature as a finite creature is at once the most unknown and the most actual to him.

Kant attempts to ground the metaphysical principles that apply a priori to any being we encounter, such as "every event has a cause." The ground that Kant provides is the human knower: these principles are grounded on the a priori resources that we bring to experience. However, if Heidegger is right about the open-ended nature of our cognition, metaphysics is based on nothing more than rules that we give to ourselves – rules to which we commit, rather than rules that are irrevocably inscribed into our cognitive psychology. This is not the solid foundation that might come from a first maxim or principle. As Heidegger later puts it: "Does not this ground-laying lead to an abyss?" (KPM 117).

5 Conclusion

Let's return to Heidegger's larger interpretive method, where two strands of argument battle throughout Kant's text: a more traditional strand of argument prioritizing the understanding and a more promising strand of argument prioritizing the imagination.

This chapter helps us see some benefits of Heidegger's preferred strand of argument, over and above the traditional strand prioritizing the understanding. These benefits appear precisely where Heidegger improves upon the German Idealists. Though several German Idealists also identify the imagination as fundamental, this is only a surface similarity of their accounts, as Heidegger differently defines the imagination. In particular, the German Idealists see the imagination as a homogeneous faculty of pure spontaneity or thinking. By contrast, Heidegger sees the imagination as pluralistic, uniting diverse capacities in a single structure. Thus, despite the surface convergence of their accounts, Heidegger's improvement upon the German Idealists helps us appreciate how an argument prioritizing a pluralistic faculty like Heidegger's transcendental imagination is superior to an argument prioritizing a homogeneous faculty like spontaneous thinking.

Because Heidegger sees the imagination as a pluralistic, multifaceted structure, he avoids positing a basic power from which Kant's dualistic faculties are supposed to be derived. Thus, he avoids the metaphysical move that Kant rejects in the Transcendental Dialectic: treating the faculties as effects that can lead us back to some fundamental cause. In so doing, Heidegger offers a foundationalism that, even as it unifies Kantian cognitive psychology, does not jeopardize Kant's insistence on the limitations on human knowledge. The human being, even if unified, is ever finite.

Heidegger's interpretation is a violent one. In order to spell out how sensibility and understanding can fit into the same unified structure, Heidegger must insist that the understanding is temporal, despite counter-evidence in Kant's text. We will see in Chapter 5 how Heidegger justifies this particular violence. Nevertheless, Heidegger achieves an interpretation that is more in the spirit of Kant's text than of German Idealism by allowing Kant's cognitive psychology its complexity and maintaining its limits.

CHAPTER 4

The Metaphysical Deduction and Schematism

Over the course of his interpretation, Heidegger attributes to Kant a standard philosophical procedure: in particular, Kant "clings first of all to the most feasible, known formulations which should lead in a preliminary way to the problem" (KPM 77). In other words, Kant attempts to get a toehold on the difficult metaphysical issues that he treats by using traditional philosophical terminology. However, Heidegger is most interested in those moments where Kant outgrows that traditional terminology and offers his own unique insights into the phenomena under discussion. The tensions that Heidegger tracks in Kant's text reveal the interplay between the "known formulations" and Kant's new, phenomenologically compelling insights.

Heidegger's portrayal of Kant's method is unsurprising in light of Heidegger's own philosophical views; indeed, we should not expect Kant to be the only philosopher who uses tradition as a crutch for framing their inquiry, by Heidegger's lights. On Heidegger's general view of understanding, our understanding of some context – whether a practical context like a workshop or the complicated theoretical space of some philosophical field – is determined first of all by others. Thus, in *Being and Time*, Heidegger introduces the concept of the they-self (*das Man*), what everyone (and no one in particular) takes to be obvious about the contents of the world and what ought to be done with those contents. When we first learn philosophy, then, we access a theoretical space that has been carved up by others. In contemporary Anglophone philosophy, for example, we might take it for granted that philosophy can be divided into the philosophy of language, epistemology, metaphysics, and so forth; we might learn the concepts common to one of those fields, using them as the starting point in our own philosophical inquiries.

However, philosophical breakthrough relies on surpassing that tradition and experiencing the phenomena in question anew. Heidegger's discussion of Aristotle in the early pages of *Kant and the Problem of Metaphysics* provides a quick illustration of this view of the philosophical enterprise. Heidegger sees Aristotle as struggling with the relationship between *beings as such* (what characterizes particular beings, such as god or the human soul) and *beings as a whole* (what it is to be, in general). In Heidegger's view, Aristotle senses that these two areas of inquiry are interconnected, but struggles to articulate how they fit together.[1] Metaphysics, for Aristotle, "is the title of a fundamental philosophical difficulty" (KPM 4). However, subsequent thinkers failed to grasp Aristotle's question, uncritically taking up the results of his line of questioning. Namely, the Scholastics adopted Aristotle's categories, taking it for granted that metaphysics is to be divided into these two areas. They sought to further divide the theoretical space they inherited from Aristotle, specifying that *metaphysica specialis* (inquiry into beings as such) is divided into theology (God), cosmology (nature), and psychology (humankind), whereas *metaphysica generalis* refers to inquiring into "the being 'in general'" (KPM 5–6). Working with Aristotle's terms more so than the phenomena he attempted to explain, the Scholastics failed to provide new insight into those phenomena.

By contrast, Heidegger asserts that Kant "is immediately brought into dialogue with Aristotle and Plato. Ontology now becomes a problem for the first time ... the first and deepest shockwave strikes the structure of metaphysics" (KPM 8). Kant is able to do this not by way of a deep dive into Aristotelian philology but rather by considering the phenomena for himself. Like Aristotle, Kant allowed himself to be disturbed by the study of metaphysics. As Heidegger outlines, Kant worried that metaphysics might lack a "binding proof" of the concepts it seeks – concepts, that is, that provide a universal and necessary characterization of beings (6). Driven by this concern, Kant inquired into the "making-manifest of beings as such" (7), leading him to argue that our access to particular beings is dependent on our understanding of Being in general (e.g., that beings conform to categories like causality, substantiality, and so forth). That is, Kant spells out the relationship between beings as such and as a whole, answering Aristotle's question: our knowledge of specific beings (*metaphysica specialis*) is grounded on our knowledge of what it means to be, in general (*metaphysica generalis*) (8). Answering Aristotle's question, Kant poses a new one that makes ontology "a problem for the first time": How is this knowledge of what it means to be in general possible – that is, how is synthetic a priori judgment possible? If traditional metaphysical divisions

---

[1] For a helpful discussion of Heidegger's reading of Aristotle, see Nir 2021.

framed Kant's inquiry, he was able to make progress in the field of metaphysics by looking into the phenomena under discussion for himself.

Heidegger's interpretive method is trained to those moments where Kant goes beyond his traditional framing and articulates a new insight into the phenomena. As I have outlined in previous chapters, he offers a two-strand interpretation of Kant. In particular, the two strands correspond to:

(a) The strand of argument that rehearses traditional terms and theses
(b) The strand of argument that surpasses tradition.

While identifying both strands, and attending to the moments where they intersect, Heidegger props up strand (b) as the line of argument that offers Kant's innovative insights into the subject matter. It is easy to see why Heidegger would see strand (b) as Kant's philosophical innovation; strand (a) offers terms and theses enumerated by others, so they are not properly Kant's own. But why think that strand (b) always offers insights? Couldn't Kant (or some other philosopher) go off-track, detracting from the insights that tradition provides? In fact, on Heidegger's view, the way we relate to tradition covers over insights; we first see the division of the theoretical space as obvious (how things are done) rather than appreciating the concerns that generated those divisions. Moreover, and as I covered in Chapter 1, anxiety drives us away from metaphysical insights. The history of metaphysics, Heidegger thinks, bears the record of those flights. Anxiety about the sort of beings that we are has driven metaphysicians away from insights into our kind of being, and humans are consistently mischaracterized as beings comparable to nonhuman entities (where we, e.g., have certain stable properties). Given our initial relationship to tradition, and the way that tradition is supposed to retreat from certain metaphysical truths, it is unsurprising that Heidegger would think that strand (b) offers greater insight than the line of argument rehearsing traditional theses. But nevertheless, Heidegger backs up his support of strand (b) by inquiring for himself into the insight provided by each strand – whether, that is, the strand does justice to the phenomena under consideration.

In this chapter, I outline Heidegger's interpretation of two sections of Kant's *Critique of Pure Reason*: the Metaphysical Deduction and the Schematism. In Heidegger's view, these two sections inquire into the source of the concepts that human understanding possesses independently of experience, or a priori: the categories. In both chapters, Heidegger suggests, Kant takes up traditional philosophical terms and theses as a first step into his inquiry. However, things start to get interesting when Kant surpasses those traditional terms; in both cases, Heidegger sees an innovative line of argument prioritizing the imagination emerge from a more traditional setup.

However, Heidegger's treatment of these two sections reveals some variety in how one can apply Heidegger's interpretive method to the different parts of a text. Heidegger suggests that the traditional strand of argument is more prominent in the Metaphysical Deduction; while Kant attempts to derive the categories from the atemporal logic of the understanding, his references to the faculty of imagination at certain critical junctures reveal the breakdown of those attempts. By contrast, the emerging, innovative line of argument is more prominent in the Schematism, which quickly surpasses its traditional framing in order to offer a phenomenologically compelling account of how the categories, as ways of interpreting time, inform our perceptual experience.

In Section 1, I outline the dominant arguments that each section provides, on Heidegger's interpretation. Section 2 offers Heidegger's account of how the traditional strand of argument unravels in the Metaphysical Deduction. Finally, Section 3 discusses the phenomenological insight that Heidegger finds in the innovative line of argument that dominates the Schematism.

1 The Metaphysical Deduction and Schematism in Context

Heidegger reads the Metaphysical Deduction and the Schematism as inquiring into the source of the categories and propping up competing answers to this question. The dominant (but not the only) line of argument in the Metaphysical Deduction suggests that the categories are generated by applying logical forms of judgment – possessed independently by human understanding – to the spatiotemporal world. By contrast, the dominant (but not the only) line of argument in the Schematism suggests that the categories are generated by way of the activity of the imagination unifying and articulating time. The categories do not come from concepts that are independently prepossessed, but are rather "guid[ed] and sustain[ed]" by time itself (KPM 63). The two lines of argument can be visualized as follows:

Path 1	Path 2
Logical judgments	*Time*
yield categories	yields categories
when applied to the spatiotemporal world	*when unified by the imagination*

Heidegger defends the second path, proposed by the Schematism, as the route that can avoid the objections dogging the first path, proposed by the

Metaphysical Deduction. Most importantly, the Schematism offers compelling phenomenological evidence for its conclusions, rather than drawing them uncritically from tradition.

The two paths represented above reflect Heidegger's general claim that the understanding and the imagination battle for priority over the course of the first *Critique*. The first path suggests the categories are generated from materials already possessed and supplied by the understanding, giving it priority in generating the categories. By contrast, the second path suggests that the imagination generates the categories, by acting on and unifying time; this path assigns the imagination the lead role in generating the categories. Reflecting Heidegger's contention that the strand of argument prioritizing the imagination represents Kant's most promising strand, Heidegger goes so far as to say that "the present interpretation, which appears to be violent, can be justified only in view of the doctrine of the Schematism" (PIK 247). Heidegger does not devote much space to the Schematism proper in the 1927–1928 lecture series, claiming rather that the Schematism is in the background of his interpretation of other sections: "in the way we set out to interpret the transcendental aesthetic and analytic, especially the transcendental deduction, we fundamentally dealt with the problem of the Schematism" (PIK 292). Nevertheless, he maintains that the Schematism shows that "Kant, in a fumbling and rough sort of way, indeed seeks the core of the transcendental deduction in time" (PIK 247). As he works out in more detail in the Kant book, it is this section that illustrates that the imagination generates the categories by acting on time.

While this chapter treats the Metaphysical Deduction and Schematism, it will be helpful to say a few words here about the Transcendental Deduction, which is the subject of Chapter 5. After all, Heidegger's interpretation of the imagination is based on primarily these three sections. But, further, Heidegger defines the two sections I treat in this chapter in relation to the Transcendental Deduction: the Metaphysical Deduction offers an "anticipation" of the Transcendental Deduction (PIK 227), whereas the Schematism "grounds" the Transcendental Deduction (PIK 292). I suggest that we understand these claims as follows: the competing strand of argument that emerges in the Metaphysical Deduction, undermining the dominant strand of argument, *anticipates* the role of the imagination that is further developed in the Transcendental Deduction, where the "manifold of intuition" is "prepared and rendered accessible" (PIK 227). By contrast, the Schematism *grounds* that role by providing a phenomenologically compelling illustration that the imagination generates categories by "working with pure temporal relations" (PIK 292). The analyses in the present chapter will show why Heidegger thinks that an argument prioritizing the understanding in the Metaphysical Deduction is unsuccessful, and why he thinks that an argument prioritizing the imagination in the Schematism has phenomenological force.

However, it is not until Chapter 5, treating the Transcendental Deduction, that we will get Heidegger's full characterization of the imagination – his argument that the imagination refers to the fundamental, temporal structure of the human being, a structure that can unite the forms of sensibility and a priori concepts. In relation to the arguments in this chapter, Chapter 5 will clarify how the second path, charted above, can begin with time. In short, time is the structure of the human being; categories are generated by acting on and articulating that structure. Thus, when Heidegger discusses – as we will see in a moment – the "ontological origin" of the categories, he means their origin in the temporal structure of the human being. Once again, Heidegger reads Kant as a fundamental ontologist, such that the ontology of objects (an ontology spelled out by the categories) is built upon the ontology of human beings.

2 Anticipation: The Metaphysical Deduction

Heidegger argues that the Metaphysical Deduction ultimately suggests that the categories are essentially related to time, despite Kant's dominant argument attempting to derive them in a purely logical manner. As Kant puts it, he aims to "research the possibility of a priori concepts by seeking them *only in the understanding as their birthplace* and analyzing its pure use in general.... We will therefore pursue the pure concepts into *their first seeds and predispositions in the human understanding*, where they lie ready, until with the opportunity of experience they are finally developed" (A66–67/B90, emphasis mine).[2] However, on Heidegger's view this argument comes undone, gesturing at the conclusion that "the time-related synthesis of the power of imagination, represented generally, yields the pure concept of understanding" (PIK 225). On Heidegger's reading, Kant himself sensed the inadequacies of his dominant argument, subtly undermining it by interjecting a different faculty, the imagination, into his explanation of the origin of the categories. These sections of Kant's work,

---

[2] Heidegger cites this passage disapprovingly as early as 1912, criticizing how it severs thought from intuition (PRMP 44).

ostensibly devoted to understanding alone, actually show that the faculty of imagination is needed to explain the origin of the categories.

In §9, Kant provides a table of judgments that lists the logical rules of thought. The categories – the basic concepts of the understanding that humans must rely on in all cognition of objects – are subsequently provided in a table of categories in §10. Kant suggests that logical rules of thought are the "origin" of the metaphysical rules for the objects we will encounter (B159).[3] As Kant puts the relationship in the B-Deduction, "the categories are nothing other than these very functions for judging, insofar as the manifold of a given intuition is determined with regard to them" (B143). In other words, one arrives at the categories by applying the forms of judgment to what we intuit; both tables can ultimately be traced back to the faculty of understanding, which is bound to certain forms of *judging* and therefore certain forms of *judging objects*. Heidegger argues, however, that the categories have a different source.

On Heidegger's interpretation, Kant's explicit aim in the Metaphysical Deduction – seeking the origin of the categories in the understanding – aligns with the strand of argument that props up the understanding as the fundamental cognitive faculty. By all accounts, Kant means to argue that the understanding is the source of the categories; this is, indeed, how the section is commonly interpreted, and Heidegger recognizes the textual support for this interpretation. However, Heidegger harbors philosophical reservations about this argument, covered in detail in Heidegger's 1927–1928 lecture series. Heidegger's reservations center on the table of judgments from which the categories are supposed to be derived. These reservations can be broken down into three different problems: I will call them the *incompleteness problem*, the *phenomenological problem*, and the *accuracy problem*.

Both the incompleteness and the phenomenological problems descend from Kant's way of presenting the table of judgments; namely, "Kant simply confronts us with the finished table of the forms of judgment" (PIK 175). Kant adopts the forms of judgment identified by previous logicians (especially Aristotle), rather than offering an argument that demonstrates that these are the logical forms of judgment. This procedure is inadequate,

---

[3] Kant's claim, in full: "In the metaphysical deduction, the origin of the a priori categories in general was established through their complete coincidence with the universal logical functions of thinking" (B159). This line continues to be taken up by secondary literature: "the whole purpose of the Metaphysical Deduction is to derive the categories of the former [transcendental logic] from the logical functions specified (supposedly on independent grounds) in the latter [general logic]" (Allison 2004: 140).

by Heidegger's lights, in two different ways. First, the *incompleteness problem* is that this argument fails to establish that the categories so derived have an independent, purely logical origin, because it is not clear that the forms of judgment (from which the categories are supposed to be derived) have such an origin.[4] Without further discussion, there is little reason to think that the forms of judgment are insulated from the world of sense, and from time in particular – little reason to think, in other words, that the forms of judgment have a logical rather than an ontological origin. Rather than settling the origin of the categories, the argument simply raises a different, purportedly earlier question: Do the forms of judgment have an independent, logical origin?

Second, the *phenomenological problem* is that Kant's account of the forms of judgment is not phenomenologically compelling, as Kant fails to demonstrate that these forms are true to our experience of judging. Kant picks up the forms of judgment from tradition, rather than exploring judgment directly, looking into the matter himself. Kant does argue that "if we abstract from all content of a judgment in general, and attend only to the mere form of the understanding in it, we find that the function of thinking in that can be brought under [the] four titles" that organize his table of judgments (A70/B95). However, Kant does not show this, and Heidegger remains unconvinced: "it is not clear at all that, if we 'consider' the mere form of judgment as such, we will 'find' something like the table" (PIK 176). Without phenomenological evidence, his account of the forms that are supposed to govern our judgment, and the forms that are supposed to govern our judgment of objects (i.e., the categories), remains unconvincing.

Finally, as I discussed briefly in Chapter 1, Heidegger points to an *accuracy problem* recognized by earlier interpreters of Kant: in particular, commentators have used formal logic to criticize the table of judgments. Lotze proposed several revisions to the table of judgments, such as eliminating modality as a heading (as this is not, in his view, properly logical) and eliminating negative judgments from the heading of quality (as all judgments, on his account, are positive). Heidegger indicates that many of his contemporary Neo-Kantians were sympathetic to Lotze's objections to the table of judgments and rejected the categories deduced from it on that basis

---

[4] In Heidegger's view, this is one place where Kant should have been more critical in his uptake of tradition. For, on Kant's own view, "logic is that philosophical discipline which is the least grounded and the least rigorously developed" (PIK 177). Heidegger outlines one of logic's ambiguities as follows: "since its inception in Plato and Aristotle logic is permeated by more or less ontological questions" (PIK 177). Therefore, even if the four moments of judgment are an accepted component of logic, they may have an ontological rather than a logical origin.

(PIK 178); if the table of judgments is faulty, then the prospect of deriving the categories from this table is a non-starter. This line of argument continues in contemporary Kant scholarship, as Henry Allison reports: "critics like Strawson, appealing to the conception of logical form operative in modern logic, question not merely Kant's catalogue of these forms but also, and primarily, the whole project of moving from them to anything like Kantian categories" (Allison 2004: 146, refering to Strawson 1966: 78–80).

While recognizing the several problems confronting Kant's dominant line of argument, Heidegger suggests that Kant's discussion hints at a different, competing source of the categories, and one that might avoid these problems. Rather than being "obtained purely logically – regardless of the *object-relatedness* of thinking," the categories could be "obtained first *transcendentally*, by relying upon judgment as an *object-related* function of unification" (PIK 176–177). On this strand of argument, the categories arise not from independent forms of judgment but rather from thought that is already related to the object – thought, as Heidegger puts it later, that is already related to intuition (181), as in the transcendental structure of the imagination.[5]

Kant gestures at this alternate explanation, Heidegger argues, in the six paragraphs between the table of judgments and the table of categories. These paragraphs point beyond the understanding and to another possible source of the categories. In particular, Kant suggests that generating the categories requires running "through the manifold of intuition" (A77/B102) and unifying that manifold by way of thought. The next paragraphs elaborate on this confrontation between intuition and thought, a confrontation that is supposed to yield the categories. In particular, conceptually unifying the manifold of intuition requires a *synthesis*: "the action of putting different representations together with each other and comprehending their manifoldness in one cognition" (A77/B103). Though this synthesis is an action – and understanding is the active, rather than the passive, faculty – Heidegger insists that synthesis could not possibly be attributed to the faculty of understanding. Synthesis here refers to putting together multiple representations "in one" and representations that are apparently intuitive in nature. Having the content and holism of intuition – capturing various parts of the manifold of intuition and holding them together in one whole – "this synthesis is something like a *spontaneous thinking* and something like *giving of an intuition*, while being

---

[5] Heidegger also provides an alternate explanation concerning Kant's starting point, the table of judgments. This table, Heidegger suggests, is not the source of the categories; it is merely an "*index* for *completeness and division* of pure concepts of understanding" (PIK 199).

neither one or the other" (PIK 187). As an action that has an intuitive character, synthesis cannot be attributed to the understanding. Indeed, Kant goes on to attribute synthesis to a different faculty, introduced for the first time in these six paragraphs: synthesis is "the mere effect of the imagination, of a blind though indispensable function of the soul, without which we would have no cognition at all, but of which we are seldom even conscious" (A78/B103). Strikingly, Kant introduces a new faculty in a section that was supposed to be devoted to understanding: the imagination.

In this anticipation of the imagination's crucial role generating the categories, Heidegger identifies multiple problems with Kant's dominant argument in the Metaphysical Deduction – some of them well recognized by the Post-Kantian tradition, and others informed by his own, phenomenological perspective on what makes a good argument. However, rather than rejecting the table of categories on this basis, Heidegger seeks out a different, more promising source of the categories in Kant's intriguing, though underdeveloped, discussion of synthesis in the Metaphysical Deduction.

The two strands of argument that Heidegger finds in interpreting this section match my portrayal of his interpretive method. Heidegger is dissatisfied with the argument that uncritically takes up ideas from tradition, rather than considering the subject matter directly. For example, by merely accepting that judgment takes certain standard forms, Kant fails to make a phenomenologically compelling case that judgment is restricted to these forms. Heidegger is intrigued, though, by those claims that depart from received tradition – from the "traditional, unfounded privileged position of logic" (PIK 279) to which Kant commits himself at the outset of the Transcendental Analytic, when he promises to seek the source of the categories in the understanding alone. These moments of inconsistency suggest that Kant begins to consider his subject matter directly and to sense that there is something lacking in the traditional accounts of logic, and indeed in the line of argument that he had so far been pursuing. These paragraphs show Kant's innovation, his departure from tradition – his recognition, if only for a moment, that something more than the understanding is needed to form the categories. While these paragraphs provide little detail on how this alternate source could form the categories, Heidegger argues that the Schematism fills in these details.

3 Ground: The Schematism

In the Schematism, Kant outlines the activity of the imagination in "schematizing" the categories of the understanding. Despite the brevity of this chapter, Heidegger agrees with Kant's 1797 remark that it is "one of the most important" (KPM 80), saying that "these eleven pages of the *Critique of Pure Reason* must constitute the central core of the whole voluminous work" (KPM 63).[6] In particular, Heidegger argues that the Schematism, and not the Metaphysical Deduction and its table of judgments, brings out the true origin of the categories: "in the Transcendental Schematism the categories are formed first of all as categories" (KPM 77–78); Schematism is "the original and authentic concept-formation" (KPM 78).[7] On Heidegger's view, the Schematism suggests that the faculty of imagination and not understanding is the actual source of the categories.

Like his reading of the Metaphysical Deduction, Heidegger's interpretation of the Schematism is supposed to answer Post-Kantian objections to the section. Heidegger declares, for example, that "The Schematism chapter is not 'confused' [*verwirrt*], but rather is constructed in an incomparably lucid way. The Schematism chapter is not 'confusing' [*verwirrend*], but rather leads with an unheard-of certainty into the core of the whole problematic of the *Critique of Pure Reason*" (KPM 80). In this passage, Heidegger characteristically (and despite the quotation marks that seem to refer to someone else's wording) does not cite the secondary sources that deem the Schematism "confused" and "confusing." However, one view against which Heidegger sets his interpretation is easy to uncover. Arthur Schopenhauer's well-known critiques of the Schematism continued to be cited among Heidegger's contemporaries.[8] Schopenhauer calls the

---

[6] Adding further evidence for the importance of the chapter that Kant remarked on in 1797, Heidegger also suggests that the "systematic place of the Schematism chapter" reveals its centrality to Kant's inquiry (KPM 63). As Heidegger elaborates in the lecture course, he takes Kant to adopt "the external architectonic of formal logic, i.e., concept, judgment, and conclusion" in his book (PIK 292). Having provided the fundamental concepts, or categories, in the Analytic of Concepts (prior to the Schematism), and in preparation for the basic principles constituting experience that are offered in the second chapter of the Analytic of Principles (after the Schematism), the Schematism chapter makes up the "judgment" that allows for the transition from categories to the world of our experience. Nevertheless, Heidegger is critical of the structure of Kant's presentation (and indeed structures his discussion of Kant differently, following the "inner movement" of Kant's thought rather than Kant's architectonic [KPM 30]). Namely, Kant takes on the "*external* architectonic of logic" when Heidegger thinks that logic is not the proper subject matter of the categories (as we saw above, Heidegger suggests that the categories have an ontological, rather than a logical, origin).

[7] Heidegger makes a similar claim in the 1927–1928 lecture series: "The 'schematism of pure concepts of understanding' basically means nothing other than elimination of the previously assumed essence of categories as notions. It even means a fundamental retracting of their initially assumed character as pure concepts of understanding, i.e., means negating the idea of pure concepts of understanding" (PIK 273).

[8] For example, Heidegger's student, Hermann Mörchen, wrote a dissertation on Kant's theory of imagination (see Mörchen 1970). In his own reconstruction of the Schematism, he paid special

Transcendental Analytic as a whole "confused" (*verworren*) but gives special attention to "the strange chapter 'On the schematism of pure concepts of the understanding,' which is infamous for its excessive obscurity, because nobody has ever been any the wiser for reading it" (Schopenhauer 2010 [WWR]: 478–479). This reception of the Schematism continues even today, with contemporary Anglophone commentators, among whom "the Schematism has a long-standing reputation for difficulty and obscurity" (Allison 2004: 202).

Given the reception of the Schematism in Heidegger's time and in our own, the lucidity that Heidegger claims to find in this chapter would be a distinct benefit of his interpretation. In particular, Heidegger thinks that his interpretation can explain why Kant motivates his chapter by raising a question about subsumption, but then departs in his discussion from traditional notions of subsumption; and it can explain why Kant appears to waffle on whether the categories have an image. Further, since commentators like Erich Adickes have suggested that the chapter is superfluous, Heidegger's ability to articulate the chapter's purpose (indeed, central purpose) marks another benefit of his interpretation; Heidegger's interpretation can appreciate why Kant not only included the chapter, but also deemed it "one of the most important."[9] In particular, Heidegger suggests that the chapter shows that the imagination forms the categories and that they are formed by articulating an a priori intuition of time.

Nevertheless, his interpretation of the Schematism faces difficulties. In particular, Heidegger's suggestion that the transcendental schema have an image is controversial, for it is in this very section that Kant explicitly *denies* that they have an image. Indeed, I think that Heidegger overstates his case when he claims to offer a univocal reading of the Schematism that can do justice to all the textual claims therein. Nevertheless, I think that his interpretive method – which was tailor-made to navigate the twists and turns of textual inconsistency – can bring out this section's support for Heidegger's overarching interpretive theses.[10] Perhaps, Heidegger's excitement at finding a portion of the first *Critique* that *nearly* said what he

---

attention to an article on the Schematism by the German philosopher and philologist Ernst Robert Curtius; Curtius, in turn, cites Schopenhauer as the leading critic of the Schematism. Curtius himself calls Kant's triangle example "confusing" (*verwirrend*) (Curtius 1916: 355). I am grateful to an anonymous referee from Cambridge University Press for bringing Mörchen's dissertation to my attention.

[9] Mörchen also cites Adickes (1924), and Karin de Boer traces the idea that the Schematism is superfluous to Adickes' reading (de Boer 2020).

[10] Thanks to Christopher Yeomans for suggesting this move.

wanted Kant to say led him to downplay the counterevidence that can be found in the Schematism. But his interpretive method tells us how to handle those claims that depart from the more compelling line of argument, even if Heidegger himself does not make these moves in his interpretation of the Schematism.

Heidegger's effusion about the Schematism resembles Schopenhauer's own reception of the Transcendental Aesthetic.[11] Schopenhauer drew a sharp contrast between his preferred section of the first *Critique* and the Transcendental Analytic:

> What a distance between the Transcendental Aesthetic and the Transcendental Analytic in this respect! In the former, what clarity, determinateness, assurance and firm conviction, openly expressed and unerringly communicated! Everything is luminous, no dark and hidden recesses remain: Kant knows what he wants, and knows that he is right. In the latter, on the other hand, everything is obscure, confused [*verworren*], indeterminate, fluctuating and uncertain, progress is timid, full of apologies and appeals to what is to come, or even what is being held back. (WWR 474)

The Transcendental Aesthetic is clear and well supported; Schopenhauer appeals especially to Kant's compelling proofs for the claim that space and time are forms of intuition. By contrast, the Transcendental Analytic is obscure and confused, lacking proof for a major conclusion: that we possess twelve concepts of understanding a priori, the categories. On Schopenhauer's view, Kant was so delighted to discover a priori forms of cognition in space and time that he went overboard identifying additional forms of cognition, forms for which he lacked proof: "pleased by this happy discovery, Kant wanted to pursue this vein even further, and his passion for architectonic symmetry provided him with a guide" (WWR 477). Having found a priori forms of cognition for intuition, Kant was determined to find them for concepts, as well, "bent on finding an a priori analogue for every empirical function of the cognitive faculty" (WWR 478).[12] Though

---

[11] Dahlstrom notes that Heidegger's interpretation of Kant is often compared to that of Schopenhauer because both prefer the first over the second edition, but remarks that Heidegger "appears to have had little regard" for Schopenhauer (1994: 295). However, Heidegger's language as well as the scholarly trail I traced in the notes above suggest that Heidegger, like many of his contemporaries, was aware of Schopenhauer's objections to the Schematism and sought to defend the section against such concerns. Note also that Heidegger in the late 1930s dismisses Schopenhauer's reading of the third *Critique* (also put forth in WWR), saying that Schopenhauer "thoroughly misunderstands" Kant (N1:107). One can also find passing references to Schopenhauer in earlier works (e.g., PRMP 46; BT 272 n. 6).

[12] At greater length, Schopenhauer says: "From this point on, Kant was no longer unbiased, no longer in a position to conduct pure research and observation of what is present in consciousness; instead

Schopenhauer does not put his problem in these terms, the issue that he has with the Transcendental Analytic is a phenomenological one; he believes that Kant lacks experiential grounds, phenomenological evidence, for his conclusions. Where the Transcendental Aesthetic convinces us in reference to our lived experience, the Analytic departs from that lived experience.

Schopenhauer takes the Schematism to play a special role in Kant's overzealous quest for a priori concepts. Because Kant lacked proof for his a priori concepts, of the sort that he provided so successfully for the a priori intuitions, Kant used the Schematism to "increas[e] the plausibility" of those concepts (WWR 478). However, his method for doing so was ultimately a confused one, Schopenhauer insists, as Kant adopted a procedure for grounding concepts that in no way could be applied to a priori concepts. In particular,

> every now and then we try to return to intuiting from abstract thinking. But we really only try this to convince ourselves that our abstract thinking has not strayed too far from the secure ground of intuition, becoming too high-flown or even turning into mere verbiage. This is something like the situation when we walk in the dark and occasionally reach out to touch the wall that guides us. (WWR 478)

Returning to schemata is a way to concretize abstract thinking; it is a way to assure ourselves that our concepts actually refer to something rather than being empty abstractions. However, Schopenhauer argues, this method for grounding concepts is appropriate only for *empirical* concepts. As he puts it,

> the purpose of the schemata in empirical (actual) thought is based solely on the material content of such concepts; specifically, since these concepts are deduced from empirical intuition, we can help and orient ourselves when we are thinking abstractly by casting an occasional, fleeting glance back at the intuition from which concepts are taken, to assure ourselves that our thought still has real content. (WWR 479)

Returning to schemata works for empirical concepts, because it involves returning to the material content from which they were initially derived. By contrast, returning to the material content of concepts that are purported to be a priori is wrongheaded:

> this obviously and necessarily does not work with a priori concepts that are utterly devoid of content, because these concepts do not emerge out of

he was directed by a presupposition and in pursuit of a purpose, namely that of finding what he had presupposed" (WWR 478).

intuition but rather approach it from within so as to acquire content in the first place; consequently, they do not have anything to look back on. (479)

A priori concepts have no material content to which to return. Where schemata can ground and help to concretize empirical concepts that have become too abstract, Kant "overlooks the fact that the purpose of the schemata is entirely absent here" (479).

Schopenhauer's criticisms, then, principally revolve around the disconnect between empirical concepts (that possess material content from experience, and thus schemata) and a priori concepts (which do not, on either count). While critical of the Schematism, Schopenhauer does claim that "its obscurity is dispelled" by his interpretation (479). With his critical reading of the Transcendental Analytic, Schopenhauer can explain why Kant included the Schematism, and what he (unsuccessfully) attempts therein. The "intention" of the section is clear, its results determined ahead of time rather than genuinely discovered: Kant is trying to convince the reader of the plausibility of the a priori forms, the categories – a conclusion demanded by his zeal for architectural symmetry.

Like Schopenhauer, Heidegger also claims to understand the purpose of the section. However, unlike Schopenhauer, who is convinced that Kant, "no longer unbiased" (WWR 478), fixes his results in advance, Heidegger argues that the section offers genuine phenomenological insight into the shape of our experience. That is, Kant *abandons* traditional philosophical biases prioritizing the understanding and looks directly into our experience of time, showing insight into how the categories shape that experience. Further, Heidegger thinks he can explain the disconnect between Kant's discussion of empirical schemata and his discussion of a priori schemata by way of his account of traditional terms in Kant's philosophy.

While Schopenhauer found Kant's language incoherent, Heidegger holds that the question about how to "subsume" empirical particulars under the categories presses a deeper issue. His discussion refers to the following passage from Kant's Schematism:

> In all subsumptions of an object under a concept the representations of the former must be *homogeneous* with the latter ... how is the *subsumption* of [appearances] under the [categories], thus the *application* of the category to the appearances possible, since no one would say that the category, e.g., causality, could also be intuited through the senses and contained in the appearance?" (A137–138/B176–177)

As Schopenhauer also recognized, in the case of empirical concepts (e.g., "dog"), the sensible content corresponding to the concept has been provided over the course of experience, enabling us to identify instantiations of these concepts in the world (i.e., the "subsumption" of objects under those concepts). As Heidegger puts this point, "the empirical concepts were drawn from experience and are therefore 'homogeneous' with the content of the being they determine. Their application to objects, i.e. their use, is no problem" (KPM 78). However, subsumption of this kind is unavailable to the categories. Categories are a priori concepts, so we cannot subsume objects under them in the way we do when those objects bear the empirical properties gleaned from previous instantiations. As we possess the concepts prior to experience, there cannot be previous instantiations that guide subsumptions. Is Kant not confused, then, when he asks about subsuming appearances under the categories?

On Heidegger's account, these terms gesture, perhaps clumsily, at deeper issues. The traditional term "subsumption" concerns how concepts and sensible content come together – how we *use* those concepts to organize what we sense. This interaction between concept and sense is precisely what Kant wants to explore in relation to those special, a priori concepts – the categories. Even if the relationship between category and sense cannot be a subsumption proper, this term "lead[s] in a preliminary way to the problem" (KPM 77). The deeper issues at stake here, groped at by this "superficial" question about subsuming sensible objects under categories, include: Do the categories even have sensible content? What sort of sensible content, and where did it come from (if not from experience)? Most basically, *what* are the categories? In short, Heidegger suggests, "in the question concerning the possible use of the categories, their particular essence itself first becomes a problem. These concepts present us with the question of their 'formation' in general" (KPM 78). Rather than a mere subsumption, the chapter inquires into the "essence" and "formation" of the categories, particularly in regard to their sensible content. With his question about subsumption, Kant only "introduces the problem in a more superficial form" (KPM 63).

In support of his claim that subsumption introduces Kant's problem only approximately, Heidegger notices that the six paragraphs leading up to the table of categories in the Metaphysical Deduction already depart from "the traditional idea of subsumption" (KPM 79). Traditional subsumption occurs when a sensible object is brought "under" a concept. However, Kant's initial paragraphs introducing the synthesis of the imagination discuss bringing this synthesis "*to concepts*" (A78/B103). This locution suggests, in Heidegger's view, that the synthesis of the imagination does not involve bringing the sensible under prepossessed concepts, but rather giving the form of sense a conceptual articulation for the first time – bringing it to concepts by conceptually articulating it. If the Schematism is supposed to expand on the synthesis of the imagination, it will comment rather on this initial formation of the categories, rather than how to subsume under prepossessed concepts. Nevertheless, in Kant's discussion and in Heidegger's reconstruction of it, considering subsumption under empirical concepts does provide a toehold, an initial entry point into this difficult issue of how a priori categories are formed.

Heidegger's reconstruction of Kant's investigation highlights the phenomenological insights he finds in this section – in posing this rough question of subsumption, Kant inquires into how concepts, both empirical and a priori, show up in our experience. Heidegger's investigation of this question takes its cue from Kant's claim that concepts are rules, and that, if they are to show up in experience – if particulars are to be subsumed under them – experience must somehow be structured by rules. Beginning with the subsumption of particulars under empirical concepts, Heidegger argues that empirical concepts show up insofar as what we experience offers a "general look." The look – sensible content – is structured by something general.

To get a grip on this *general* look, Heidegger offers two contrasting looks: the this-here and the copy. Keeping in mind that, for Kant, an experience that is unmediated by concepts is an impossibility ("intuitions without concepts are blind"), seeing something as a "this-here" means seeing it in a way that appreciates its singularity, how it is incomparable to others. Heidegger provides the example of seeing a person as a this-here. This example is particularly apt given the familiar experience of noticing the particularities of the people to whom we are closest; for example, how their cheek dimples *just so* when they make a joke. When we see a this-here, we appreciate this person as an individual, rather than as a type of person (e.g., a train conductor). Heidegger's morbid example of a death mask provides a look that is still more general than a this-here, but does not rise to the generality of a concept; it refers to something else, but does not yet give a rule-governed kind. When we see the mask as a stand-in for some individual (i.e., as something that looks like someone we once knew), we still do not have a general look (something that can be found across multiple individuals).[13]

---

[13] However, just as we can see someone, more generally, as a type of person, we can have a general look at the mask, too. For example, we could see the mask as representing a particular type of person (e.g., an ancient Roman) or even as a typical example of a death mask (noticing its material and so forth).

With the general look, the being is not a this-here (KPM 65) or a copy of a this-here. Rather, it is an instantiation of something general – say, a house.[14] Heidegger's point is perhaps better appreciated not in reference to a familiar concept like "house" but rather in relation to those fine-grained concepts possessed by experts. For example, the architectural enthusiast might see something as a Tudor Revival house, where I see just a house. Their possession of the concept of Tudor Revival means that they notice certain features – a particular bend to the roof, certain patterns of brickwork – that do not stand out to me. The expert's intake of these characteristic features is still holistic in nature; to notice, for example, that the roof has a particular bend, one must appreciate that this is the roof of the structure of the whole, standing in a certain relation to the other parts (e.g., above and not below the walls). The expert's perception is schematic, appreciating a whole whose parts fit together in a certain way. The expert appreciates not a checklist of items, or one-off features, but how these features fit together to make this whole item an instantiation of such and such a kind. Similarly, the birdwatcher might notice the particular, subtle markings characteristic of a certain species, which I overlook. The possession of certain concepts, like those of particular kinds of houses or particular kinds of birds – or, indeed, the more general concepts of "bird" and "house" themselves – make a difference to our representations of particulars. We notice how they conform to certain standards; we see them *as* conforming to those standards.

When we form a general look, Heidegger suggests, we represent a particular *as* instantiating a concept. When we represent something *as* a house, for example, those features that qualify it as a house are salient; the house is not a singularity, but a familiar construct of doors, windows, and so forth. Concepts show up in our experience by shaping our representation of what is given, such that we see it *as* something of a particular kind. Heidegger suggests that, with this "as," "what we have perceived is the range of possible appearing as such, or, more precisely, we have perceived that which cultivates this range, that which regulates and marks out how something in general must appear in order to be able, as a house, to offer the appropriate look" (KPM 67). Concepts, in short, add something to our

---

[14] Along these lines, Heidegger also says that "what is essential to the schema-image first becomes clear: it does not get the character of its look only or first of all from the content of its directly discernible image ... it gets the character of its look from the fact that it springs forth and how it springs forth from out of the possible presentation represented in its regulation; thus, as it were, bringing the rule into the sphere of possible intuitability" (KPM 70).

experience; not the look of the this-here but the look of the general. When we represent something we see *as* a house, we represent it as meeting certain standards. This look, as Heidegger indicates in the passage above, incorporates our expectations of what is possible – the "range of possible appearing as such." The look sees not only characteristic features, such as the way something must appear at a single time slice in order to appropriately be classified as a house. It also carries certain expectations: the door *could* open; the window *will not* begin to melt; if I were to circle the house, I *would* see exterior walls all around it. With this attention to characteristic features coming together in one whole, and the expectation of a temporal range (i.e., future occurrences of some kind), the object before us "has assumed one determinate [appearing]" (KPM 67).

On Heidegger's reconstruction, concepts show up in our experience by shaping what we experience *while* we experience it. The general look is not, say, a picture that one has in mind ahead of time, before one perceives a particular (e.g., a paradigmatic case to which a particular might be compared); the general look is a way that a particular shows up for us.[15] This idea likewise appears in Heidegger's interpretation of the new terms that Kant introduces in this section: schema and image. "Schema" is Kant's answer for how concepts can be located in the sensible world, despite their apparently non-sensible format. Concepts are made sensible in a schematism – in becoming schematized. In ordinary empirical cases, Heidegger reconstructs, the imagination provides a schema "representing the rule" of a concept that determines "how"[16] the concept is to be located in the sensible world. Heidegger suggests that the schema represents "the rule governing the specific making-sensible" (KPM 68). According to this schema, a "schema-image" is formed in the representation of an object. The way the concept attains an image is by shaping the image of some particular object, at the moment of perceiving the empirical object; as Heidegger puts it, "the making-sensible of concepts is a completely specific procuring of characteristic images" (KPM 71). Ahead of time, we have

---

[15] This claim departs from Sacha Golob's argument that Heidegger offers a "prototype theory" of concepts (see Golob 2014: 3.4 and 3.5), insofar as such a theory sees concept application as being guided by a prior image (prototype) of the concept. According to my reconstruction here, empirical concepts procure images *only* when they are applied to empirical particulars.

[16] The following is the larger passage using this language: "The representing of the 'how' is the free 'imaging' of a making-sensible as the providing of an image in the sense just characterized, an imaging which is not bound to a determinate something at hand" (KPM 68).

only the "ability" to represent the empirical object in light of the concept (KPM 67). The schema refers to that ability, rather than an image.[17]

Stepping back from the finer details of Heidegger's reconstruction, it's important to note that the schema-image procured by the schema plays an important role in grounding the schema. That is, schema-images provide evidence that we have certain abilities. Our seeing an object not as a "this-here" but as a "general look" shows that we possessed an ability prior to this encounter – the ability to see something *as* this general kind (e.g., house). Less technically, our particular experiences provide evidence of the structures that we bring to experience – our prior abilities to shape experiences in certain determinate ways. In empirical cases, these experiences of seeing-as would show that I did in fact figure out how to apply the concept (e.g., house) at some point. However, if there were certain structures that permeated our experiences – structures that show up in our encounters with any particular, and not just particulars of this or that kind – this would evidence a more fundamental ability. They would provide evidence, that is, not of an ability acquired over the course of experience, but an ability possessed independently of experience. On Heidegger's view, the categories are schemata of this kind, possessed in a "preliminary" way but phenomenologically evidenced "constantly" over the course of our experience as we form schema-images (KPM 63). The schemata that for Schopenhauer were wholly divorced from experience are for Heidegger only evidenced by experience.

Therefore, even as Heidegger discusses the schemata of a priori concepts (e.g., the schema for substance, the schema for causality), Heidegger continues to interpret "schema" as the ability to procure characteristic images. As with the concept "house," even the a priori schemata are supposed to shape how things show up for us. As he acknowledges, this reading appears to face a glaring piece of counterevidence. In particular, Kant argues that "the schema of a pure concept of the understanding is something which can never be reduced to any image whatsoever" (A142/B181, KPM 72). However, Heidegger reads this claim not as a complete denial that the schema of a category can procure *any image at all*, but rather as a denial that it can procure a *certain kind* of image. The image procured by a priori schemata is not the image procured by empirical schemata; it does not shape our perception of some particular kind, making particular characteristics

---

[17] Heidegger differentiates the schema from an image, for example, in this passage: "The schema is indeed to be distinguished from images, but nevertheless it is related to something like an image, i.e., the image character belongs necessarily to the schema" (KPM 68).

salient. Rather, a priori schemata shape all of experience, giving structure to any object whatsoever. The a priori schemata do not procure a general look of some particular kind, but they procure an image nonetheless – an image that amounts to what Heidegger calls "the horizon of objectivity" (KPM 92) or "the preliminary turning-toward an object" (KPM 63).

Heidegger recommends this tortured reading of Kant's passage due to a reference that Kant makes just a few lines later to a "pure image" (A142/B182).[18] Of course, this could not be the image obtained by an *empirical* schema (which would be impure). The pure image to which Kant refers must be the image obtained by an a priori schema. Therefore, Heidegger suggests we read Kant's claim that a priori schemata "can never be reduced to any image whatsoever" as a partial rather than categorical denial. This reading would make Kant's denial consistent with his subsequent reference to a "pure image."

This reading is, admittedly, a stretch; it is difficult to interpret Kant's passage as anything but an outright denial that a priori schemata have an image. However, I think we can arrive at better support for Heidegger's account if we use his interpretive method – a method that seems to fall by the wayside in this part of his interpretation, as he (perhaps overzealously) attempts a univocal reading of the Schematism. Heidegger's interpretive method does not demand that an interpreter establish consistency among the author's many claims. Rather, Heidegger's method is tailor-made to cope with inconsistencies.

On Heidegger's larger interpretive method, inconsistencies show us that an author is struggling with some subject matter. Kant's inconsistency in this section shows us that he is struggling with how the categories show up in our experience; can they be linked to some sort of sensible content (such that they frame a general look), or can they not? Kant's denial that the a priori schemata can obtain an image speaks to a broader tradition in philosophy that attempts to insulate concepts from the sensible world. Yet Kant's ensuing reference to a "pure image" provides an intriguing departure from that tradition. On Heidegger's interpretive method, we can decide between these two strands of argument by determining which strand is more convincing – which strand does justice to the phenomena under discussion. And Heidegger will argue that the strand of argument assigning an image to a priori schemata provides a phenomenologically

---

[18] In context, Kant asserts that the "pure image … for all objects of the senses in general" is time (not space, which is only external). His ensuing discussion suggests that a priori schemata, like the schema of magnitude, "generate time itself in the apprehension of the intuition" (A142–143/B182).

rich and compelling account of how categories show up in our experience. Heidegger's aim is "to show that Kant's doctrine of the Transcendental Schematism is no baroque theory but instead is created out of the phenomena themselves" (KPM 75).

In particular, Heidegger argues that the a priori schemata articulate a pure image of time, taking his cue from the very passage that refers to a pure image (KPM 73–74). Given its support for Heidegger's account, the passage is worth quoting at length:

> The pure image of all magnitudes (*quantorum*) for outer sense is space; for all objects of the senses in general, it is time. The *pure schema of magnitude* (*quantitatis*), however, as a concept of the understanding, is *number*, which is a representation that summarizes the successive addition of one (homogeneous) unit to another. Thus number is nothing other than the unity of the synthesis of the manifold of a homogeneous intuition in general, because I generate time itself in the apprehension of the intuition. (A142/B182)

In this passage, Kant reminds us of his familiar claim that time is the more universal form of intuition in comparison to space. Space is only the form of "outer sense" (external objects), whereas time conditions both inner and outer sense (extending to internal, mental experience). Therefore, if the pure schemata are to shape all of experience (inner *and* outer sense), then they must inform the "pure image" of time. While the passage distinguishes the schema of magnitude from this pure image, Kant goes on to suggest that, through the schema of magnitude (and, presumably, the other a priori schema), "I generate time itself in the apprehension of intuition." In particular, time apparently gains a number-like form, where homogeneous moments succeed one another. On Heidegger's reading, this passage suggests that pure schemata, such as the schema of magnitude, articulate a pure image of time, and that this articulation occurs over the course of experience (as intuition is apprehended).

Indeed, Heidegger argues, time offers a flexibility that corresponds to all four moments listed on the table of categories. Time, Heidegger argues, "is formable in a variety of ways. Through internal self-regulation in time as pure look, the schemata of the notions pass their image off from this and thus articulate the unique pure possibility of having a certain look into a variety of pure images" (KPM 74). Time, Heidegger elaborates, is articulated as a "pure sequence of nows" (KPM 75) when schematized by the imagination. This is a complex understanding of a unitary phenomenon – moments follow one another, moving in one direction (from past to future), at a uniform rate – and Heidegger thinks that the "schemata of the notions" pick out different aspects of this unified articulation of time. Hence Heidegger's claim that the categories are "artificially isolated elements of the pure synthesis" (KPM 104). The categories, "transcendental determinations of time" (75), break down the articulation of time into its various elements.

To show in detail that each category articulates some aspect of time as a pure sequence of nows, Heidegger uses the category of substance as an example, arguing that "what is meant by the notion Substance can itself procure a pure image a priori in time" (KPM 76). Paraphrasing the First Analogy, Heidegger reports that "substance, as a notion, signifies first of all just: that which forms the ground (subsistence)" (KPM 75). More specifically, it "signifies that which forms the ground for a 'thing which adheres'" (KPM 76). The pure image of time as a sequence of nows, Heidegger argues, reflects this character. First, "time, as pure sequence of nows, is always now. In every now it is now" (KPM 75). Even as the moments of time flow forward, time retains its character as a now. For this reason, "time gives the pure look of something like lasting in general" (KPM 76). Second, "time, however, is as a sequence of nows precisely because in every flowing now it is a now, even another now. As the look of what lasts, it offers at the same time the image of pure change in what lasts" (KPM 76). As a sequence of nows, time continuously undergoes change as its moments tick by; therefore, change adheres in time. Time as a sequence of nows, then, is a subsisting ground of change. The category of substance articulates this aspect of time.

As in his discussion of empirical concepts, Heidegger sees the categories as procuring this image of time not at some separate t_o, but rather *while* we experience particulars. We bring the category to experience, making experience by way of the categories. The schema is an ability to procure an image, and these images are procured only over the course of our experience. However, Heidegger does insist that the images procured by the categories are different in character from those procured by empirical concepts – they are pure images. We can understand this difference as follows. Empirical schemata procure particular images – something that might be found in one part of our experience, but not others. A priori schemata procure images that are common to all experience. Whatever empirical particular that we encounter, we place it in time; we see it as having a past of some kind, a future of some kind, and persisting between that past and future. Remember, for example, the temporal appreciation of the house, where the features we currently perceive are laden with possibilities; for example, the door *could* open. This basic experience of appreciating something's place in time (e.g., having expectations for future states) is formed by the categories; these are the images that the categories procure. These ground rules that we bring to experience, and with which we form experience, make time not as something separate from the objects that we experience but as the very form of objectivity. Our basic understanding of what it means to be an object concerns its regular, temporal properties. The categories articulate time *and* objectivity, or time *as* objectivity. The categories give a "horizon of transcendence" that informs each and every one of our experiences (KPM 76).

Thus, the category of substance articulates not only an image of time (as something that persists as a now despite changes in moments), but also the whole of experience. Heidegger argues that "the objectivity in the letting-stand-against becomes discernible and distinct a priori, provided that substance belongs to [objectivity] as a constitutive element ... in this preliminary view of the pure image of persistence, a being which as such is unalterable in the change can show itself for experience" (KPM 76). Substance partially constitutes objectivity (what it means to be an object), providing a sense of lasting through change.[19] The category of substance shows up in experience – procures an image – when we see something *as* persisting despite change. Seeing something *as* a substance means appreciating its comparatively stable properties and expecting those to stay put in ensuing moments. For example, I expect the shape of the house to persist even as light and shadows play across it. In seeing the house this way, I see it not only as a house comparable to other houses (walled, roofed, and so forth), but as a substance comparable to other substances (having stability despite changes). In so doing, I appreciate the house not only *as* an object of some (empirical) kind, but *as* an object, full stop. The articulation of time as a sequence of nows is not some separate thing, a timeline hovering over or beyond or behind our experience. It makes or forms our experience, framing or shaping our experience. But that form is a temporal one, such that everything we encounter has a basic temporal form.

Heidegger has argued that a priori schemata are an ability; they are an ability to procure images ("schema-images"), that is, to see something *as* an object. Seeing something as an object means seeing it as having a basic temporal form (rather than having particular properties specific to one kind of thing). This ability is not carried out separately from our

---

[19] As Kant says, "to time, therefore, which is itself unchangeable and lasting, there corresponds in appearance that which is unchangeable in existence" (A144/B183).

experience of empirical particulars; it is an ability that shows up in our experience, fundamentally shaping every one of our experiences. Heidegger claims further that these schemata provide the genuine origin of the categories: "in the Transcendental Schematism the categories are formed first of all as categories" (KPM 77–78), making Schematism "the original and authentic concept-formation" (KPM 78). Categories are formed by articulating time in a certain way; time "guides and sustains" this articulation (KPM 63). (On a better presentation of his view, Heidegger implies, Kant would have drawn the categories "systematically through and out of time itself" [KPM 74].) The unified articulation of time can be broken into separate schemata; and one can, further, abstract away from the sensible content of those schemata to list rules (unschematized, pure notions). Yet Heidegger suggests that these levels are isolations, abstractions, derivations of those structures that actually show up in our experience; they do not represent the genuine origin of the categories.

There are a few different reasons why Heidegger prefers his origin story, where the categories are formed by articulating time, to the one offered in the Metaphysical Deduction, where the categories have an independent, logical origin. Doubtless, Heidegger finds this to be a more elegant explanation. The categories as time-determinations are already discernible (KPM 74). The way that they contribute to experience (i.e., by determining time in certain ways) is already apparent; they do not require some mediating element that translates atemporal notions into sensible terms. But I think we find the most important argument for Heidegger's preferred origin story in the claim that "in the Transcendental Schematism the categories are formed first of all *as categories*" (KPM 77–78). That is, an origin in time better fits the critical role that the categories are supposed to play in Kant's system. In particular, categories are supposed to be basic rules that guide and structure our experience. Categories *constrain* us, providing some sort of "resistance" in our experience, such that experience can take some forms and cannot take others.[20] The categories regulate experience – providing something like a "check" (KPM 76) – *because* they are articulations of time. Time is the thoroughgoing form of our experience, and moreover, it is something that can be determined by the articulations of the categories; it is, so to speak, a clay that can be sculpted and can hold that shape. Time, as receptive, accepts and sustains their

---

[20] In his reading of the Transcendental Deduction, Heidegger lauds Kant's recognition that the categories provide resistance ("contrary to the haphazard"), calling it an "immediate find" (KPM 52) – again, genuine insight into how the categories show up in our experience.

Ground: The Schematism

determinations (rather than taking haphazard forms). Put differently, one does not have a rule until one has something that submits to its governance. The categories as logical notions lack precisely what makes them regulative. Without temporal content, one has a list of take-'em-or-leave-'em logical notions; one does not have *rules*.

The comparison to clay helps, I think, bring out one more important feature of the origin story that Heidegger defends in this part of his interpretation. Like clay, time offers some limitations concerning how it can be formed; the material itself limits its possible forms of articulation. However, these possible articulations are also underdetermined. Time does not prescribe one determinate set of articulations; making sense of time is to some extent (i.e., within its material boundaries) open to interpretation. Thus, Kant's categories (magnitude, substance, etc.) offer one way to make sense of time – one version of time to which we could commit ourselves, time as a sequence of nows – but not necessarily the only one. It is for this reason that the activity of the imagination articulating time is a "free 'imaging'" (KPM 68), and not mechanical. Some liberties are being taken. This means that time could be differently interpreted, for example, across historical periods, such that those periods were committed to different sets of categories, and different synthetic a priori truths.[21] Nonetheless, across those periods, it would remain a constant that those categories were drawn from time itself, being used to construct a particular image of time (e.g., time as a sequence of nows) over the course of our experience. The Schematism reveals the "innermost occurrence of transcendence" (KPM 77) by showing how the way we make sense of beings bottoms out in the way we make sense of time, however that may be articulated.

To conclude our treatment of the Schematism, let's return to the problems that Heidegger identifies with the dominant line of argument in the Metaphysical Deduction. First, that line of argument faced the *incompleteness problem*: arguing that the categories descend from a premade table of judgments is unsatisfying and fails to establish whether the categories have a logical or ontological origin (for the status of the table of judgments is itself obscure). Heidegger's preferred line of argument clarifies that the categories are ontological in origin: they are derived from time, as ways of determining time. Further, we have the notions (and this number of notions) on the table of judgments because they provide a complete characterization of time, specifying it as to "time-series, time-content, time-order, and time-inclusiveness" (KPM 74, A145/B184). This

---

[21] I will return to this idea at the end of Chapter 6.

solution is perhaps unwelcome for philosophers who wish to insulate logic from ontology – to assert the independence of logic from ontology – but it is explanatorily superior in that it actually attempts an explanation. It attempts to explain where the notions come from rather than positing them as theoretical basics.

One might worry that Heidegger's preferred origin story also reaches an unsatisfying moment where it must posit a theoretical basic. On this story there is a form of time that is schematized by the categories; is it not just as mysterious where this form of time comes from? We will see in the ensuing chapters, though, that time is not posited as a theoretical basic. Heidegger argues that we are ultimately temporal beings; he thinks that Kant recognizes this, too, and provides a rich characterization of our threefold temporality that can be made richer still. On this construal of Kant's argument, time is not a mysterious theoretical basic; the buck stops with us, with the temporal beings that we are. The categories determine and make sense of the time that we are.

Turning to the other problems with the Metaphysical Deduction, Heidegger's preferred origin story also solves the *phenomenological problem*. Where Kant's presentation of the table of judgments provided no evidence that these forms in fact determine our judgment, the account in the Schematism identifies precisely where the categories show up in our experience. Our experience of empirical particulars betrays a determinate understanding of time, where we make assumptions about their past and predictions about their future. The traces of these temporal expectations are found, for example, in how the difference between stable and ephemeral properties is salient in our experience. We get the categories from a unified understanding of time that shows up in our experience. Seeing the categories first and foremost as time-determinations avoids the problem that Schopenhauer identifies, keeping an eye on how the categories show up in our experience.

Finally, Heidegger's preferred origin story provides some guidance concerning the *accuracy problem*, though not a full solution. The accuracy problem was introduced by Lotze, who argued that Kant was wrong about the taxonomy of logical judgments, and therefore about the table of categories (purportedly) derived from that taxonomy. Heidegger's reconstruction cannot fully solve this problem, because he does not dig into every category and corresponding notion. He focuses exclusively on the category of substance and does not, for example, treat the modal categories that Lotze challenged. However, Heidegger's story provides new guidance for testing the accuracy of Kant's taxonomy. On his account, the accuracy of the notions cannot be determined by logical considerations alone. Rather, the question is whether these notions can determine time, and whether they accurately capture how we determine time over the course of our experience (i.e., whether they are supported by phenomenological evidence). This method would allow one to revise the categories, but in a way that is still in the spirit of Kant's inquiry (as Heidegger sees it). With an explanation for the table of categories – of what they are supposed to capture, namely, the way we determine time – rather than a dead-end that stops at a mysterious, prepackaged table of judgments, one can continue to work out the concepts relevant to synthetic a priori judgment.

Heidegger offers a close reading of the Schematism chapter in order to argue that the imagination's determination of time is the actual origin of the categories. Articulating an image of time as a pure sequence of nows, the categories are formed as categories – that is, rules constituting experience, by determining the time of that experience.

4 Conclusion

Substantively, Heidegger's readings of the Metaphysical Deduction and the Schematism suggest that the imagination, and not the understanding, is the source of the categories. On an interpretive level, both readings demonstrate Heidegger's distinctive interpretive method, where two strands of argument battle it out over the course of Kant's text. These readings, however, reveal some variety in how one can apply this interpretive method to the different parts of a text.

The Metaphysical Deduction, by all appearances, attempts to demonstrate that the understanding is the source of the categories. Yet Heidegger sees this argument unraveling over the course of Kant's discussion, as Kant senses that understanding is inadequate for explaining their origin. By contrast, the Schematism outlines the imagination's schematization of the categories, and in so doing provides an account of the categories' origin that is more phenomenologically compelling. To be sure, the chapter contains some traces of a competing line of argument that prioritizes logic (though Heidegger downplays these moments), for example, when Kant attempts to insulate the categories from sensible conditions by denying they have an image. But the argument does not unravel in the way that the Metaphysical Deduction does (e.g., by introducing other faculties that might help with the work of the imagination). Rather, it finally spells out how the categories show up in our experience.

On Heidegger's two-strand interpretation then, a line of argument might dominate one part of the text, whereas a competing line of argument dominates another. The two lines of argument, in other words, need not be in equal footing in every part of the text. Either way, Heidegger recommends that we navigate inconsistencies by attending to the convincingness of the arguments: where they unravel, on the one hand, and where they show insight into the phenomena, on the other. This method, as applied to the *Critique of Pure Reason*, shows that the dominance of the understanding unravels, whereas the dominance of the imagination provides insight.

CHAPTER 5

The Transcendental Deduction

While Heidegger's interpretation of Kant lingers on the Transcendental Aesthetic, the Metaphysical Deduction, and the Schematism, it is Heidegger's interpretation of the Transcendental Deduction that has earned him the most criticism. Several commentators suggest that Heidegger ignores counterevidence to his interpretation, instead cherry-picking claims that fit with his idiosyncratic way of reading Kant. Daniel Dahlstrom and Dieter Henrich both focus on Heidegger's account of transcendental apperception in particular, the form of self-consciousness that Kant introduces in the Transcendental Deduction. Dahlstrom argues that Heidegger's claim that apperception is temporal "discount[s] Kant's conception of the spontaneity of self-consciousness" (Dahlstrom 1991: 358). Moreover, Henrich suggests that Heidegger's claim that the imagination is the source of apperception sits uneasily with Kant's portrayal of the imagination as a (mere) mediator between apperception and intuition (Henrich 1994: 34).[1] Recently, Karin de Boer and Stephen Howard have suggested a response to Henrich, noting that Henrich "does not deal with passages [in the Transcendental Deduction] that seem to support Heidegger's view" (2019: 373 n. 33). Building off their suggestion, I would like to argue that Heidegger, in addition to offering a reading that is supported by textual evidence, also addresses the counterevidence to his reading.

My reconstruction of Heidegger's interpretation, which highlights his two-strand method of interpreting Kant, replies to Dahlstrom's and Henrich's objections by showing that and how Heidegger deals with counterevidence in his reading of the Transcendental Deduction. As with the earlier parts of his interpretation, Heidegger picks out two different strands of argument in the text and attempts to motivate why his preferred strand of

---

[1] Dahlstrom is himself critical of Henrich's objection (see 1991: 358 n. 81). Nevertheless, I take both commentators to offer the same sort of criticism: Heidegger's interpretation is objectionable because it fails to address counterevidence in Kant's text.

argument, prioritizing the imagination, is philosophically superior to the strand of argument prioritizing the faculty of understanding. My reconstruction shows that Heidegger both acknowledges the counterevidence to his interpretation and argues that this counterevidence is in tension with Kant's most compelling line of argumentation in the Transcendental Deduction. Finding inconsistency among Kant's claims, Heidegger presses us to pursue the line of argumentation that best answers Kant's main questions. In what follows, I will show that Heidegger systematically traces these two strands of argument over the course of interpreting the A-Deduction and explains why his preferred strand is superior. This approach becomes especially clear when one turns to the extended treatments of the argument found in the 1927–1928 lecture course.

In order to appreciate the basic shape of Heidegger's interpretation, it will be instructive to outline the basic shape of Kant's argument in the A-Deduction. The earlier sections of Kant's treatise separately treat the faculties of sensibility (our faculty for passively sensing) and understanding (our faculty for actively conceptualizing what we sense). The Transcendental Deduction brings them together, attempting to reconcile the receptive, sensing aspect of human cognition with the spontaneous, conceptualizing aspect. In the A-Deduction, Kant outlines three sorts of syntheses (or "putting together"): the synthesis of apprehension, the synthesis of reproduction, and the synthesis of recognition. The synthesis of apprehension constitutes our ability to apprehend what is immediately before us, viewing multiple elements as one (i.e., putting together the multiple elements of what we are currently looking at, say, a glove on the floor). The synthesis of reproduction constitutes our ability to recall previous apprehensions (what we saw on the floor earlier today) and put it together with what we currently apprehend. The synthesis of recognition constitutes our ability to reidentify what we apprehend (e.g., recognizing the glove the next time we see it). Kant maintains that all three syntheses are required for us to have any perceptual experience at all, and he discusses these syntheses with the aim of establishing that the categories of the understanding apply to the world we sensibly intuit. To carry out this aim, Kant also appeals to a third faculty, the faculty of imagination (our ability to represent what is not present), presented as a mediator between sensibility and understanding.

According to the titles of Kant's sections on each synthesis, it is tempting to think that Kant attributes the synthesis of apprehension to sensibility (after all, it is "apprehension in intuition"); reproduction, to the imagination ("reproduction in the imagination"); and recognition, to understanding ("recognition in the concept") (A98–103). On this line of argument, the three syntheses are divvied up among three different faculties. Heidegger, however, thinks that Kant's analyses of each synthesis point to another conclusion: each synthesis, he suggests, ultimately stems from the faculty of imagination. Heidegger intends to develop and defend this latter line of argument: "Kant considers primarily the synthesis of reproduction as the synthesis of the power of imagination. But our interpretation goes further and tries to take all three syntheses back into the originally conceived transcendental power of imagination" (PIK 232). The "transcendental power of the imagination," Heidegger argues, is responsible for all three syntheses. In particular, Heidegger suggests that Kant's "point of departure" in each section is to begin with an "empirical" synthesis and then transition to a "transcendental" or "pure" synthesis that makes the empirical synthesis possible (PIK 232; KPM 125). That is, Kant begins with a synthesis that must take place for us to have a particular perceptual experience (e.g., an empirical synthesis required to apprehend the glove), and then elaborates a transcendental synthesis that grounds the empirical synthesis, and therefore every particular perceptual experience. In each case, Heidegger attributes the transcendental synthesis to the transcendental power of the imagination (dubbed "transcendental" because it is a condition for the possibility of any experience at all). While Heidegger's interpretation is at odds with some of Kant's explicit claims, Heidegger suggests that it allows Kant to achieve his aim in this argument: if the transcendental imagination grounds all three syntheses, sensibility and understanding can be reconciled successfully.

1 The Two Strands of Argument

Heidegger thinks that many of Kant's explicit claims – making up one strand of argument – offer an unsuccessful answer to Kant's question in the Transcendental Deduction.

This more traditional strand of argument is linked to the way Kant poses his problem in the Transcendental Deduction. On Heidegger's view, and as I reviewed in Chapter 4, Kant often borrows traditional terminology that only approximates his inquiry, in order to get traction on unwieldy philosophical problems. As Heidegger puts this point, Kant "clings first of all to the most feasible, known formulations which should lead in a preliminary way to the problem" (KPM 77). Thus in the Transcendental Deduction Kant poses his problem as a *quaestio juris*: Do the categories of the understanding – the a priori concepts we possess in advance of experience – have jurisdictional authority over our sense experience? This question gets at Kant's main concern, to show that and how sensibility and understanding are in contact a priori. However, it has the potential to lead readers astray. In particular, readers might think of the categories as being separate from the world of sense – as rules that might be compared to an independent sense experience in order to establish their legitimacy (as accurately capturing that experience). But on Kant's transcendental idealism, we have no independent access to the world of sense, such that the categories could be measured against it; the categories enable and structure our sense experience through and through. If the reader avoids assuming the independence of the categories, then Kant's real inquiry can be appreciated, exploring the a priori connection between sensibility and understanding.

But Heidegger suggests that the juridical question likewise leads Kant astray, as his quest for legitimacy drives him to insulate the categories from the condition of time, a move that hinders his attempt to reconcile sensibility and understanding. In particular, Kant locates the categories in the faculty of understanding, and suggests further that the understanding is removed from time. Time is, of course, the a priori form of sensibility, and not understanding; but Heidegger cites further Kant's claim that pure reason in general "is not subject to the form of time" (A551/B580; KPM 129) and his claim that the principle of contradiction – "which delimits the essence of pure thinking," per Heidegger (KPM 129) – cannot be "affected by the condition of time" (A152/B192). Moreover, the Transcendental Deduction proper makes no mention of time when Kant turns to the synthesis of recognition, making this conceptual synthesis an outlier among the other syntheses in this section. In attributing the categories to an atemporal faculty of understanding, Kant takes a traditional path toward establishing their legitimacy, where legitimacy can be conferred only by permanent, stable laws.[2]

On Heidegger's view, Kant's painstaking work connecting the synthesis of apprehension in sensibility to the synthesis of recognition in understanding (by way of the synthesis of reproduction in imagination) leads ultimately to a gridlock. The synthesis of apprehension is conditioned by time, as is the synthesis of reproduction: apprehension takes in the manifold at a single time slice, and reproduction recalls past intuitions. Yet the synthesis of recognition is rendered atemporal. Kant's discussion does

---

[2] According to Heidegger, "Kant retains the ontologically unclarified point of departure from the subject as inaugurated by Descartes" (PIK 258).

identify the deeper capacity required for recognition: reidentifying the same *object* requires a stable *subject* – that is, a subject who will draw on the same concepts over the course of experience, thereby ensuring the same standards of individuation across multiple experiences. Yet because apperception has no temporal dimension, it is unclear how to unite these two disparate elements, time and apperception. How do two unlike things come together – time and not-time?

Thus, on Heidegger's view, Kant ends up in the Transcendental Deduction with a more fine-grained account of what must be combined for sensibility and understanding to be in contact a priori: namely, time and apperception. Yet the argument still lacks the finer details about how such a synthesis – where "pure intuition and pure thinking meet one another a priori" – could occur (KPM 49). Here we spy the problem that Heidegger credits the Neo-Kantians with articulating (as I reviewed in Chapter 2): "Cohen and Natorp noticed as clearly as no one else before that the *Critique* lacks an ultimate encompassing unity, in the sense namely that this unity and *the ground of this unity of the transcendental aesthetic and logic was not explicitly brought to light by Kant*" (PIK 54). Kant does not successfully unify sensibility ("aesthetic") and understanding ("logic"), as he does not identify the ground that allows for their unity. Indeed, and as I also reviewed in Chapter 3, one can see some of the Post-Kantian reception as an attempt to identify the commonality that allows for their combination, with Reinhold identifying "representation" as the common denominator between intuition and concept, and the Neo-Kantians themselves attempting to reduce a priori intuitions to concepts. Heidegger joins these Post-Kantian interpreters in trying to bridge time and apperception, but his reading of the Transcendental Deduction claims to find a different answer on what unifies them, in Kant's second, more innovative strand of argument.

As I have already indicated, Heidegger thinks the imagination unifies sensibility and understanding. The three empirical syntheses that Kant distributes across the three faculties ultimately rely on three transcendental syntheses that are carried out by the transcendental power of the imagination. But Heidegger's reading of the Transcendental Deduction also identifies the deeper structure that allows them to be unified: *temporality*. In fact, Heidegger argues of the imagination that "this power *itself* is time understood as original time, which we call *temporality*" (PIK 232).

Though Kant does not suggest that the synthesis of recognition is temporal, Heidegger insists that Kant's analyses of the three syntheses points to the conclusion that the final synthesis, the synthesis of recognition, is in fact temporal in character. And if recognition is temporal, this makes it easier to see how it could hang together with the two other syntheses, apprehension and reproduction, which are explicitly temporal. In particular, each of the transcendental syntheses distinguishes or articulates a dimension of time, with the synthesis of apprehension articulating the present moment, the synthesis of reproduction articulating the past, and the synthesis of recognition articulating the future. The transcendental imagination, as temporality, unifies these three syntheses. This complex unification strategy can be visualized as follows:

Empirical synthesis	Synthesis of reproduction	Synthesis of apprehension (in intuition)	Synthesis of recognition (in concepts)
relies on	relies on	relies on	relies on
Transcendental synthesis	Synthesis articulating the past	Synthesis articulating the present	Synthesis articulating the future
	└─────────── make up ───────────┘		
	The Threefold Structure of Temporality (Transcendental Imagination)		

If successful, this strategy unifies intuition and concepts by showing their dependence on two modes of temporality, which are unified within the deeper structure of temporality (i.e., the transcendental power of imagination). The success of the argument depends on establishing dependency relations of two kinds: first, vertical dependency relationships between the empirical synthesis that Kant invokes, and the deeper, transcendental (and temporal) synthesis that Heidegger identifies; and second, horizontal dependency relationships between the three transcendental syntheses, establishing their unity at this deeper level. My discussion in what follows will reconstruct both kinds of dependency relationships, bringing out what Heidegger takes to be the more promising response to Kant's inquiry in the Transcendental Deduction. But before I get to those reconstructions, two remarks are in order regarding Heidegger's discussion of time in these sections.

First, the temporality that Heidegger claims to find in the Transcendental Deduction is a model of time different from the one that Kant explicitly invokes. In particular, Heidegger suggests that his account of the temporality of the imagination "go[es] beyond Kant" in conceiving of time as "original time" or "temporality" (PIK 232). Kant, he argues, offers only an "ordinary sense" of time: "for Kant time is the pure succession of the sequence of nows given in pure intuition: now, and now, and now – that is, a constant sequence of nows" (PIK 232). For

Kant, time is an infinite timeline where we always occupy the present "now" (seeing past moments, in Heidegger's terms, as "no-longer-nows" and future moments as "not-yet-nows"). While Kant explicates time as a sequence of nows, Heidegger suggests that Kant's discussion of the three syntheses gestures at original temporality. The transcendental syntheses articulate the understanding of time as a sequence of nows, but this articulation is enabled by a deeper structure, the structure of temporality, where the temporal modes of past, present, and future are held together.

Second, in offering this model of time – and suggesting that time as a sequence of nows depends on this deeper model of time – Heidegger's interpretation of Kant resembles his own account of temporality in *Being and Time*. There, Heidegger argues that original temporality is the structure of Dasein, or the human being, differentiating it from other sorts of beings, like those nonhuman entities found in the natural world. At its base, Heidegger argues, Dasein is fundamentally a being who is "being-already-in-a-world" – Dasein already has a personal history, a cultural and historical location, and projects in which it is already invested. Moreover, Dasein is a being that is "ahead-of-itself" – it is always oriented toward what it would like to be or accomplish. Heidegger calls this fundamental structure of Dasein's existence, that of previously being immersed in a world and oriented toward future projects, "care" (BT 192). Heidegger argues that "*the primordial unity of the structure of care lies in temporality*" (BT 327). Temporality is the process of interpreting the *present* in light of *future* projects and *past* traditions, and this process characterizes human existence. He suggests that, within this structure of "ahead-of-it-self-already-being-in," the future has priority (BT 326). In order to pursue a project, we must take one up from the space of possibilities that is offered by our cultural and historical moment (i.e., we must *already* be in the world); but moreover, we must carry out that project concretely in the present. Since the future requires the other two moments, it unifies them, bringing them into contact with one another.

If Heidegger were to find this temporal structure as the transcendental basis of Kant's three empirical syntheses, then he could spell out the unity between intuition (apprehension) and concept (recognition). In original temporality, the dimensions of time are unified; they refer to one another, forming a whole. Yet it must be underscored that Heidegger does not invoke his own conceptual machinery when interpreting the Transcendental Deduction. Indeed, Heidegger's interpretive remarks leading up to this section preclude such an approach: he deems it "unjust" to "force upon the Kantian philosophizing a standard which remains foreign to it" and commits rather to "interpretation," which draws on Kant's own inquiry (KPM 89). Heidegger thinks that original temporality is implicated by Kant's discussion – that one can arrive at this structure by working within the confines of Kant's conceptual apparatus. Indeed, Heidegger's remarks at the close of his 1927–1928 lecture series indicate that he takes Kant to provide independent confirmation of Heidegger's findings: "When some years ago I studied the *Critique of Pure Reason* anew and read it, as it were, against the background of Husserl's phenomenology, it opened my eyes; and Kant became for me the crucial confirmation of the accuracy of the path which I took in my search" (PIK 292). Heidegger's task when interpreting the Transcendental Deduction is not one of import, but of excavation – excavating the ideas in Kant that converge with his own work, confirming Heidegger's own ideas (here, about temporality and its foundational character). Therefore, in the reconstruction that follows, it remains to be seen which dimensions of temporality are implicated in the Transcendental Deduction and how these implicated dimensions are unified.

2 The Synthesis of Apprehension

The synthesis of apprehension is the first synthesis that Kant offers in the A-Deduction as a basic requirement for us to have any perceptual experience at all. Heidegger aims to show that the empirical synthesis that Kant identifies is grounded in a transcendental synthesis that is carried out by the transcendental power of imagination. Heidegger is sensitive to the challenges of his reading. First, he seeks to elucidate a transcendental synthesis that Kant mentions – "pure apprehension" (A100) – but does not develop in detail. While Heidegger's account of pure apprehension is therefore heavily reconstructive, Heidegger develops it with an eye toward Kant's strongest possible argument. He seeks an account of pure apprehension, where pure apprehension refers to something that is actually required for the empirical synthesis that Kant outlines.

Second, while Heidegger aims to show that pure apprehension is grounded in the transcendental power of the imagination, he admits that Kant entitles this section "On the synthesis of apprehension in the intuition" (A98). It might be tempting, therefore, to attribute this synthesis not to imagination but to the faculty linked to intuition – sensibility. Yet, as Heidegger notes, Kant also claims that the imagination is "an active faculty for the synthesis of the manifold" and "its action, when immediately directed upon perception, I entitle apprehension" (A120). With textual evidence pointing in two different directions, Heidegger's interpretive method demands that we determine which line of argument is most convincing. Heidegger will argue that pure apprehension is most convincingly attributed to imagination.

Heidegger draws on Kant's claims about the empirical synthesis of apprehension in order to develop his account of pure apprehension. Kant suggests that in the empirical synthesis, we intuit a manifold (A99), taking in multiple elements or features in one intuition. Heidegger argues that intuiting a manifold requires "an already operative regard for the now" (PIK 234) or the "immediate look of the now as such" (KPM 126). This prior sense of the now, which enables empirical apprehension, is provided by the transcendental synthesis of apprehension.

Empirical apprehension requires a prior appreciation of the now, on Heidegger's view, because an intuition containing a manifold requires (a) that we individuate it and (b) that it is unified. Beginning with (a), Heidegger recounts Kant's claim that a manifold "would not be represented as such (i.e. a manifold) if the mind did not distinguish the time in the succession of impressions on one another" (A99; PIK 233). Heidegger argues we should read this passage as saying that time is not only intuited a priori, but is also *distinguished* a priori, articulated specifically as a succession or sequence of nows. This a priori differentiation of time allows one to then appreciate the sequence of impressions: "only on the background of a now which is always already said – only in an advance view of the differentiated succession of nows – can the offer of impressions as a sequence of impressions be made" (PIK 233). It is not the case that we deduce the sequentiality of time from the sequentiality of impressions (i.e., deducing that moments follow one another because impressions change).

Heidegger insists on this interpretation, because a prior appreciation of the now enables us to differentiate impressions even where their content is identical; "even when the same impression with the same content returns, this second impression is necessarily another impression and different from the preceding one, insofar as it originates in a new now" (PIK 233). All content being equal (as, say, when one sees a house one day and then sees it again the next), we differentiate impressions on the basis of their positions in time. This interpretation helps to explain Kant's idea that each intuition is immediate, offering something singular that is not yet related to others – as Heidegger puts it, "in-itself simply unique, isolated, for-itself dissociated, absolute this" (PIK 234). Even if impressions are identical, they are at a unique moment in time, in a unique location on the sequence of nows. If we distinguish time as a succession of nows a priori, this enables us to take each impression as unique, content notwithstanding; as Heidegger summarizes this point in the Kant book, "in distinguishing time, our mind must already be saying constantly and in advance 'now and now and now,' in order to be able to encounter 'now this' and 'now that' and 'now all this in particular'" (KPM 126).

In addition to enabling us to individuate our impressions, Heidegger suggests (b) that a prior appreciation of the now enables us to appreciate the unity of each impression. Heidegger supports this leg of his argument by recounting Kant's claim that "for each representation, insofar as it is contained in a single moment, can never be anything but absolute unity" (A99; PIK 234). In Heidegger's view, the single moment of the now provides a basis for unifying the various elements or features that are encountered in that moment. In advance, we appreciate the now itself as a plurality: it spans from "just now" to "right now," buttressing a "just-now-no-longer" and a "right-now-not-yet" (234). Therefore, "the now has a span and is related to the many that can occupy that span" (234). Because the now is appreciated in advance as spanned, "the many can be traversed and taken together on the basis of directedness to a now" (234).

Therefore, for empirical apprehension, the advance appreciation of the now is required for both differentiating an impression as unique and unifying its various elements as a manifold. Since pure apprehension is supposed to enable empirical apprehension, Heidegger argues that pure apprehension carries out a synthesis that provides this advance appreciation of the now. While empirical apprehension "is directed to what is offered affectively in sensation," pure apprehension "is that which a priori unifies a manifold" (PIK 235).

In Heidegger's view, "the pure, apprehending synthesis does not first take place within the horizon of time, but instead it first forms precisely the like of the now and the sequence of nows" (KPM 126). In particular, nows are put into succession and related to one another. As Heidegger details this synthesis:

> pure intuition is not simply an isolated grasping of a whole lot of nows that simply have no relation to each other. Rather each now as now, in order to be intuited as what it is, requires to be taken together with other nows. This taking-together has the character of a unification and in fact in each case unifies the just-now as no-longer-now and right-now as not-yet-now unto a now. (PIK 235)

In the transcendental synthesis of apprehension, a sequence of nows is unified such that each individual now is flanked by a no-longer-now and the not-yet-now.

The Synthesis of Apprehension

Because pure apprehension actively unifies time as a sequence of nows, it betrays a spontaneity; the receptive faculty of sensibility could not be its source. Therefore, to argue that the (receptive and spontaneous) faculty of imagination is its source, Heidegger, working within Kant's transcendental psychology, focuses on eliminating the spontaneous faculty of understanding. The spontaneity of apprehension, he argues, is to be differentiated from the spontaneity of the understanding: "This synthesis of apprehension is pure *syndosis*, that is, spontaneity of reception. In this synthesis of apprehension, there is nothing like a conceptual determination in the sense of comparison, reflection, and abstraction – nothing like the logical function of the understanding" (PIK 235). The transcendental synthesis of apprehension involves setting nows into a successive relationship with one another, where each now is a *part* of the larger *whole*, time. This is not spontaneity of the understanding, which unites particulars as instantiations of some abstract rule; for example, all of these particular chairs are united by the concept "chair," but they are not parts of it. Rather, this spontaneity unifies parts of a larger whole. To have part-whole relationships, *many* must be given in *one* look or image.

Heidegger attributes the spontaneity of apprehension rather to the imagination; pure apprehension "is a *mode of the pure power of imagination*" (PIK 235–236), which "only now *develops* time as a pure succession of nows" (PIK 236). Rather than unifying with a rule, Heidegger suggests, the imagination unifies by "forming an image" (PIK 236).[3] In so doing, the transcendental imagination forms the advance appreciation of the now that is required for empirical apprehension.

In offering this interpretation of the synthesis of apprehension, Heidegger develops Kant's claims about what it means to have a manifold of intuition, and attempts to put the strongest version of the argument forward (where the sequence of nows is appreciated in advance of any impression). However, in considering the transcendental requirements for having such a manifold, Heidegger describes a transcendental synthesis and attributes this synthesis to the imagination. This description and attribution are less than explicit in Kant's text, as Heidegger acknowledges: "Kant does not say what [pure apprehension] is and how it functions as a mode of the power of imagination" (PIK 236). Instead, Heidegger expands on Kant to offer an interpretation of what he might mean by "original

---

[3] Heidegger also alludes to the simultaneous spontaneity ("creating") and receptivity ("giving") of pure apprehension in KPM: "what the pure intuiting offering (forming as giving a look) produces (forming as creating) is the immediate look of the now as such, i.e., always the look of the actual present as such" (126).

receptivity" and "pure apprehension," based on Heidegger's understanding of what is required for intuiting a manifold empirically. While this is an expansion, it is not a tangent; it is an attempt to further develop those places where "Kant proceeds summarily and crudely," using Kant's preceding analysis as a guide (PIK 236).

3 The Synthesis of Reproduction

As with the synthesis of apprehension, Heidegger takes Kant's discussion of reproduction to begin with an empirical synthesis, and then transition to the transcendental synthesis on which the empirical synthesis relies. Again, Heidegger attributes the transcendental synthesis grounding the empirical synthesis to the transcendental imagination. On this point, he agrees with Kant, as Kant also attributes the synthesis of reproduction to the imagination in his section title. Therefore, in this part of his interpretation, Heidegger is not at pains to rule out the other faculties in order to prove that the imagination is behind the synthesis of reproduction; the involvement of the imagination is not in question.

However, one aspect of Heidegger's interpretation is controversial. Heidegger argues that the synthesis of reproduction is merely one "mode" of the imagination's transcendental activity. Heidegger acknowledges that, in Kant's discussion of the transcendental synthesis of reproduction, "it is not clear whether this pure synthesis of reproduction is to be the only accomplishment of the power of imagination, or only one mode [of it]. If Kant means the former, then the power of imagination here is not yet grasped in its originality" (PIK 240). While Heidegger agrees with Kant that the pure synthesis of reproduction ought to be attributed to the transcendental power of the imagination, he insists that this is only one mode of the transcendental power of imagination. He acknowledges here the very idea that Henrich uses to object to Heidegger's interpretation – that at this point in Kant's analysis, the imagination is presented merely as a mediator between apprehension in intuition and recognition in concept, between sensibility and understanding. As Heidegger baldly puts it in the Kant book, "by naming the second of the three modes of synthesis 'Synthesis of Reproduction in Imagination,' Kant already says that the power of imagination is just one element among others and that it is in no way the root of intuition and concept" (KPM 124). But Heidegger argues nevertheless that developing and expanding the role of the imagination in a way that is suggested by other parts of Kant's analysis (e.g., his attribution of apprehension to imagination at A120) can lead to a more satisfying

The Synthesis of Reproduction

account of how sensibility and understanding are unified. Heidegger acknowledges the counterevidence, but suggests that there is good reason to disregard it, in the quest for a better argument.

However, Heidegger does not explain why the imagination has more than one mode in his discussion of reproduction. This justification, rather, is left to the discussions of apprehension and recognition that flank the discussion of reproduction, which reveal the other modes of transcendental imagination. Therefore, Heidegger offers a more straightforward interpretation of reproduction than of the other two syntheses; his claims do not require so extensive a justification. However, the interpretation reflects his larger arguments that the imagination, because spontaneously receptive, is the fundamental root of human cognition and that the imagination is identical with what Heidegger calls "temporality."

Notice, then, two points of emphasis in his interpretation: First, his language indicates the simultaneous spontaneity and receptivity that is required for the transcendental synthesis of reproduction. As Heidegger argues throughout his interpretation that the spontaneity and receptivity of the imagination secures its place as the fundamental root of human cognition, his language fits well with the larger moves of the interpretation. Second, Heidegger's interpretation argues that "the pure synthesis [of reproduction] again proves to be time-related," as was the synthesis of apprehension before it (PIK 236), in support of Heidegger's larger argument that the transcendental imagination is temporality. To fit the interpretation of reproduction into the broader argument, my reconstruction will bring out these elements.

Heidegger reviews that Kant's empirical synthesis of reproduction reproduces "something which was already once brought-forward, that is, was offered – in the apprehending unity of reproduction" (PIK 237). In other words, the empirical synthesis of reproduction brings forward something that was apprehended in the past. However, the representation that it reproduces is not "freely invented" by the imagination; rather, it "has a certain necessity" (237). Namely, the imagination reproduces representations that "are associated with each other" (237), representations that are relevant to or connected with what one is intuiting presently. Heidegger notes that "here we are confronted with a peculiar intuiting which does not immediately go back to an affection. Rather this intuiting of a manifold offers something by itself from out of itself" (237). While sensibility intuits what is immediately presently before oneself, imagination can intuit something that is no longer present.

Heidegger argues that, prior to any empirical case of reproduction, the "mind must be capable of retaining what is represented," whatever it may be (PIK 237). Because the empirical synthesis of reproduction relies on this prior ability to retain, it points to a transcendental synthesis: "this possibility of empirically retaining presupposes the possibility of an a priori retaining" (238). Heidegger suggests that Kant "argues indirectly" for the claim that this ability to retain is required for experience (237). Kant, on Heidegger's construal, argues that experience would not be possible *were it not the case* that we have a prior ability to retain. Kant supposes that we have no ability to retain; our representations "simply slip away," coming and going with the presence of what we perceive (238). As Kant puts this thought experiment, he imagines what experience would be like "if I were always to lose the preceding representations ... from my thoughts and not reproduce them when I proceed to the following ones" (A102). We would not be able to reach "out and back," as Heidegger puts it, for some object that we have encountered before; "mind would be tied firmly to each phase of the now" (PIK 238). If this were the case, "an experience in the sense of a progressive retaining determination of the region of objects would remain impossible" (238). In other words, we would be unable to learn from experience, unable to develop any sense of the "region of objects" beyond what currently confronts us. Since we surely learn from experience, appreciating how the past bears on the present, it cannot be the case that our intuitions simply slip away; we must have the ability to retain.

Heidegger argues that the transcendental synthesis of reproduction creates "the overall possibility of going back into the past" where I have "an open horizon of the past at my disposal" (PIK 238). In the transcendental synthesis of reproduction, "time *as* past offers itself immediately – not as the present but immediately as it itself, as past" (238–239). In particular, the past is given as something that can be retained. In pure reproduction, the past is immediately given, but also unified with the present; there is a "unification of each [no-longer-now] with each actual now" (238). The past is given, therefore, as something that can be relevant to the present.

The transcendental synthesis of reproduction has both a receptive and a spontaneous component. One receives the past as past, with its distinctive character of being no longer. Further, one actively unifies the moments of time, such that the present moment can be put into contact with any moment past; "we can place ourselves quite freely at any given point in time. That is why for Kant pure intuition is a pure *play* of the power of imagination" (PIK 239). As Heidegger describes the spontaneity and receptivity of the transcendental synthesis of reproduction, "this synthesis of the pure retaining of the no-longer-now is an immediate offering as well as a free and constant, possible reaching back" (PIK 238–239).

With apprehension and reproduction, then, we have two modes of the imagination, which provide, respectively, "*the manner in which pure time is disclosed a priori in its now and no-longer-now, as present and past*" (PIK 240). The synthesis of recognition will provide the third mode, disclosing the future.

4 The Synthesis of Recognition

Heidegger's interpretation of the synthesis of recognition, and the "I think" of transcendental apperception, is the most controversial part of his interpretation of the A-Deduction. Heidegger acknowledges that

> we must explicitly emphasize that *in interpreting the third synthesis we go way beyond Kant*, because now the problem of the common root of both stems of knowledge becomes acute. We are concerned with understanding time and the I-think more radically and in the direction which is certainly visible in Kant, but which is not taken by him, i.e., in the direction of the synthesis of the power of imagination. (PIK 243)

Rather than examining the letter of Kant's text in regard to the synthesis of recognition, Heidegger orients his interpretation to the prior two syntheses; based on the synthesis of apprehension and the synthesis of reproduction, what sort of synthesis remains as a requirement for perceptual experience? Further, Heidegger keeps in view Kant's goal of reconciling sensibility and understanding. Heidegger suggests that his own interpretation can successfully unify sensibility and understanding, achieving the goal that Kant set out.

Controversially, Heidegger insists that the synthesis of recognition is related to time. Heidegger argues that this conclusion is already suggested by the tight link that Kant draws between the three syntheses, and the relation to time that is established in the first two syntheses. In particular, Kant argues that the three syntheses are interdependent, and specifically (as Heidegger paraphrases) that "the synthesis of reproduction, too, in turn will not be possible without the synthesis of recognition" (PIK 240). Since the synthesis of apprehension requires reproduction (as I will detail in Section 5 below), the synthesis of recognition "too belongs to apprehension" (240). Due to the interdependence of the three syntheses, and the direct relationship to time of the synthesis of apprehension and synthesis of reproduction, Heidegger argues that "obviously the third synthesis of recognition cannot be without an essential relation to time" (241).

However, Kant does not make this sort of argument. Accordingly, Heidegger remarks, "precisely this relation to time is not brought to light in the Kantian interpretation of the synthesis of recognition" (PIK 241). Heidegger argues that Kant's failure to address time leads him to encounter "special difficulties" in his account of the third synthesis. These "special difficulties" are apparent from the disproportionate length of the section in comparison to the sections treating the prior two syntheses, and from Kant's failure to clearly follow his "customary procedure" of beginning with an empirical synthesis and transitioning to a transcendental synthesis (241).

While the first two syntheses are related to time, in Kant's discussion of the synthesis of recognition "*the inner rupture in the foundation of Kant's problem becomes clear: the lack of connection between time and transcendental apperception*" (PIK 242). Heidegger indicates that the solution Kant offers to connect intuition and concept in the A-Deduction ultimately reproduces the opposition between them; "in the end he again places intuition on one side and concept on the other" (242). Instead of establishing the unity of intuition and concept, Kant's solution redescribes the problem. We are therefore left, in Kant's text, with an "unresolved problem of transcendence" (252); with the understanding cut off from time, it is not clear how our concepts come into contact with the sensible world.

Rather than following Kant's atemporal treatment of recognition, then, Heidegger infers the character of this synthesis by considering its fit with the other two syntheses. He develops his interpretation of the synthesis of recognition in two steps: first, he discusses an empirical synthesis of identification, creating the possibility to identify the same being again; second, he discusses an a priori synthesis of pre-cognition, establishing our relationship to the future. Heidegger's proposal of new terms for the synthesis ("identification" and then "pre-cognition") reflects his suggestion that Kant was misguided even in his naming of the synthesis; Kant provides a "wrong interpretation which is already announced in calling this third synthesis 'recognition'" (PIK 241).[4]

Heidegger first proposes that we interpret the synthesis of recognition as a synthesis of *identification*, since identification provides the final element needed to complete the prior two empirical syntheses. Here he follows Kant's suggestion that, without a synthesis of identification, the synthesis

---

[4] Heidegger objects to this term because it contains "cognition" in it, yet the three syntheses are supposed to secure the possibility of one cognizing at all; cognition cannot figure as part of the transcendental conditions for cognition (PIK 245).

of recognition would fail to be informative: "Without consciousness that that which we think is the very same as what we thought a moment before, all reproduction in the series of representations would be in vain" (A103; KPM 129). As Heidegger reconstructs the idea, reproducing "what is past" is only informative if we can identify something that is present before us as something we have experienced before (rather than, say, something entirely new) (PIK 244). The synthesis of recognition provides this ability to *identify* the same thing again (e.g., the same glove that I saw on the floor yesterday).

Heidegger argues that the synthesis of identification cannot be done subsequently to the synthesis of apprehension and reproduction, such that "we first take up and apprehend, then reproduce, and then identify what we perceived with what is brought again" (PIK 245). Rather, in order to re-identify – to take what is perceived right now (i.e., apprehended) to be the same as what we perceived before (which is now reproduced) – our initial apprehension must pick out something discrete that can maintain an identity across multiple moments of time. As Heidegger puts this point, "we cannot identify what is brought forth again with what is offered at first, if we do not hold on to this from the beginning already as one and the same" (246). Identification of an individual must be carried out at the moment of apprehension, rather than coming subsequent to apprehension.

Turning to the transcendental synthesis that allows us to identify an individual in particular empirical cases, Heidegger argues that picking out a discrete individual requires a prior familiarity with a "unified interrelation of beings" (PIK 246). We must have a basic, "ontological" sense of what differentiates one being from another – how beings are set against one another (248). This prior familiarity allows one to select the individual. As Heidegger puts this point,

> what is offered in apprehension shows itself each time already against the background of that which is present to us in advance. Factually and essentially, we never begin with the simple grasping of something present as though prior to this grasping nothing had been given. We never begin with a now. Rather in beginning, that is, in apprehending, there is already present to us an interrelation of beings which is somehow unified without its unity's being conceptually clear to us. (246)

In other words, when we apprehend an individual, we pick it out against a background. This background is not just the background noise of our current perception (e.g., everything that is not the glove), but an "advance" background appreciation – even if it is not "conceptually clear to us" – of an "interrelation of beings." This background allows us to appreciate how one being could be differentiated from another, allowing us to pick out the individual. We do not "begin with a now," having "grasped nothing." When we identify something, we do it "against a background" that has been grasped "in advance."

Therefore, Heidegger traces the synthesis that is required to complete the synthesis of apprehension and the synthesis of reproduction to a transcendental synthesis of *pre-cognition*. The synthesis of pre-cognition "opens up and projects in advance a whole;" it is "an advance awaiting of a regional unity of offerable beings" (PIK 246). Due to this advance awaiting, we can pick out an individual; "this taking-in-advance of a regional totality makes possible for the first time the identification of individual objects of this region" (248). Picking out an individual allows us, in turn, to reidentify those individuals, complementing the syntheses of apprehension and reproduction.

As Heidegger's heavy use of the phrase "in advance" throughout this argument suggests, he takes the transcendental synthesis of pre-cognition to relate to the future. In particular, the synthesis of pre-cognition relates to the future by projecting a whole in advance: "by tracing recognition back to identification and this again back to an advance taking of a regional totality, it becomes clear ... the moment of time (the temporal moment), to which the synthesis of *re*-cognition relates, is precisely the future, having in advance" (PIK 246). By way of the synthesis of pre-cognition, we await or expect to find certain beings (individuals, set in certain regular relationships). The transcendental synthesis of pre-cognition opens up the future, such that it is "await[ed]" in any experience that we have.

In particular, the beings that are awaited are those that conform to Kant's categories. One expects to find, for example, enduring substances in causal relationships with one another (such that, for example, an object would never pop into existence without a prior causal impetus). The synthesis of pre-cognition establishes a certain stance on experience, where one anticipates unifying one's experience with certain stable concepts – the categories.

Kant claims that the "I think" of transcendental apperception is the "vehicle of all concepts" (A341/B399; PIK 255). Though, as Heidegger acknowledges, Kant depicts transcendental apperception as atemporal – "pure, original, unchanging consciousness" (A107; PIK 252) – Heidegger maintains nevertheless that apperception fills out the futural character of this third synthesis. It is this step of Heidegger's argument to which Dahlstrom objects, arguing that Heidegger misreads Kant's claims about the spontaneity of apperception, for these claims preclude a temporal character. However, Heidegger acknowledges these troublesome claims, arguing that we should disregard this strand of argument in favor of an argument that can better meet Kant's aims – spelling out the relationship between time (sensibility) and apperception (understanding). Moreover, Heidegger thinks that the temporal character of apperception can be developed out of Kant's own descriptions of it. Let us see how Heidegger develops this account.

Transcendental apperception refers to a basic form of self-consciousness, where one's various experiences are brought under the umbrella of one "numerically identical" consciousness (A107). In addition to experiencing certain content (glove laying on the floor), one experiences oneself as the owner of that experience, as the haver of that representation (*I* see the glove laying on the floor). One is co-present in any experience, providing a unifying perspective on a multiplicity of experiences. Kant's elucidation of transcendental apperception, Heidegger admits, does not acknowledge that it has a temporal character; transcendental apperception is a stable point from which multiple moments can be unified, standing opposite to time. But Heidegger worries that at this level of analysis, apperception is portrayed as wholly other to time, stymying explanation for how intuition and concept can combine. Indeed, Heidegger suggests that Kant's explanation is incomplete: "the unity of time and the I-think is only intimated in the expression 'synthesis.' And it is not *shown* how these syntheses spring from a common root" (PIK 242; see also 247). Simply claiming that apperception and time synthesize does not explain *how* they combine, and what enables their combination. Heidegger proposes that spelling out the temporality of apperception – "a direction which is certainly visible in Kant, but not taken by him" (243) – will enable this deeper explanation: "only then do *we* have the possibility of rendering all three syntheses visible in their unified ground with respect to time" (243).

Heidegger argues that developing Kant's characterization of transcendental apperception, in addition to his claim that apperception is the vehicle of concepts, leads ultimately to its relationship to the future. Heidegger agrees that it is a kind of self-consciousness, as Kant suggests, but argues that it is a consciousness of one's own abilities – "a grasping of oneself with respect to abilities" (PIK 254). This development follows Kant's intriguing comment in the B-Deduction that apperception is an ability (*Vermögen*) (B158). Heidegger reads this ability as an *interpretive* ability, where one is open for certain possibilities and not for others. This consciousness of one's own abilities provides a stable stance – in Kant's terms, a "fixed and abiding self" (A107) – such that one anticipates finding a world of a certain kind. In his own philosophical terminology, Heidegger argues that transcendental apperception is a future-oriented "comportment" (*Verhalten*) (PIK 254). It is only apperception in this sense, Heidegger reasons, that can provide a "vehicle" of concepts.

Heidegger's example of a moral disposition can help elucidate what he means by a comportment. On Heidegger's view, a moral disposition is not a "quality" that we possess, but an orientation: "moral disposition of a human being is a basic position toward a realm of possibilities which the human being controls on the basis of his moral disposition" (PIK 254). A moral disposition – say, being charitable – means taking a certain stance, being oriented to opportunities for exercising charity (as opposed, say, to opportunities for growing one's bank account). Charitability is a stance that governs how one takes a situation. But moreover, it is an *ability*, an ability to discern a charitable course of action and to take that action. A person who cannot discern others' neediness, or cannot begin to fathom how to respond to that neediness, is not charitable. A charitable person is someone who can interpret the world in a certain way – who can take on this particular stance. Having a comportment means "openness for" certain possibilities (277).

But moreover a moral disposition is an *abiding* stance. A moral disposition is not based on a one-time action; one is not charitable having performed a single charitable act (this could, after all, be some fluke in one's normal way of proceeding). One is not even charitable if one has performed a great deal of charitable acts in the past, for one could have a change of heart. Rather, someone has a charitable disposition only if possibilities for future action are open. As Heidegger puts this general idea, "In the field of subjectivity, where freedom primarily determines the mode of being of the subject and this mode of being is characterized by the 'I can,' the faculty, i.e., possibility, is higher than actuality. Here it is not actuality that constitutes existence but rather the 'I can' as 'I am able to'" (PIK 256). The single charitable act that one has actually carried out (or the sum of charitable acts from the past) does not establish one's having a charitable disposition; one only has such a disposition insofar as these possibilities continue to be available to oneself. If one no longer has access to the charitable way to proceed, then one's disposition has changed; one is no longer charitable, despite the number of charitable acts that one has, in fact, carried out. The future, then, is crucial for a comportment. The self is fixed and abiding when it projects itself into the future.

Heidegger argues that any comportment, such as charitability, relies on a "free self-binding" (PIK 255). One must bind or commit oneself to a certain vision of the world, but also a certain vision of one's own place in that world. But further, one must actively or freely enact this stance, interpreting the world in light of it. One is *conscious* of oneself as a certain kind of self (e.g., a charitable one), as having a certain "mode of being" (256), adhering to and working out this self-understanding.

Transcendental apperception, like charitability, is also on Heidegger's view a comportment. It is the ability to interpret the world in a certain way, namely, by way of the categories; these delimit the possibilities for organizing and unifying one's experience, thereby delimiting the sort of objects that one can find over the course of one's experience. Transcendental apperception means that one is open for certain possibilities – for example, that an object might alter in accordance with a causal rule – and closed to others – for example, that an object might pop into existence with no causal antecedent. Transcendental apperception is, moreover, an abiding stance – one that is projected into the future, as standing expectations for the objects that one will encounter. Actively committing oneself to these rules, one is aware of oneself (though perhaps only implicitly), as a knower who knows by way of these categories – as a knower who unifies experience using certain stable rules, rules that one will continue to rely on in the future – as a subject, facing a stable world of objects.

Heidegger traces the ability that underlies our employment of the categories back to a more basic ability, the ability to take up a comportment at all. He argues: "Experience and object-relatedness is only possible when the resistance of a binding regulation of all syntheses springs from that which is fundamentally pure possibility, i.e. from the free 'I can.' *Thus the 'I' in its actuality is pure possibility; this 'I can' is just existing existence*" (PIK 258). Because we can take up an orientation, making sense of the world by way of a comportment, we can relate to a resisting, rule-governed object. In particular, transcendental apperception binds itself with the rules offered by the categories; these rules are "understood in advance and accepted as binding – these rules are nothing but unities which lie in the possible free forms of synthesis as such" (259). The categories rely on transcendental apperception, because they offer rules that limit or constrain our taking of the objects that we encounter. In order to be in operation, these rules must be taken up. However, rules can be taken up only by a being capable of being limited, that can bind future actions by anticipating the rule; the categories can be taken up only by a being that is "open" for possibilities (259). Transcendental apperception freely binds itself with the categories, taking up a constrained comportment toward the future objects that it will encounter.

In short, Heidegger argues that, if the categories are to be employed, the subject is required to take a certain stance on the makeup of its world and its own place in that world. Construing transcendental apperception as a future-directed comportment, Heidegger argues that this specific, knowing comportment is dependent on a further, more fundamental ability to take up a comportment at all. Taking a stance relies on *existence*, where one anticipates a world of a certain kind, and one's own place within that world (e.g., one experiences oneself as a knower who can determine the properties of rule-governed objects). Therefore, Heidegger argues that our employment of the categories is ultimately dependent on a future-oriented self – a being who can project into the future.

While Heidegger's analysis of the synthesis of recognition might seem like it goes two steps further than his analysis of the other syntheses – burrowing deep underground, descending from an empirical synthesis to a transcendental synthesis to transcendental apperception to existence – it is helpful to recognize that Heidegger is not offering a string of deeper conditions but, rather, attempting to spell out the transcendental synthesis in its entirety. The so-called synthesis of pre-cognition projects a totality or interrelation of objects, but in opposition to a stable, knowing subject. The expectations held up for objects are intimately connected with the expectations held up for the subject; we do not get a stable (e.g., causal) object absent a stable subject (i.e., one who abides by the concept of cause). The projection of subject and object are two sides of the same coin, both a part of the same synthesis of pre-cognition that opens up a future of a certain kind. Further, the synthesis of pre-cognition provides a concrete way to *exist*, one way of temporalizing the future. The synthesis of pre-cognition opens up the future in a particular way (where a "now-not-yet" is populated by stable objects opposite a knowing subject), just as the synthesis of reproduction opens up the past in a particular way (i.e., as a "no-longer-now" that can be retained and set in relation with a present now), and the synthesis of apprehension opens up the present in a particular way (i.e., as a now that is distinct from other moments, and contains an inherent unity).

If the transcendental synthesis of pre-cognition is time-related, opening up the future in a particular way, this provides a quick reason to attribute that synthesis to the imagination. After all, Kant relates the imagination to time, yet portrays the spontaneous faculties, pure reason in general, as removed from the condition of time. But further, the synthesis betrays the dual spontaneity and receptivity that characterizes the imagination. The synthesis of recognition is a free self-binding – expectations are both actively *formed* and receptively *submitted to*. The latter moment of receptivity or submission precludes attributing the synthesis to a purely spontaneous faculty, as Kant portrays the understanding. In the section that follows, we will finally put together the transcendental structure of the imagination, and explore whether that structure is indeed unified.

5 The Unity of the Three Syntheses

The previous sections have developed one set of dependency relations: dependency relationships between the empirical synthesis that Kant invokes and the deeper, transcendental (and temporal) synthesis that Heidegger identifies. To review, the synthesis of apprehension is dependent on opening up the horizon of the present, by articulating it as a distinct and unified now. The synthesis of reproduction is dependent on opening the horizon of the past, by articulating it as a retainable and relevant no-longer-now. Finally, the synthesis of recognition is dependent on opening the horizon of the future, a not-yet-now where a stable subject continues to encounter a stable object.

Yet we still need to develop the second set of dependency relations: dependency relationships between the three transcendental syntheses, establishing their unity at this deeper level. This second set requires development, because Heidegger motivates his preferred strand of argument by arguing that it can unite intuition and concept, sensibility and understanding, time and apperception. And it is supposed to unite them by showing the deeper transcendental unity that holds between apprehension in intuition and recognition in concepts. So, how are the transcendental syntheses underlying apprehension, reproduction, and recognition unified?

Heidegger suggests that these three interdependent transcendental syntheses are unified in the transcendental power of the imagination (see, e.g., PIK 283). However, while Heidegger has argued that each synthesis, on its own, ought to be attributed to the transcendental power of imagination (as spontaneous and receptive), these arguments do not establish that the syntheses themselves are unified – internally referring to one another, being dependent on one another, forming a whole. So, another way to put the question is: Why do the three transcendental syntheses belong together in one faculty (again, what unifies them)?

It might be tempting to affirm that these transcendental syntheses are unified because each spell out a dimension of time, and the dimensions of time are unified. That is, the transcendental syntheses are unified just because past, present, and future are unified. However, given the deep analyses of time offered by both Heidegger and Kant, it would be unsatisfying to take the unity of the dimensions of time for granted. Indeed, Heidegger's own analysis of temporality in *Being and Time* does not take this unity for granted, but rather works out how the dimensions of time refer to one another (as one can appreciate from the perspective of the future, which requires a past possibility and present activity to work out any projection). Are the dimensions of past, present, and future that Heidegger unearths in the Transcendental Deduction similarly unified?

The empirical syntheses that Heidegger adopts from Kant are interdependent. On Heidegger's reconstruction, the synthesis of recognition unifies the other two syntheses, thereby having priority among the empirical syntheses.[5] Namely, recognition establishes the relationship between an apprehended intuition of something present before oneself and a reproduced intuition of something seen in the past – establishing, for example, that they represent one and the same object (e.g., a glove). Without this recognition, where multiple time slices are unified under a concept, an apprehension and reproduction could be set side by side, but would bear no relation to one another. The first two syntheses call for the third; the third synthesis completes them. These syntheses are unified and complementary at the empirical level, though Kant's aims in the Transcendental Deduction call for more: he wants to show that intuitions and concepts are in contact a priori, such that the categories form the sensible world.

This interdependence and unity are supposed to be visible at the a priori level, with the help of Heidegger's violent interpretation of recognition. We have now seen the pieces that are to be united: an a priori apprehension that seizes the present now as distinct and internally unified; an a priori reproduction that opens up the past as a no-longer-now that is retainable and relatable to the present now; and an a priori recognition that opens up the future as a not-yet-now that is had in advance, maintaining some resemblance between the present and future (not identical beings, but an identical interrelation of beings). Are these syntheses interdependent?

On Heidegger's account, the internal unification of the apprehended now already refers to the horizons of the past and future, being dependent on them. The pure now contains a plurality, such that it can morph from not-yet-now to now to no-longer-now. Appreciating this plurality requires that one grasp the past as no-longer-now and the future as not-yet-now. As Heidegger puts this point in regard to the horizon of the past in particular: "Already in seizing what is immediately given as intuitive there occurs a *reaching beyond and*

---

[5] I'll say more about temporal priority in Chapter 6.

reaching back to something which from out of the moment-phase of a now each time necessarily flows or is about to flow into the very next no-longer-now" (PIK 239). Similarly, apprehending the pure now requires also *reaching beyond and reaching forward*, such that the now is seized as something that was previously not-yet. The a priori synthesis of apprehension requires the a priori syntheses of reproduction and recognition.

The a priori synthesis of reproduction also requires the a priori synthesis of apprehension; these "two primordial acts ... belong to one another" (PIK 240). The now-no-longer that the a priori synthesis of reproduction opens up offers a moment that was once a now; it internally refers to the present that is opened up by a prior apprehension. As Heidegger puts this point, "everything retainable which can be brought forth must be capable of being displayed in each actual case of the now of apprehension" (PIK 239).

The a priori synthesis of reproduction requires the a priori synthesis of recognition, too. In fact, a priori recognition is needed to establish the relationship between a priori reproduction and the other a priori synthesis that it requires – apprehension. Here is how Heidegger explains this dependency: "this *pure-taking-in-advance*, this *pure synthesis of recognition*, is simultaneously the sustaining ground of the pure synthesis of apprehension and reproduction" (PIK 248, see also 263). Recognition unifies the other two dimensions because the expectations that it holds up – the interrelations that it has in advance – are essentially temporal expectations. Pure recognition projects expectations about how time will flow, and how objects will show up within that time. It projects expectations about how present nows relate to past nows, and what is and is not possible for objects that are bound to such nows (e.g., the present object cannot pop up arbitrarily, but must follow from some past state). Put otherwise, what the subject expects from itself and the objects that it encounters are not expectations that are limited to a single time slice. These expectations are more complex, drawn out across multiple moments of time; they are expectations about how a subject will act, how an object will behave. These expectations span and connect the now offered up by the synthesis of apprehension and the no-longer-now offered up by the synthesis of reproduction.

From here, one can see why the a priori synthesis of recognition also requires the other two syntheses, apprehension and reproduction. The "regional totality" or "unified interrelation of beings" that pure recognition awaits is complex, already temporally differentiated; it is a projection of how objects can be expected to behave across multiple moments, of how time itself will behave across multiple moments (of how the subject will unify experience across multiple moments). Such expectations refer not to a single time slice (an anticipated future moment) but rather to multiple temporal dimensions. They are expectations, say, about how past moments bear on present moments, about how past objective states bear on present objective states. These temporal dimensions are baked into the expectations that the pure synthesis of recognition forms. Awaiting a regional totality already makes reference to the other two syntheses.

This discussion provides a more complete view of transcendental apperception. Though Kant invokes apperception only to explain the synthesis of recognition, apperception as a comportment relates to all three transcendental syntheses – "sustains in an originary way the entirety of the three names [syntheses]" (PIK 242). These three syntheses spell out our expectations for time – as a sequence of nows – and the objects that can be found within time – for example, as enduring across multiple moments despite their (rule-governed) changes. Indeed, the categories articulate those expectations we have for time (and the objects found therein), their content cashed out in terms of time relations (as the Schematism elucidates in more detail). These categories are the very abilities that we have for uniting the moments of time (and the objects found therein), the abilities of which we are conscious in apperception, keeping them fixed. The expectations that we hold up for ourselves and for the world that we find ourselves in are cashed out in terms of time.

With this argument, Heidegger solves the problem he posed to Kant, spelling out the unity between apperception and time (as a sequence of nows), and thereby understanding and sensibility. Apperception articulates and sustains time as a sequence of nows, carrying this interpretation of time forward into each of its encounters with empirical objects. Apperception is not removed from time or opposite to time. Rather, it holds up a certain vision of time, certain capacities for making sense of time, sustaining that vision across the moments of time.

6 Conclusion: Heidegger's Interpretive Strategy Revisited

Let's return to the interpretive approach that we have now seen worked out in Heidegger's interpretation of the Transcendental Deduction. Heidegger reads Kant as offering two competing strands of thought. The first strand, more prominent and embraced by other Post-Kantian interpreters, treats understanding as the primary faculty, bringing unity to experience by way of its atemporal standpoint. The counterevidence that

Conclusion: Heidegger's Interpretive Strategy Revisited   159

Dahlstrom and Henrich pose against Heidegger's interpretation belongs to this strand of argument; Heidegger recognizes these counterclaims, but suggests that they should be disregarded, as this strand of argument opens an "inner rupture" between the faculties that the argument is intended to unify. Heidegger, sensitive to the challenges that this strand of argument faces, brings out another strand of thought in Kant, where the imagination is fundamental, and its temporal structure brings unity to our experience. The benefit of Heidegger's preferred strand of argument is that it carries out the aim of the Transcendental Deduction; it unites the faculties that Kant first analyzed in isolation from one another, showing how the categories of the understanding inform the world of sense. If the syntheses are grounded in the structure of original temporality, then this avoids reading the Transcendental Deduction such that it concludes with transcendental apperception opposed to time, reproducing the duality between understanding and sensibility that the argument was initially supposed to resolve. While Heidegger's interpretation does not maximize agreement, it does attribute a strong, radical argument to Kant, offering its own kind of charity.

According to some commentators, Heidegger's interpretation of the Transcendental Deduction betrays his characteristic violence; here, Heidegger goes beyond Kant, rather than uncovering a strand of argument that reasonably could be attributed to Kant. However, my work here has shown that the strand of argument that Heidegger attributes to Kant – where Kant identifies the threefold, temporal structure of the imagination in his discussion of the three transcendental syntheses – is based on a few different kinds of evidence. First, some of Kant's explicit claims imply that all three syntheses are temporal in character: two syntheses are explicitly temporal, suggesting that the third one, as their complement, would also be temporal. Second, in Heidegger's view, of all the human faculties that Kant introduces, the imagination seems the best suited to serve his purposes (uniting the three syntheses) in the Transcendental Deduction. While Heidegger's interpretation goes beyond Kant's explicit claims, taking some liberties – such as surveying Kant's critical system for a solution, rather than accepting the solution that Kant articulates – it does not import Heidegger's views into Kant's text. It does not, that is, amount to hermeneutic ventriloquism.

CHAPTER 6

The Form of Time and Self-Affection

In Chapter 5, we saw that Heidegger thinks his account of Dasein has something to offer Kant. Heidegger summarizes how his account helps Kant in the 1927–1928 lecture series when he cites the sections of *Being and Time* developing Dasein's temporality, saying:

> It was only on the basis of that investigation that the possibility arose for me to understand what Kant is actually seeking, respectively must seek. Only from out of that [investigation] can we grasp the unity of receptivity and spontaneity, of time and the transcendental apperception, as a possible problem. (PIK 267)

Heidegger's fuller development of the structure of the human being – specifically, how the human being's capacities are interlaced in a threefold, temporal structure – spells out the unity between Kant's dual faculties of sensibility and understanding. Posing Heidegger's Dasein as the "common root" of Kant's faculty psychology explains the possibility of synthetic a priori judgment that combines sensible and conceptual components. Now that we have seen what Heidegger has to offer Kant, we will in this chapter see what Kant has to offer Heidegger.

I've argued that Heidegger goes to Kant with philosophical questions that he takes Kant to pursue, as well. In particular, on Heidegger's understanding of Kant's main question – "How are synthetic judgments a priori possible?" – Kant also wants to inquire into the human being as the foundation for other ontologies. In Chapter 5, I introduced a quote suggesting that Heidegger also found something in Kant that confirmed his own philosophical work. Recall Heidegger's claim that

> When some years ago I studied the *Critique of Pure Reason* anew and read it, as it were, against the background of Husserl's phenomenology, it opened my eyes; and Kant became for me the crucial confirmation of the accuracy of the path which I took in my search. (PIK 292)

This quote could be read as saying that Heidegger independently took some philosophical path, and Kant subsequently confirmed the accuracy of that path. However, I argue in this chapter that interpreting Kant does not simply confirm a path that Heidegger has already traveled; rather, interpreting Kant allows Heidegger to walk further down that path. To speak less metaphorically, interpreting Kant allows Heidegger to make progress on the philosophical questions that they both share.[1] This chapter will turn to Heidegger's own philosophy to consider what progress has been made. I will argue that interpreting Kant helps Heidegger make progress on his account of Dasein and, more broadly, his fundamental ontology.

In *Being and Time*, Heidegger clarifies precisely what intrigues him about Kant's philosophy. In the second introduction, Heidegger identifies Kant's Schematism as the site of deep insight, saying: "The first and only person who has gone any stretch of the way towards investigating the dimension of Temporality or has even let himself be drawn hither by the coercion of the phenomena themselves is Kant" (BT 23). This clarification, along with the previous chapters of the present study, suggest that interpreting Kant helps Heidegger make progress on his account of time: specifically, Dasein's temporal structure, and how that structure is a basis for other temporalities, like Kant's form of sequential time ("now-time"). Accordingly, this chapter will turn to Heidegger's account, offered at the end of the second division of *Being and Time*, that Dasein is characterized by the structure of temporality and that now-time has its "origin" or "source" in the fundamental temporality of Dasein (BT 405).

I will endorse a temporal idealist interpretation of that account, where the time that organizes our experience descends from the human standpoint. That is, the now-time that structures the beings we encounter is derived from the temporality of the human being; temporality produces or creates the model of now-time. Indeed, I will argue that interpreting Kant allows Heidegger to develop more fully his own account of temporal idealism, in conversation with a thinker who also defends that theory. Heidegger deepens the temporal idealism he finds in Kant, where time is a form of intuition; Heidegger presses ahead to the source of that model of

---

[1] We also cannot think of Kant as confirming a path that Heidegger traveled independently, because Heidegger's engagement with Kant began well before the Kant book. As Theodore Kisiel (1993) has explored in great detail, this engagement informed Heidegger's work in *Being and Time*. I am indebted to a brief discussion in Truwant (2022) for reminding me of this point (pp. 214–215). One can also consult Engelland (2017), especially chapter 2, for a broader account of Heidegger's engagement with Kant over the course of his career.

time, arguing that it springs from a deeper model of time, which in fact constitutes the human being.

However, some interpreters defend a temporal realist reading of Heidegger's Kant interpretation. These readings suggest that Heidegger finds a temporal realism in Kant, where time is a real feature of the world around us, and we derive our understanding of now-time from external reality. To defend and develop my own temporal idealist reading of Heidegger's Kant interpretation, I respond to the temporal realist readings of it. I introduce two reasons why some interpreters find temporal realism in Heidegger's Kant interpretation. First, Heidegger's opening discussion of intuition claims that we intuit beings that are already "at hand" (KPM 18), seeming to place us in a world of preexisting beings with their own spatiotemporal natures – natures that we must access and grasp, and of which we are not ourselves the author. Second, Dasein's temporal structure can be interpreted as an enabling condition – something that allows us to appreciate the spatiotemporal natures of other beings, without itself producing that nature.

To respond to the first argument, I compare the account of time at the end of *Being and Time* with the account developed in the Kant interpretation. I first outline the three models of time that Heidegger identifies at the end of *Being and Time*: temporality, world-time, and now-time. Confirming the tight connection between Heidegger's magnum opus and the Kant interpretation, I show that Heidegger's treatment of time in the Kant interpretation can be mapped onto these three models. This comparison sheds new light on Heidegger's opening discussion of intuition. In particular, I argue that the Kant interpretation proceeds recursively: Heidegger begins with an experience that is *already* structured by a model of time, and he goes on to dig into the deeper conditions for that experience, landing ultimately on the temporal structure of the human being. This means that when we intuit beings already "at hand," the human standpoint is already operative. Since we are already interpreting the spatiotemporal natures of these "at hand" beings (e.g., taking it that they have a causal history in their own right), Heidegger's locution does not suggest that those beings possess a spatiotemporal nature independently of the human standpoint.

To respond to the second argument, I turn to the account of self-affection in Heidegger's Kant interpretation. According to my interpretation, self-affection describes the process where human temporality *produces* the now-time that organizes objects (rather than simply *enabling our appreciation* of that time). This discussion will also find a remarkably different argumentative strategy from the one found at the tail end of *Being and Time*, revealing a more sophisticated version of Heidegger's temporal idealism. In particular, we will see that Heidegger shifts from tracing the characteristics of other models of time back to Dasein's fundamental temporality, to explaining the process whereby temporality "temporalizes" itself – that is, where the interaction between our fundamental, temporal capacities produces another model of time. This shift helps Heidegger foreground a gap between temporality and the model of now-time that it produces: now-time is not a necessary derivation from temporality, an interpretation of time that we must adopt. Rather, now-time is a "free" interpretation, merely one possible way of making sense of time. Heidegger thus proposes that historical developments explain why we interpret time as we do, anticipating his account of the "history of Being" in the 1930s.[2]

1 Heidegger's Temporal Idealism

In reading Heidegger as a temporal idealist, I follow William Blattner, who finds temporal idealism in the second division of *Being and Time*.[3] I also follow Beatrice Han-Pile, who finds temporal idealism in Heidegger's Kant interpretation (though she does not focus on Heidegger's account of self-affection, as I will).[4] The temporal idealist reading suggests that Heidegger thinks that the human standpoint (itself a kind of time) is the source of the time that organizes our experience. Further, time is not an incidental or occasional part of our perspective, but a central and thoroughgoing part of it. From this, two things follow: First, we do not know what beings are like outside our temporal perspective. All our encounters with beings are temporally structured; we lack any other access to beings. But second, we can guarantee that everything we encounter will be temporal – for we cannot otherwise experience beings.

I take Heidegger's temporal idealism to resemble, but deepen, Kant's temporal idealism. According to Kant, time, as a form of our intuition, is a

---

[2] Centrally, Heidegger provides this account in his 1936–1937 work, *Contributions to Philosophy* (CP).
[3] See Blattner (1994 and 1999). Blattner's account has faced criticism from Carman (2000), Cerbone (1995), and Philipse (1998), and Blattner responds to these critics in Blattner (2004). More recently, Rousse (2022) defends a temporal realist reading of Heidegger against Blattner.
[4] Han-Pile (2005), more generally, compares Heidegger's position to Kant's transcendental idealism, for example, by developing his take on the distinction between appearances and things in themselves. I focus specifically on the analysis of time in the Transcendental Deduction, thereby adding to the evidence that she introduces.

feature of the human standpoint (a way in which we are constrained to experience beings). However, for Kant, the form of time is only one of the conditions of our transcendence: time, in addition to the form of space and the categories of the understanding, is but one component of our perspective. Heidegger deepens Kant's temporal idealism, because, for Heidegger, time is the heart of the human standpoint, encapsulating the human perspective.[5] Though deepening the role of time, Heidegger can nevertheless make the Kantian claim that all the beings that we experience will be in time – though not because time is one a priori condition among others, but rather because the human perspective is fundamentally temporal.[6]

The deepened role of time in Heidegger's temporal idealism is reflected throughout the Kant interpretation. On Heidegger's reading of the Schematism, time is presented as the condition for the possibility of experience that sustains and organizes all the other conditions (save space, which he mostly ignores). The categories determine the form of time, such that time is articulated as being a constant that undergoes change (substance), having moments that follow one another irreversibly (causality), and so forth. Time, so determined, forms the horizon guiding our uptake of empirical particulars. But further, on Heidegger's reading of the Transcendental Deduction, the form of time that Kant outlines – the linear, unidirectional time that shapes our engagement with the natural world – is dependent on another model of time: the human temporality comprising three interlaced temporal capacities. In my view, Heidegger concurs with Kant that the form of time is relative to the human standpoint, but offers a deeper account in that he explains where that form of time comes from – that is, how it derives from the very structure of the human being. In comparison to Kant's temporal idealism, Heidegger identifies another model of time as the basis for the more superficial model

---

[5] Han-Pile also outlines this idea in her treatment of Heidegger's temporal idealism: "Heidegger does not criticize Kant for claiming that entities are transcendentally determined (as spatio-temporal): on the contrary, *he blames him for not developing the idea of transcendental determination far enough*, and in particular for not having seen (or rather having 'shrunk back' from the idea) that temporality is not only an *a priori* form of sensibility, but also underlies the 'I think' of transcendental apperception and the syntheses of transcendental imagination" (2005: 90).

[6] Both Blattner and Han-Pile affirm this point (Blattner 1999: 234; Han-Pile 2005: 91). However, both notice an important difference between Heidegger's idealism and that of Kant: where Kant denies that things in themselves are spatiotemporal (i.e., space and time are forms of human sensibility only), Heidegger makes no such denial. That is, on Heidegger's view, we cannot know the spatiotemporal properties of things in themselves either way. Thus, both shy away from attributing transcendental idealism to him. For Blattner, Heidegger is an ontological idealist (1999: 246), and for Han-Pile "his position is most of the time (but not always) analogous to [Kantian transcendental idealism]" (2005: 95).

of now-time. Insofar as that original model of time is the very structure of the human being, time for Heidegger is not just one a priori element among others; it is the ultimate condition for any transcendence at all.

To support my claim that Heidegger defends and develops a temporal idealist position in his Kant interpretation, I must address readings that find in the Kant book a temporal realism instead. Daniel Dahlstrom and James Kinkaid both suggest that, in Heidegger's reading of Kant, we gain access to the thing itself – including, on Kinkaid's account, its own temporal nature.[7]

Dahlstrom draws his reading primarily from Heidegger's opening discussion of intuition, which suggests that, in order to intuit, we must be affected by beings "already on hand." According to Dahlstrom, Heidegger "proceeds from the realist standpoint that entities are already on hand. In order for them to be taken up, the subject must turn toward them in the appropriate way, making the encounter possible in advance" (2010: 394). On Dahlstrom's reading, Heidegger begins with the idea that beings are "already on hand" (or, on Taft's translation, "at hand") and then outlines the transcendental, horizon-forming activities of the subject – the turning-toward – that allow us to encounter this being as the being that it is.[8] This process, where we turn toward these entities "in the appropriate way," leaves us with a horizon that is only "co-constituted" by the subject's activities (2010: 399). This means, if I understand Dahlstrom correctly, that the entities toward which we turn contribute to the horizon that we form; the horizon incorporates or reflects what those beings are really like.

It is important to see where and how Dahlstrom's reading strikes the temporal idealist reading, since the temporal idealist reading does make some room for entities to contribute to our experience of them. The form of time that structures our encounters with entities guarantees that entities will have a certain ontological structure; for example, if it is now-time that structures our experience, it guarantees that entities will persist across time slices and change according to causal laws. However, the form of time that we bring to experience does not predict simply everything about those

---

[7] Dahlstrom and Kinkaid draw different conclusions from this finding, though. For Dahlstrom, the realism that Heidegger finds in Kant is at odds with Heidegger's philosophical position in *Being and Time*, which is neither realist nor idealist (2010: 383–384). For Kinkaid (2018), the Kant interpretation reflects a broader commitment to realism. To the contrary, I read the Kant interpretation as reflecting (and developing) a broader commitment to idealism.

[8] Similarly, Sacha Golob argues that "Heidegger presents Kant as beginning from the assumptions both that the objects of experience are 'present-at-hand' and that they are so independent of any facts about the human mind" (2013: 348).

entities. As Han-Pile puts this point, "what is must conform to the conditions of transcendental determination to be disclosed as entities; but conversely, such conformity is not something that can be determined solely by those conditions" (Han-Pile 2005: 93). That is, we know in advance that any being we experience will persist across moments of time, but we do not know the precise form that this persistence will take (e.g., that an orange, three-legged object persists); we know in advance that any being will change in accordance with causal laws, but we do not know which changes (e.g., that it will begin to emit a strange odor), or which causal laws (e.g., laws pertaining to decomposition). In brief, we do not know in advance which incidental, empirical, or ontic features entities will have. If we bring the ontological structure to experience, entities contribute the ontic particularity (though these ontic particularities are processed or rendered according to that ontological structure, fitting into its spatio-temporal framework). Dahlstrom, however, argues that these entities do more than contribute ontic features; they contribute *ontologically*, co-constituting the *horizon* that structures our experience. And Heidegger's opening discussion of intuition is supposed to suggest such a view, for it introduces entities already "at hand" that can contribute to the formation of a horizon as we are "directing [ourselves] toward" them (Dahlstrom 2010: 394 n. 34).

Kinkaid builds on this account, spelling out how it offers a specifically *temporal* realism.[9] According to Kinkaid, the transcendental activities of

---

[9] This dimension may be implied by Dahlstrom's account, because Dahlstrom compares Heidegger's realist interpretation of Kant to that of Alois Riehl. Riehl, as Frederick Beiser explains, rejected the idea that "space and time would disappear if there were no human beings with their characteristic sensibility" and therefore attempted to recover realist elements in Kant's Transcendental Aesthetic (Beiser 2014: 538). Beiser agrees that "the heir of Riehl's interpretation, though it was never acknowledged, was Martin Heidegger" (533).

However, Heidegger has little and primarily critical things to say about Riehl's interpretation of Kant: though he lists Riehl's *Der philosophische Kritizismus* among "some important secondary literature" in the lecture series (PIK 5), Heidegger in the Davos debate identifies Riehl as one of his Neo-Kantian "opponents" (KPM 193) and in the Kant book nitpicks (wrongly, as the translator notes) Riehl's rendering of a Kantian passage (KPM 59 n. 118). Moreover, as Heidelberger and Nordmann reconstruct, Riehl's realism rests on the idea that the thing in itself is the "cause" of appearances (Heidelberger 2006: 235; Nordmann 2006: 254) – that is, on a two-world view. As I argued in Chapter 3, Heidegger defends a two-aspect view of the distinction between appearances and things in themselves.

In a 1912 essay, Heidegger approvingly reconstructs the position of Oswald Külpe, another prominent realist of this period. Heidegger argues that Külpe "sees the external world as 'the basis of the externally determined, lawful relations of our sense impressions' . . . that this is still a causal relation is clear" (PRMP 47). Once again, this sounds like a two-world view, though Heidegger here endorses the view (and moreover positions it against Kant): "a causal relation between the external

the subject create a space where the being can reveal its own spatiotemporal properties. He bolsters his reading by arguing that the temporality of the human being is only an *enabling condition*. That is, the temporal structure of the human being *enables* the object to show up as it is in itself, allowing us to appreciate the spatiotemporal characteristics that beings independently possess: "By emphasizing that these structures are enabling, I suggest, Heidegger intends to reject the understanding of form that leads to idealism by emphasizing that intentional form allows spatial and temporal objects to be given without thereby contributing or grounding their spatial and temporal natures" (Kinkaid 2018: 16). Thus, Kinkaid's temporal realist reading of Heidegger takes him to inquire into the existential structures (i.e., temporality) that allow objects to show up as just the sort of (temporal, spatial) objects that they are. Temporality is not the *source* of now-time, but merely the structure that gives access to it.

These readings of the Kant interpretation raise two difficult questions for a temporal idealist reading: First, in line with Dahlstrom, how can the idealist account for Heidegger's starting point in the Kant book, where beings are already "at hand"? Second, in line with Kinkaid, why think that the temporality of the human subject exhaustively determines the temporal natures of the beings that we experience? I take on these questions *seriatim*, in Sections 2 and 3.

2 Convergence with *Being and Time*

In this section, I will compare the models of time that Heidegger introduces in *Being and Time* with the models of time to which Heidegger appeals in the Kant interpretation. In addition to noticing the convergence between these two treatments of time, this comparison will pave the way for answering Dahlstrom's question.

---

world and sense impressions must undeniably exist" (PRMP 46). Heidegger's defense of the two-aspect view in the Kant book indicates that Heidegger has moved on from this early view. Indeed, Heidegger is explicit about his departure from Külpe: as the translators of the essay note, Heidegger "in 1916 argues for the need to critically supplement [Külpe's 'critical realism'] with the viewpoint of 'transcendental idealism' ... but then in 1922 he dismisses it completely as a 'misbegotten epistemology'" (PRMP 40 n. 5).

Notably, both Riehl and Külpe insist on an external cause, because according to them such a cause ensures the communicability of knowledge – that is, that multiple people would agree about the same object (Nordmann 2006: 254; PRMP 46). In the Kant book, and as I discussed in Chapter 2, Heidegger rather argues that it is *understanding* that ensures communicability: "the intuited is only a cognized being if everyone can make it understandable to oneself and others and can thereby communicate it" (KPM 19). Even in the opening discussion of intuition, Heidegger departs from Riehl and Külpe in his two-aspect view and in his treatment of communication.

In *Being and Time*, Heidegger outlines three models of time: now-time, world-time, and temporality. I endorse a temporal idealist interpretation of his argument connecting these models; that is, I think Heidegger argues that now-time and world-time are derivative models of time in that they are derived from (created or produced by) temporality. Insofar as temporality refers to the structure of the human being, or Dasein, this argument renders Heidegger's fundamental ontology in temporal terms: Dasein's own ontology is captured by a model of time, and it forms a basis for the models of time that encapsulate other ontologies. Thus, Heidegger's argument that temporality founds other models of time is an argument that Dasein founds other ontologies.

However, my response to Dahlstrom does not hang on a temporal idealist interpretation of Heidegger's argument. Rather, reviewing Heidegger's three models of time will lend credence to my interpretation of the opening discussion of intuition, where Heidegger argues that "cognizing is primarily intuiting" (KPM 15) and that we intuit beings that are already "at hand" (KPM 18). As I argued in Chapter 2, I think that the opening discussion of intuition describes a sort of experience, where we encounter independent, "at hand" beings. The discussion does not attribute independent, metaphysical properties to beings (indeed, even Heidegger's account of "affection" is metaphysically indeterminate). It treats an experience where we find metaphysically determinate beings, and then presses forward to the deeper conditions for that experience. These deeper conditions are, ultimately, an ontological understanding that we bring to those beings, rather than the independent, metaphysical properties of those beings.

Reviewing Heidegger's three models of time from *Being and Time* will lend credence to this interpretation because it will shed new light on the opening discussion of intuition. In particular, paying special attention to the temporal moment that is primary in each model – that is, past, present, or future – will provide new vocabulary for appreciating Heidegger's claim that "cognizing is primarily intuiting" (KPM 15).[10] I will argue that, in Heidegger's opening discussion of intuition, he is describing an experience that is framed by an interpretation of time; specifically, the model of now-time is already in play when we intuit (and, more broadly, cognize). If intuition encounters "at hand" beings, then, this does not mean that they exist independently, possessing certain spatiotemporal properties on their

---

[10] My understanding of this priority is indebted to many conversations with Christopher Yeomans, especially as we coauthored Lambeth and Yeomans (forthcoming).

own, as Dahlstrom would have it. It means rather that we experience them as existing spatiotemporally from within our spatiotemporal framework – from within the horizon of now-time. The opening discussion of intuition, therefore, does not support a temporal realist reading of Heidegger's Kant interpretation.

We begin, then, with the model of now-time. Now-time refers to the model of time that has dominated the philosophical tradition, with Kant being no exception. Heidegger already remarks on Kant's traditional conception of time in *Being and Time*, when laying out his planned destruction of the philosophical tradition: "in spite of the fact that he was bringing the phenomenon of time back into the subject again, his analysis of it remained oriented toward the traditional way in which time had been ordinarily understood" (BT 24). Even though Kant brings time into the subject as a form of intuition – as a way that we sense the world, rather than the way the world is structured in itself – he continues to conceive of time as a sequence of nows, where the moments of time follow one another on a timeline. Heidegger repeats this charge in the Kant interpretation when he says, for example, that Kant is "orient[ed] toward the nonoriginal essence of time" (KPM 136; see also PIK 58). Kant is oriented, that is, toward the derivative model of now-time, rather than the more original time, temporality, from which now-time is derived.

At the end of *Being and Time*, Heidegger characterizes now-time, where "time is understood as a succession, as a 'flowing stream' of 'nows'" (BT 422). This sort of time is quantifiable and public (425); that is, the passage of time can be measured in seconds, hours, days, and so forth, and these measures sync up across different people (e.g., 3 pm EST does not happen at different times for different people). The moments of now-time are continuous or uninterrupted; there is no gap in the succession of moments that make up now-time (423). Further, this model of time is infinite, with no end point when looking either forward or backward in time; it is also irreversible, progressing only forward and never backward (424).

According to Heidegger, the present moment dominates the model of now-time: "the basic phenomenon of time is seen in the 'now'" (427). That is, although now-time also includes past and future moments, these moments are characterized by their relation to the present moment. On the sequence of nows, we occupy the present "now"; "no-longer-nows" are past and "not-yet-nows" are future. The other moments are moments *of time* in virtue of the fact that they *will be* present (future moments), or at one point *were* present (past moments). Becoming present is a basic feature of each moment of time, wherever it figures on the timeline.

Heidegger suggests that the model of now-time is in fact an abstraction, derived from another model of time, world-time, by "level[ing] off" much of its richness (BT 422). The model of world-time structures our rich, concrete, everyday projects. The moments of world-time are indexed to what we find ourselves alongside in that moment. They are not just empty moments, but moments when something happens – not simply a "now" but a "now that – a door slams" and "now that – my book is missing" (408). That is, in Heidegger's terms, the moments of world-time are "datable." These moments are also significant – either *appropriate* or *inappropriate* for certain activities (414). For example, it is inappropriate to host dinner at the first light of dawn; appropriate to say "Gesundheit!" immediately after someone sneezes, but not sometime later. As these examples suggest, world-time is also public (413f.). World-time is not a personal construction, but something accessible to others, such that they can likewise appreciate the ill-timing of your dinner or "Gesundheit!" utterance. Finally, the moments of world-time are spanned according to the happening or activity that dates the moment, "with the width of the span varying: 'now' – in the intermission, while one is eating, in the evening, in summer" (409).

Heidegger argues that the present also has a "peculiar importance" for world-time (BT 407). World-time does incorporate the past and future. In the experience of world-time, we retain an "on that former occasion" and await an approaching "then." However, Heidegger argues that each of those moments is understood in relation to the current "now": "the 'then' and the 'on that former occasion' are understood with regard to a 'now'" (406–407). That is, the past that is retained and the future that is awaited are determined by one's present involvement. So, for example, when one is hammering in the workshop, one retains past steps of the construction project and awaits the project's completion. As with now-time, the present sets the standard, dictating how the other two dimensions of time are understood.

The model of world-time is conspicuously absent from the Kant interpretation. While the interpretation finds Heidegger discussing both a "sequence of nows" (e.g., KPM 123, 135, 140) and "original time" (e.g., KPM 123, 137), "world-time" does not appear. This omission is consistent with Heidegger's claim in the lecture series that Kant "fail[s] to recognize the phenomenon of world and to clarify the concept of world" (PIK 14). Kant misses the "world" of our practical pursuits and the time that organizes it, and Heidegger does not read this model of time into him.

However, Heidegger's reading of the Transcendental Deduction does offer a version of time that is existential in the way that world-time is; that is, Heidegger considers not just the model of now-time, but what it is like to live out that model, to encounter beings in light of that model. In this encounter, time is experienced through what we are "alongside" (rather than as a pure, empty sequence). However, we are not here engaged in practical, everyday activities, defining the moments of time accordingly. This time is narrowly tied to one activity, mere observation, with the past that we recall and future that we anticipate being determined by what is presently observed (e.g., whatever is relevant to my current apprehension of a glove on the floor). At any rate, in both world-time and in the empirical syntheses of the Transcendental Deduction, Dasein lives out a model of time that is dominated by the now. Indeed, the experience described in the Transcendental Deduction is comparable to Heidegger's discussion of the "existential conception of science" (BT 357), which he likewise differentiates from the "making-present" proper to world-time: "Being which objectifies and which is alongside the present-at-hand within-the-world, is characterized by a distinctive kind of making-present. This making-present is distinguished from the Present of circumspection in that – above all – the kind of discovering which belongs to the science in question awaits solely the discoveredness of the present-at-hand" (BT 363).[11] This is a pared-down version of world-time, where we remain alongside the world and an understanding of time shapes our encounter with it. However, this encounter is tied to one activity and one activity alone: mere observation.

Heidegger argues, finally, that the model of world-time, in which we carry out everyday activities, arises from the model of "primordial time" or "temporality" (BT 405, 420), which provides the broader identity structuring those everyday activities. Temporality refers to the ontological structure of the human being – more technically, Dasein, which is characterized by three interlaced temporal capacities: *coming toward*, *having been*, and *making present*.[12] As coming toward, Dasein is "ahead-of-itself"

---

[11] See also Heidegger's discussion in the 1927–1928 lecture series of the "existential concept of science" (PIK 13) – i.e., the "scientific comportment" of "*mere* looking at and observing" (PIK 18).

[12] Heidegger also translates these three temporal dimensions into the language of the first division, where he defined Dasein's constitution not as temporality but as care: "The schema in which Dasein comes toward itself *futurally*, whether authentically or inauthentically, is the '*for-the-sake-of-itself*.' The schema in which Dasein is disclosed to itself in a disposedness [*Befindlichkeit*] as thrown, is to be taken as that *in the face of which* it has been thrown and *to which* it has been abandoned. This characterizes the horizonal schema of *what has been*. In existing for the sake of itself in abandonment to itself as something that has been thrown, Dasein, as Being-alongside, is at the same time making present. The horizonal schema for the *Present* is defined by the '*in-order-to*'" (BT 365). Thus, the dimension of the future aligns with projection toward a for-the-sake-of-which (in

(337), "projecting toward some potentiality-for-Being for the sake of which any Dasein exists" (336). That is, Dasein takes up some identity or existential commitment, such as being a carpenter or writer; parent or friend; or even a knower who merely observes. This identity provides not only a sense of self (e.g., the activities and standards prescribed by this identity) but also a sense of world (e.g., the beings and interrelationships relevant to the identity) (324). As "having been" (340), Dasein finds itself already in a world with certain features, customs, and limitations, and Dasein must contend with this world into which it has been thrown. Finally, as "making present" (326), Dasein encounters beings, "Being-alongside" them. These three "ecstases" represent ways in which Dasein is outside itself: in the past with which one contends, among the beings out there in the world, and toward the self that one is trying to be.

This model is comparable to the three temporal capacities that Heidegger finds in the Transcendental Deduction: reaching back into the past, seizing the present, and coming toward a self (and beings) of some kind. Indeed, toward the end of his reconstruction of the three syntheses, Heidegger explicitly links the imagination (which, as we know from Chapter 5, carries out the three syntheses) to the constitution of the human being: "the transcendental power of imagination is able to support and form the original unity and wholeness of the specific finitude of the human subject" (KPM 131). Even more baldly, Heidegger in the lecture series equates the imagination with his own term for the human being, Dasein: "The productive power of imagination is the root of the faculties of subjectivity; it is the basic *ecstatic constitution of the subject*, of *Dasein* itself" (PIK 417–418).

In *Being and Time*, Heidegger argues that the future has priority for temporality: "In enumerating the ecstases, we have always mentioned the future first. We have done this to indicate that the future has a priority [*Vorrang*] in the ecstatic unity of primordial and authentic temporality.... *The primary* [primäre] *phenomenon of primordial and authentic temporality is the future*" (BT 329).[13] This passage affords a special role to the future: it

---

understanding); the dimension of the past aligns with thrownness (in disposedness); and the dimension of the present is aligned with falling (in Being-alongside). This passage does not map discourse onto temporality, despite the claim in the first division that discourse is equiprimordial with understanding and disposedness (BT 161). As Blattner reconstructs, Heidegger briefly links discourse to the present, but has little to say about it (1999: 121–122).

[13] As this passage reflects, the discussion of temporality in *Being and Time* refers to both primordial and authentic temporality (*ursprünglichen und eigentlichen Zeitlichkeit*). I take it that Heidegger refers to two different things here. Primordial temporality refers to Dasein's fundamental, temporal

secures the "ecstatic unity" of the structure of temporality (i.e., Dasein's very structure). That is, it unifies the three ecstases, thereby unifying temporality as a whole. In particular, I argue that the future unifies the three ecstases because it requires the other two in order to be "projecting towards a potentiality-for-being" (BT 336).[14] By roping the other two ecstases into its project, it likewise determines the character of those ecstases, making it the "primary phenomenon" for temporality (BT 329).

The ecstatic future requires the other two ecstases, because projecting toward a potentiality-for-being is the *working out* of a *concrete identity*. To start with the latter requirement, a projection needs determinacy – to be "distinctive" (BT 325). One could not attempt to be an empty potentiality; after all, what would such an attempt look like – what sort of activities or standards could it prescribe? Further, pursuing a future project requires "taking action" (BT 326), and not just idle hopes and dreams; I get to claim an identity as a writer not because I *could* sit down and write one day but because I am actively working out that identity. Thus, pursuing a potentiality-for-being needs, in the first place, some content – a particular identity to pursue. That is, this pursuit requires *reaching back into the past* for that content, taking up some identity that is (contingently) possible at one's historical moment. But further, that concrete potentiality must be *worked out* in the present, in order to be an actual pursuit of that potentiality.

Thus, the dimension of the future calls out for the other elements, in order to be what it is. In so doing, it ropes the other dimensions into the pursuit of a potentiality-for-being. But further, it sets the other two moments in relation to one another. That is, a projection is taken up from the past, and then the present is revealed in light of both moments, past and future: one finds in the present the beings and interrelationships relevant to one's future project, as informed by tradition. Thus, the present dimension is likewise shaped by the past (and not only the future). The dimension of the future, therefore, unifies the whole structure:

---

structure – the basic constitution of any Dasein, whether authentic or inauthentic. For any Dasein, then, the mode of the future unifies its temporal structure. By contrast, authentic temporality refers to the constitution of authentic Dasein alone: this is, as Blattner argues, a "mode" of fundamental temporality (1999: 99). In this mode, Dasein is oriented primarily toward the for-the-sake-of-which upon which it has resolved, rather than being wrapped up in the present like inauthentic Dasein. This follows the theme that authentic Dasein is more aware of itself (more authentically Dasein) than inauthentic Dasein; in prioritizing the future, authentic Dasein recognizes the fundamentally temporal (and primarily futural) being that it is. Since authentic temporality does not figure into Heidegger's interpretation of Kant, I leave it aside here.

[14] Again, my account here is indebted to many conversations with Christopher Yeomans; see Lambeth and Yeomans (forthcoming).

the character of "having been" arises from the future, and in such a way that the future which "has been" (or better, which "is in the process of having been") releases from itself the Present. This phenomenon has the unity of a future which makes present in the process of having been; we designate it "temporality." (BT 326)

The dimension of the future brings the three dimensions of time in concert with one another, unifying the structure of temporality. In so doing, it determines the character of the other two ecstases: the past and present are sites for claiming and enacting a potentiality-for-being. More specifically, the projection determines how we reach back into the past – taking up this possibility and not that one; carrying forward this tradition, and not that one – and how we make present – seeing beings in light of the project (e.g., as tools for writing).

Since the other two models of time arise from the model of temporality, the priority of the future is also supposed to appear, if only covertly, at the other levels. As Heidegger puts this point, "the priority of the future will vary according to the ways in which the temporalizing of inauthentic temporality itself is modified, but it will still come to the fore even in the derivative kind of 'time'" (BT 329). For example, the priority of the ecstatic future is supposed to explain the irreversibility of now-time (we are oriented first and foremost toward what we're becoming and not to what has been) (426), as well as its infinitude (which betrays a fleeing from the finitude of the ecstatic future) (431). Thus, the future covertly affects the characteristics of other models of time (in varying "ways"), and not just fundamental temporality. Further, I argue that the ecstatic future has a unique, unifying function that reverberates across the models of time: the future links the three dimensions of time. As I will show through an example below, the ecstatic future unifies the moments even in derivative models of time.

Through this reconstruction, we can appreciate how the "primary" (*primär*) dimension of time – or, equivalently, the one with "priority" (*Vorrang*) – can shift between different models of time (i.e., the primary dimension can vary from model to model). Admittedly, Heidegger uses these precise terms only when discussing the status of the future for temporality. However, the passage where Heidegger assigns priority to the ecstatic future indicates that the terms generalize: "The nature of the temporalizing can be determined primarily in terms of the different ecstases. Primordial and authentic temporality temporalizes itself in terms of the authentic future and in such a way that in having been futurally, it first of all awakens the Present. *The primary phenomenon of primordial and authentic temporality is the future*" (BT 329). While the future is the "primary phenomenon" of temporality, this status can go to "the different ecstases." That is, each of the ecstases – not just future, but also past and present – can determine "the nature of the temporalizing." More specifically, according to the generalized account of temporal primacy, a dimension counts as the primary phenomenon when it determines the other dimensions – having-been is a "having been futurally" and the future "awakens the present" – thereby dominating the model as a whole. This reason for affording the future this status for temporality extends easily to the status of the present for world-time and now-time. In now-time, the present moment determines the character of the past and future, as no-longer-nows or not-yet-nows. In world-time, the present moment determines the content of the retained past and anticipated future, such that what is retained and anticipated is determined by one's present involvement.

With this generalized account of temporal priority in view, we can now appreciate the significance of Heidegger's claim in the Kant interpretation that "cognizing is primarily [*primär*] intuiting" (KPM 15).[15] Using the same language that he uses to assign primacy to dimensions of time, Heidegger here assigns primacy to intuition. Recall that Heidegger goes on to link intuition to the present moment in his analysis of the Transcendental Deduction. That is, the empirical "synthesis of apprehension in the intuition" (A98) apprehends a manifold in the present moment, taking in and synthesizing the multiple elements that are present. This synthesis in the present, further, is based on an a priori synthesis articulating the present, where the present moment is a "now" in sequence with other nows. Given Heidegger's later, temporal analysis of intuition, we can now read Heidegger's claim that "cognizing is primarily intuiting" as asserting the primacy of the present moment – and, importantly, asserting its primacy for cognition. In line with Heidegger's claim that the future has primacy for fundamental temporality, I argue that this claim asserts the primacy of intuition for a derivative level of time: the pared-down world-time where a subject merely observes objects.

Like the present moment for world-time in *Being and Time*, intuition (the present) is primary in the sense that it determines the other dimensions of time. Intuiting is primary not in the sense that cognizing is *only* intuiting but in that it determines the other elements of cognition.

---

[15] A marginal note on the same page likewise remarks "priority [*Vorrang*] of intuition!" (KPM 15), showing how Heidegger refers to what is primary or has priority interchangeably. See also PIK 152: "Here too the priority [*Vorrang*] of intuition in all cognition is revealed in a definite form."

Primacy in Heidegger's sense holds only if there are other elements or moments to which intuition is primary in relation.[16] Indeed, Heidegger's opening discussion of intuition attempts to show that the primacy of intuition does not threaten the heterogeneity of cognition; intuition requires understanding. Further, this is a place where we can see how an identity (i.e., the ecstatic future) unifies another model of time. In this case, projecting toward a potentiality-for-being unifies the pared-down world-time where a subject tracks the past, present, and future of some object. On its own, it is not clear why intuition requires understanding, as Heidegger claims in the Kant book. Yes, intuition is partial, but this hardly seems like a problem from the perspective of intuition alone; why go beyond the partial, blind chaos of sensations? However, if one pursues the potentiality-for-being a knower, intuition is insufficient, for it does not yet provide cognition. The project aiming for cognition explains why intuition needs understanding.

How intuition (the present) determines the other moments of time becomes clearer in Heidegger's explicitly temporal analysis of cognition in the Transcendental Deduction. Consider the empirical syntheses with which Kant begins in the A-Deduction: empirical apprehension, reproduction, and recognition. On Heidegger's analysis, the "now" of intuition dominates these syntheses. That is, the empirical manifold that is apprehended determines the content of the other two syntheses, and thus dominates the pared-down world-time that accompanies mere observation. The reproductive synthesis reproduces previous states of what is currently apprehended (or, at least, that are relevant to what is apprehended). The synthesis of recognition recognizes the same, making sense of what is currently apprehended: it relates what is apprehended to what was apprehended before, and more broadly identifies a being with certain anticipated regularities. In the encounter with the being that Kant outlines, the present now (and the being experienced therein) determines the other dimensions of time.

Arguably, intuition (the present) also has priority for the sequence of nows – that is, the model of pure, empty time that is articulated by the a priori syntheses, on Heidegger's analysis, and that enables the experience of empirical observation. As we saw in Chapter 5, the past and future are articulated in reference to the present moment. The past is articulated as a

---

[16] Again, this sets Heidegger in contrast with the Marburg Neo-Kantians who insist that cognizing is only thinking, as well as the German Idealists, who (at least on Henrich's account) identify something that is primary in the sense of preceding and generating other elements of cognition.

now that can be brought back and that has relevance to the current now: a "dimension of the no-longer-now" (PIK 238). The future is a "now-not-yet" that follows predictably and necessarily from the present (PIK 234). The dimensions, considered in themselves (and not by what is encountered in them), are defined in relation to the now. The now sets the standard for the moments of time.

However, for the primacy of intuition in the Kant interpretation to remain consistent with Heidegger's treatment of time in *Being and Time*, intuition can be primary only for a derivative level of time – not for temporality itself. That the account stays consistent in this way is supported by the fact that Heidegger specifies that intuition is primary *for cognition*. When we cognize, a subject faces an object, taking in and understanding that object. While this experience provides an important moment of phenomenal contact (after all, Heidegger wants to do justice to this sort of experience), Heidegger's interpretation ultimately presses, with Kant, to the deeper conditions for that experience: the deeper "turning toward" that enables the cognition of objects. Cognition is what is grounded; it is not the ground. That ground, for Heidegger, is the fundamental, temporal constitution of the subject.

Further, Heidegger's reading of the Transcendental Deduction explicitly assigns priority to the future.[17] More technically, Heidegger maintains that the third synthesis, which "explores the horizon of being-able-to-hold-something-before-us in general" (KPM 130), has priority. The future, that is, is primary among the three syntheses or "primal activities" (PIK 267) that articulate time, even if the time that they articulate gives primacy to the present moment. Using the exact same terms that he used to mark the priority of the future in *Being and Time*, Heidegger says that the third synthesis,

> according to its inner structure, even exhibits a priority [*Vorrang*] over the other two, with which at the same time it essentially belongs together. In this Kantian analysis of pure synthesis in concepts ... when exactly does the most original essence of time [*ursprünglichste Wesen der Zeit*], i.e., that it is developed primarily [*primär*] from the future, come to the fore? (KPM 131)

---

[17] Likewise, the lecture series extolls "the legitimate priority of the transcendental apperception in the explication of subjectivity in Kant" (PIK 270). Heidegger also attributes a unifying function to transcendental apperception (which, recall, he links to the future): "Transcendental apperception is not something standing next to or behind the three transcendental syntheses, but is the unity of that wide-ranging encompassing which as such generally constitutes a dimension of resistance or what is representable" (PIK 263).

Heidegger does not directly answer this question, perhaps because he thinks that Kant, in failing to see the relationship between the third synthesis and the future, never fully brings the "most original essence of time" to the fore. However, in the immediately foregoing discussion, Heidegger does indicate one place where Kant nods to the priority of the future – or, at least, the "synthesis of recognition" that Heidegger takes great pains to link to the dimension of the future. This discussion clarifies that Kant recognizes the priority of this synthesis precisely because he recognizes that it unifies the other two syntheses.

In particular, Kant suggests that the empirical synthesis of recognition establishes the connection between what we apprehend and what we reproduce; without this synthesis, "all reproduction in the series of representations would be in vain" (A103). By recognizing that we are once again faced with the same object, for example, the synthesis of recognition allows us to see our past reproduction and present apprehension as representing two views of one and the same thing.[18] Therefore, Heidegger recounts, "at the ground of both syntheses [of perception and recollection], and directing them, a unifying (synthesis) of the being with respect to its sameness is already found" (KPM 130). In recognizing the same object across multiple time slices, the synthesis of recognition recalls the past reproduction that is relevant to a present apprehension. But further, the synthesis informs how we take up the present: picking out the stable identities that can be reidentified and reproduced. The third synthesis unifies the others, and in so doing directs their activities: "it pops up in advance of them, so to speak" (KPM 130). At this juncture, Kant recognizes how the projection of a stable object determines how we reach back (what is carried forward as relevant) and make present (how the being shows up). If the moments of time that we seize out there in the world are dominated by a present "now," the abilities that discover those moments are determined by a future projection.

On my interpretation of the opening discussion of intuition, where intuition is primary, Heidegger begins with an experience that is structured by a derivative model of time – one, that is, where the present moment has priority. On my reading, Heidegger then unveils the deeper model of time that makes that experience possible: the temporal structure of the subject, which in fact gives priority to the dimension of the future. That is, the

---

[18] As Heidegger summarizes this argument: "only by anticipating something beforehand is a foothold gained with reference to which what is to be seized and seizable, what is reproduced, can be grasped and comprehended as one and the same thing" (PIK 263).

much remarked-on priority of intuition in the Kant book[19] in fact gives way to a (less celebrated) priority of projection.

Indeed, Heidegger already anticipates the direction of his Kant interpretation in *Being and Time* when he first analyzes projecting toward a potentiality-for-being (the more capacious meaning of "understanding" that Heidegger uses in this passage): "By showing how all sight is grounded primarily in understanding ... we have deprived pure intuition of its priority, which corresponds noetically to the priority of the present-at-hand in traditional ontology. 'Intuition' and 'thinking' are both derivatives of understanding and already rather remote ones" (BT 147). Even the mere observation of present-at-hand beings is guided by one's projection toward a potentiality-for-being. The taking-up of intuition and the thinking of what is intuited are guided by a perspective that looks out for regularities among spatiotemporal beings – seeking to know those beings. They are derived, then, from the fundamental capacity to project toward some identity. Heidegger's Kant interpretation shows that an observational experience dominated by the present moment nevertheless relies on the projection of an identity, tracing the ordinary understanding of time to the human temporality from which it springs.

My analysis here shows how the temporal idealist reading can address Heidegger's opening discussion of intuition, and more specifically his claim that we intuit beings that are already "at hand." Cognition – the cognition where intuition is primary, and we experience beings already "at hand" – occupies a derivative level of time. Our cognition of an independent being is an *achievement*, built on fundamental temporality. By interpreting ourselves as knowers, we likewise anticipate a world of causally interacting substances, projecting the horizon of now-time. Only by so projecting do we encounter beings that are already "at hand"; these temporal expectations allow us to appreciate that something is causally independent from us, such that it affects us. Thus, on my reading, Heidegger does not proceed from the assumption that beings are already "at hand," independently of and prior to our turning toward them; he begins with a sort of experience, where we experience an "at hand" being, and then brings to light the prior turning toward that makes that experience possible. That is, Heidegger proceeds *recursively* in the Kant book: he begins with the (primarily intuitive) encounter with an independent being, and then presses ahead to the conditions that make that experience

---

[19] See, e.g., Dahlstrom 1991: 340; Dahlstrom 2010 (quoted above); de Boer and Howard 2019: 363; Piché 2000: 201; and Truwant 2022: 103.

possible, landing on the fundamental temporality of the human being. The being is not independently "at hand," but "at hand" in light of the temporal horizon that we bring to it.

This reading of the Kant interpretation is consistent with the "empirical realism" that both Blattner and Han-Pile find in Heidegger. Han-Pile underscores that Heidegger does not defend a "subjective idealism" that takes the human perspective to be the cause of those beings that we intuit (2005: 91). Heidegger's idealism, rather, takes us to be the source of the ontological framework (i.e., the horizon of time) within which beings appear. As Heidegger repeatedly insists, we are not ontically creative, like the infinite knower who creates beings by representing them; we are ontologically creative. Further, the ontological framework that we create allows for an experience of beings that are independent. According to the horizon of now-time, these beings "stand over against us," as beings with a causal history in their own right. Comparable to how Kant pairs his transcendental idealism with empirical realism, Han-Pile argues that for Heidegger "entities (like phenomena for Kant) cannot be defined as such independently of the conditions of their disclosure," but "we can know phenomena/entities as they are at the empirical level/from Dasein's perspective" (Han-Pile 2005: 91). We can say what entities are like from within our ontological framework; we can, for example, affirm that they are "at hand." The temporal idealist reading can accommodate, then, the realist moment that Dahlstrom identifies at the outset of the Kant book: when we intuit a being, our ontological framework is in play, such that we can appreciate that we are faced with an already "at hand" being.

3 Progress beyond *Being and Time*

I turn now to the second question raised by temporal realist readings of the Kant interpretation: Why think that we exhaustively or comprehensively determine the temporal characteristics of the beings we encounter, drawing their temporal characteristics from our own temporality? Why not think, rather, that our temporality enables an experience of their inherent temporal natures? More robustly, why not think of temporality as capturing *our* temporal structure, and now-time as (at least in part) capturing *their* temporal structure?

The answer to these questions lies in Heidegger's interpretation of self-affection in Kant. This interpretation builds on Kant's passage claiming that "the form of intuition can be nothing other than the way in which the mind is affected by its own activity" (B67; KPM 133).[20] Accordingly, Heidegger takes self-affection to be the process where now-time, as a whole, is articulated – the articulation of past, present, and future that the Transcendental Deduction treats piecemeal. Since this process for Heidegger characterizes the "essential structure of subjectivity" (KPM 132), his account of self-affection offers the main bone of contention between the temporal idealist and temporal realist readers of Heidegger: the sense in which now-time is built upon the structure of the subject. Some of Heidegger's claims about self-affection are ambiguous between an idealist and realist reading. For example, he says that "time as pure self-affection allows the pure succession of the sequence of nows to spring forth for the first time" (KPM 135). This claim could mean either that pure self-affection is the source of now-time (as on the idealist reading) or that it allows us to appreciate the external time that governs objects (as on the realist reading). However, there are other claims that are not quite so ambiguous.

For example, in his account of self-affection, Heidegger insists with Kant that time is a "pure intuition" and explains that "Time is only pure intuition to the extent that it prepares the look of succession from out of itself ... this pure intuition activates itself with the intuited which was formed in it, i.e., which was formed without the aid of experience" (KPM 132). When time is formed as a succession, or sequence of nows, it is "formed without the aid of experience" – it is therefore pure, completely a priori. It is tempting to read this passage as saying that now-time is formed separately from beings, independently of whatever their inherent natures might be. Nevertheless, the realist reading could reinterpret Kantian terms like "pure"; indeed, Kinkaid offers such a reinterpretation of "a priori." On Kinkaid's reading, Heidegger does not endorse a "subjectivist understanding of the a priori" where the a priori refers only to what the subject brings to experience (2018: 17). Rather, he endorses "a phenomenological conception of the a priori" articulated by Max Scheler. Here, the a priori includes the subjective activities that make experience possible, along with (quoting Scheler) "the essences ... of the qualities and other thing-contents given in acts," as well as the "essential interconnections" between these two sources (Kinkaid 2018: 17). Thus, the a priori is a meeting of subjective structures and the essential characteristics that things themselves

---

[20] This passage was not added until the second edition of the first *Critique*, but according to Heidegger that edition "simply formulated more explicitly" an idea of self-affection already contained in the first edition (apparently, a rare moment of clarity for the second edition) (KPM 133).

possess. Therefore, something "pure" and free of experience could nevertheless incorporate the inherent spatiotemporal nature of things.

However, Heidegger is even more explicit about the a priori source of now-time. In a passage from the lecture series worth quoting at length, Heidegger explains that

> if self as such should proffer to itself the primal resistance as time – and a priori – then this means that this resistance cannot be grabbed up from the empirical realm as something empirical. Resistance, that is, pure time, must come from the self through the self itself. But self *is* only as ability, as the I can – the primal activity of the articulated three syntheses is to be accomplished only as ways of reaching out and encompassing. In and through these primal activities, that is, in and through the peculiar way of being a self, self must derive pure time from out of itself. As a self-possessing freedom, the self must be a priori laden with time. The articulated primal activity of the transcendental apperception must as such be the origin of pure time as pure sequence of the relation of nows. This time as pure sequence of nows must spring from the three primal activities themselves. Pure time springs from the three ecstases which determine the selfhood of the self in its free self-possessing. (PIK 267)

In this passage, Heidegger reiterates that the sequence of nows lacks an "empirical" basis; it is developed "a priori" and is thus a "pure intuition." But he is more specific about the a priori sources from which this model of time "springs" – from which it is "derive[d]." Heidegger does not appeal to the essential nature of things; rather, pure time "must come from the self." Even more specifically, and reflecting Heidegger's ecstatic conception of the self, pure time is derived from "ability, as the I can" – "the primal activity of the three syntheses" – "in and through these primal activities" – "articulated primal activity ... as such." Not appealing to any other a priori source, this passage finds the origin of now-time in a self that is already "laden with time." This evidence therefore suggests that Heidegger in his Kant interpretation develops and defends the same thesis that Blattner finds in the second division of *Being and Time*: the human being is the source of the time that organizes our experience.

Nevertheless, the argument for that thesis is remarkably different, pointing the way toward the progress Heidegger accomplishes in the Kant interpretation. On Blattner's characterization of Heidegger's argument for temporal idealism in *Being and Time*, the characteristics of now-time are explained by the characteristics of temporality. These explanations are routed through the model of world-time, which therefore has an intermediary status: the characteristics of temporality explain the characteristics of world-time, which in turn explain the characteristics of now-time. This "chain of dependencies" is supposed to show that now-time is derived from world-time, which is in turn derived from temporality – making temporality the fundamental or original model of time (Blattner 1999: 28).

For example, according to one of Heidegger's arguments, the "stretchedness" of original temporality explains the "spannedness" of world-time, which explains the continuity of now-time (Blattner 1999: 220–222). That is, temporality stretches across three ecstases; these ecstases interact with, codetermine, and cooperate with one another. This makes way for an experience of the present "now" of world-time, where the present moment (e.g., where I carry out some task) is set into relief with a past moment from which it arose (e.g., earlier stages setting up this task) and the future moment toward which it tends (e.g., the completion of the task); thus, the present moment spans from past to future. Once these moments are stripped of their rich, practical content, in the abstraction of now-time, the moments remain continuous (with no gaps), though the inner relations giving texture to their continuity are gone. This provides one string of derivations showing that now-time is ultimately (if mediately) derived from fundamental temporality.[21]

Like Blattner's reading of the second division of *Being and Time*, Heidegger's Kant interpretation tells a story where the human being's temporality is the source of now-time. However, Heidegger's way of telling this story takes a different form. In the Kant interpretation, Heidegger does not focus on the particular characteristics of now-time. Heidegger, in his treatment of the Schematism, does explain how the concept of substance forms now-time, as what endures despite change. However, Heidegger declines to detail the remaining characteristics encompassed by the categories; the category of substance is the only example. Rather, I suggest that Heidegger in the Kant interpretation shifts from explaining the one-off characteristics of now-time in reference to the one-off characteristics of temporality, to explaining the *process* of derivation – *how* temporality forms now-time. This means explaining how each dimension of temporality (i.e., each temporal ability) contributes to that process. In so doing, he offers a more fine-grained account of the complex process that generates now-time, if not how each characteristic of now-time is generated.

---

[21] Blattner argues that there is one feature of now-time that fundamental temporality is unable to explain: its sequentiality. Temporality is nonsequential, comprising three equiprimordial ecstases, leaving the derivation of successiveness from temporality a mystery. I will not take on this objection here, as I argue elsewhere (with Chris Yeomans, forthcoming) that *Being and Time* has resources for explaining this derivation.

Heidegger suggests that temporality is a self-realizing or a self-activating structure: "if it belongs to the essence of the finite subject to be activated as a self, then time as pure self-affection forms the essential structure of subjectivity" (KPM 132). In the Kant interpretation, Heidegger uses the term "self-affection" to name how temporality realizes or activates itself by way of a particular articulation of time. In *Being and Time*, though, his word for this process is "temporalizing." Since temporality is a self-realizing structure, and it realizes itself through an interpretation of time, it is not possible to have temporality alone, absent another model of time; temporality is not a structure that sits dormant, but one that actively interprets itself. Even more evocatively, Heidegger speaks of the "ripening of time itself" – a ripening that is supposed to occur through "the original, threefold-unifying forming of future, past, and present in general" (KPM 137). Temporality is a *self-ripening* structure, and Heidegger's Kant interpretation details how this self-ripening works.

Now-time is formed, namely, in the interaction between the three temporal ecstasies – or in the language of the Kant interpretation, the "three modes of transcendental synthesis – transcendental apprehension (seizing), transcendental reproduction (reaching back), and transcendental precognition (reaching ahead)" (PIK 263). This is a "threefold articulated synthesis" (PIK 284), where the synthesis associated with the future (reaching ahead) leads the way in articulating time as a sequence of nows.

The interaction between these three ecstases is sometimes difficult to track, as Heidegger sometimes focuses on only two ecstases – present and future (i.e., intuition and thinking, time and apperception) – in an attempt to show that his narrative successfully unites the two elements that Kant's Transcendental Deduction attempts to unite. However, a number of compressed passages, as I read them, spell out the interaction between the three ecstases. For example, Heidegger (once again channeling Kant's claim that time is *pure* intuition) argues that "Time is only pure intuition to the extent that it prepares the look of succession from out of itself, and it *clutches* this as such to *itself* as the formative taking-up" (KPM 132). I submit that this passage makes reference to each of the three temporal ecstases (in, indeed, the exact order that Heidegger likes to treat them), providing each of their contributions to the process of self-affection. That is, the dimension of the future actively forms, prepares, or articulates time, creating "the look of succession." However, it creates this look "from out of itself" – that is, from the sort of being that it *already* is. It "clutches" or "takes up" this interpretation, operating with this interpretation of time.

A passage from the lecture series, offering a similarly compressed account of the three ecstases, sheds more light on the dimension of the past, or what has already been: "But whatever is thus originally laden with time and as such releases time from itself while simultaneously comporting itself to time, whatever deals with time and simultaneously binds itself to time, that must itself be temporal in an entirely original sense" (PIK 267). The first clause, I suggest, proceeds in the typical temporal order, from past to present to future. Once again, Heidegger gestures at something that the self already is: though here, in more detail, he specifies that it is "originally laden with time." That is, we are *already* temporal beings; we find ourselves already as beings who reach forward, reach back, and make present. The process of self-affection is the process of trying to make sense of the temporal beings that we already are. That is, we interpret ourselves – each of the temporal dimensions that we already are – and in so doing create an interpretation of time. The present dimension "releases" that interpretation of time, whereas the future dimension directs it, by "comporting itself" toward time.

We know from *Being and Time* that projection (i.e., the dimension of the future) has a complex structure. Interpreting myself means interpreting other things, too. Entities who exist like Dasein does "sight 'themselves' only in so far as they have become transparent to themselves with equal primordiality in those items which are constitutive for their existence" (BT 146). The same idea plays out in the Kant interpretation. Committing to the project of being a knower means more precisely committing to the ground rules of the categories (i.e., to using those categories to make sense of beings). These ground rules, in turn, guarantee that the beings we encounter will themselves have a certain structure. More simply, seeing myself as a knower means seeing myself as being among beings that can be known (e.g., possessing regularities that I can track). These beings, which stand opposite me, are constitutive for my identity as a knower; I cannot know, if there is nothing to be known.

The Kant interpretation, moreover, renders this idea in explicitly temporal terms. In particular, transcendental apperception captures the complex structure of projection, specifically as it is realized relative to now-time. It captures the structure where we offer a determinate interpretation of our own temporal capacities and in so doing interpret the time that we will find out there, among the beings we encounter. For example, in the projection specific to transcendental apperception, we see ourselves as being able to reach back into a past that sets up later nows, and seize a present that follows necessarily from the recollected past. By so determining our temporal capacities, we also form an image of time: time is a series of nows, following one another in a single direction.

In the explicitly temporal terms of the Kant interpretation, then, the projection toward an identity is not a one-sided interpretation of the time that I am, myself (i.e., my temporal capacities alone); it is also an interpretation of the time I expect to find out there among beings. More generally, an interpretation of my own reaching-back, seizing, and reaching-ahead is accompanied with an interpretation of what I reach back, out, and ahead into. That is, interpreting the time that I am – my temporal capacities – invites two levels of interpretation: determining those capacities themselves (the distinct way that I will reach back, seize, and reach ahead) and determining the horizon toward which those capacities reach (what my reaching-back, seizing, and reaching-ahead will find). Committing to being a temporal being of some distinct kind – who reaches back, out, and ahead in certain determinate ways – leaves me also with a distinct vision of the time that I will find out there, and the beings that populate it.

This horizon then guides the dimension of the present, which "releases" this vision of time, "clutch[ing]" it to itself as it encounters beings. That is, this horizon operates in the background as a guide to what we see those beings as being (e.g., as causally interacting substances). As we saw in Heidegger's reading of the Schematism, we form our a priori image of time not separately from our experiences, but in those experiences. For example, we see a house not only as having the ontic or empirical features proper to its being a house (e.g., exterior walls), but also as having an ontological structure: it is stable, persisting across moments of time, and changing (e.g., weathering) according to certain physical laws. In so doing, we reveal a being in the present in light of now-time; we take up this image of time while we take up the being.

In the process of self-affection, as I've outlined it, each temporal dimension has a distinct role to play. The past dimension refers to the fact that we are already laden with time; the future dimension interprets that time; and the present dimension enacts that interpretation. Despite their distinct contributions, each dimension implicates – and in a certain sense, contains – the other two. The interpretation (the ecstatic future) gives a unified understanding of past, present, and future; the fact of that we are laden with time (the ecstatic past) is the temporal capacities we already find ourselves with; and together they enact some interpretation of time in the ecstatic present. Put differently, each temporal dimension is rendered thrice: the bare fact of reaching-ahead, reaching-back, or seizing; formed, interpreted in some determinate way; and enacted, structuring our encounter with some being (which we likewise experience as having a past, present, and future of some kind).

This process is supposed to give us the form of now-time. Indeed, now-time offers a unified (though one-sided) interpretation of what we reach into. The past is a no-longer-now, the present is a now, and the future is a not-yet-now, these moments being united (e.g., following one another necessarily, in one direction) on a successive timeline. This interpretation, moreover, guides an experience of the present, serving as a horizon against which beings appear, as Heidegger's analysis of the Schematism works out. But finally, as Heidegger argues in painstaking detail in his treatment of the Transcendental Deduction, the interpretation depends on our already having those temporal capacities that it articulates one side of: reaching-back, seizing, and reaching-ahead. Like the argument at the tail end of *Being and Time*, Heidegger continues to argue that temporality is the source of now-time.

However, in the Kant interpretation (and in contrast to *Being and Time*), Heidegger does not focus on the characteristics of standing models of time – a procedure that has the danger of ossifying the models of time, such that they seem to be inevitable features of human life (and the trick is only to figure out how they relate to one another). By focusing rather on how fundamental temporality might produce or develop another model of time – indeed, by working recursively from what seems like a stagnant model of time to the dynamic capacities that produce it – Heidegger foregrounds a gap between the productive time and the time produced. Far from suggesting that now-time is an inevitable derivation, Heidegger presents it as just one possible interpretation of time. Our temporal capacities are capacious, allowing for multiple interpretations; if temporality is the point of departure, now-time is not necessarily the destination. Now-time is only one of many possible interpretations of time.

In the lecture series, Heidegger describes self-affection as "the primal activity of *freely* transposing oneself into the self which as such should constitute the unity of syntheses, that is, objectness" (PIK 266, italics mine). That is, the act of unifying past, present, and future – in a projection of both myself and the constitutive items for my identity – is in some sense free. Some pages later, Heidegger clarifies this remark by linking freedom to the "ontological creativity" of the imagination: "it *freely* forms the universal horizon of time as the horizon of a priori resistance, i.e., of objectness" (PIK 283, italics mine). That is, when the imagination forms time into the time of independent, causally interacting objects, this is a *free* formation. I take it, then, that time could be otherwise formed; the time of resisting objects is one possible interpretation among others, only one possible result of the "free and creative play of time relations" (PIK 283) that makes our experience of beings possible.

The final pages of the Kant book, which render Heidegger's interpretive findings in his own vocabulary, confirm and add depth to this idea. Here, Heidegger discusses the "Metaphysics of Dasein," which gives a determinate interpretation of not only the sort of beings that we are but also the beings we expect to encounter ("the metaphysics which necessarily occurs *as* Dasein") (KPM 162). He claims that, in contrast to a "zoology" of some animal, "The Metaphysics of Dasein is no fixed and ready-for-use 'organon' at all. It must always be built up anew amid the transformation of its idea in the working-out of the possibility of metaphysics" (KPM 162). That is, our interpretation of ourselves, of the sort of beings that we are (and those, conversely, that we can expect to encounter), cannot be fixed but is rather continually transformed and worked out. A throwaway comment sheds perhaps the most light on why this metaphysics lacks fixedness: "how from time to time the [Metaphysics of Dasein] is rooted historically in factical Dasein cannot be discussed" (KPM 163). That is, our interpretation of ourselves is contingent, apparently the result of historical developments. For example, the possibility of being a knower (who knows according to Newtonian physics, no less) arises at a certain historical moment.

These passages reveal a gap between the temporal beings that we are and the interpretation that we develop of that temporality. This is not an incidental gap: it is not that we provide a bad interpretation of our temporal capacities. It is, rather, that any interpretation fails to capture the temporal beings that we are. The temporality that we are is underdetermined; any act of determination distorts it. Necessarily, our interpretation of ourselves reveals and conceals at the same time.

Heidegger's reading of self-affection opens up a gap between the time that we are and the categories that we adopt to form that time. Outside of suggesting that the metaphysics we adopt has some "factical" and "historical" basis, Heidegger does not explain how this space is filled – that is, how one interpretation of time is selected over another. The interpretation could be impacted by broad social developments, everyday practices, lifechanging encounters with certain anomalous beings. This remains open as a mystery, a lacuna that could easily be seen as a motivator for the history of Being that Heidegger goes on to develop in the 1930s. But nevertheless the space that this reading opens up provides insight into Heidegger's temporal idealism.

Heidegger has made it clear that our metaphysics can be propelled by factical developments. That is, the interpretation of time at which we arrive is affected by the concrete situations in which we find ourselves –

by the beings out there and not the bare structure of Dasein in here. However, surprisingly, these findings do not force a temporal realist reading. First, the fact that our interpretation of time changes – and changes in accord with *historical* developments – speaks against the idea that our interpretation of now-time gloms onto real (presumably, stable) spatiotemporal features of beings. But second, despite the freedom of interpretation that Heidegger recognizes, and the factical input informing that freedom, this recognition in fact does not make room for beings to contribute temporal content to our interpretation of time.

To see this, notice where factical input enters the process of self-affection – that is, where there is room for freedom. To return to evidence from the lecture course, the imagination "freely take[es] together the horizons of time as one" (PIK 282); "freely reaches out into the future, into alreadyness (the past), and into the present" (PIK 282); "freely forms the universal horizon of time" (PIK 283). These passages suggest the factical input does not *provide* temporal content; rather, it *contributes to interpreting* the temporal content that is already there. The dimensions of time are already provided by our own being, by the sorts of beings that we are; we reach back, out, and ahead, giving a past, present, and future that we reach into. The fact that we are already laden with time provides a basis for, and constrains, any interpretation of time that we might adopt; for example, any interpretation is constrained to unify three (and not two or four) temporal horizons. Nevertheless, the temporality that we are is, evidently, flexible; despite its constraints, it can be interpreted in a number of different ways. The factical input helps us home in on an interpretation – but an interpretation of the time that was already there.[22] Heidegger's admission of factical input does not make room for temporal realism, since we remain the source of the time to be interpreted. We generate the temporal content, which goes on to be interpreted (with the help of factical input).

---

[22] These features of how we interpret time provide some tools for answering Barash's worry (following Karl Löwith) that Heidegger's late 1920s interpretation of Kant reflects a "political decisionism" – a decisionism that anticipates Heidegger's political decision to join the Nazi Party in the 1930s (Barash 2012: 446; Löwith 1995: 159f.) and that Heidegger eventually abandons following the "turn" in his thinking in the 1930s (Barash 2012: 449). However, the freedom that we find here is not a random or completely autonomous choice. Our creation of an ontology is constrained by the sorts of beings that we are: ontology must interpret time, for example, and more specifically three dimensions of time. Further, it is supposed to respond to historical shifts, though this point is underdeveloped. This notion of freedom, as I will outline in the conclusion to this chapter, points forward to Heidegger's research in the 1930s rather than representing a break with it.

My interpretation retains Heidegger's temporal idealism, while making some admissions to the realist readings that I canvassed above. Like Blattner and Han-Pile, I maintain that human beings are the source of time; temporal content (at least, the temporal content that we experience) comes from us and us alone. However, that does not mean that the ontology that guides our experience of beings – which, for Heidegger, is always an articulated understanding of time – comes entirely from our ecstatic structure.[23] The development of ontology is not a closed system. While our ecstatic structure predetermines that we will experience in terms of a past, present, and future, the particularities of those moments – the specific rendering of past, present, and future – admits of external or factical input. Thus, I agree with the temporal realists (though perhaps not in the way they would like) that our *interpretation* of time does not descend solely from the structure of the human being. Nevertheless, *time* does issue from the structure of the human being. When we interpret time, we interpret our own triad of temporal capacities, and the horizons toward which these capacities reach.

4 Conclusion

What does Heidegger learn through interpreting Kant? I've argued that Heidegger further develops his own account of temporal idealism. He goes beyond Kant by taking time to be the very structure of the human being, rather than just one a priori structure possessed by the human being. Indeed, his procedure in the Kant book is to work backward from an experience structured by Kant's form of time to the deeper temporal structure that makes that experience possible. Through this engagement with Kant, he develops an account of how the elements of that structure interact to produce the more superficial form of time that Kant discusses. This account also goes beyond the argument in *Being and Time*, which traces the characteristics of now-time back to the characteristics of temporality, lending support to the origination of now-time in temporality. The

---

[23] Thus, even as I maintain Heidegger's *temporal* idealism, I recognize that Heidegger distances himself in these comments from *ontological* idealism. Time comes from us, but ontology (the interpretation of time that we articulate, the rendering of temporal dimensions that we select) is open to other inputs – though which inputs, and how, remains underdeveloped. I think my conclusion here is consistent with Mark Wrathall's suggestion that Heidegger in the 1930s abandons a commitment to ontological idealism in favor of "keep[ing] open" questions about it (Wrathall 2022: 547). Indeed, Heidegger's account of self-affection in the Kant interpretation tends toward this development.

Kant interpretation, rather, spells out *how* ecstatic temporality could be such an origin – the process by which it produces a certain interpretation of time. This argumentative strategy makes room for a gap between the temporal structure of the human being and Kant's form of time, propelling the conclusion that time could be otherwise interpreted.

This finding anticipates the historical shifts in ontology that Heidegger goes on to trace in the 1930s. Indeed, the year after publishing his Kant book, Heidegger would go on to teach a lecture course, *The Essence of Human Freedom*, that turned to a new topic in Kant: the account of freedom provided in the Transcendental Dialectic and in Kant's practical philosophy. This indicates, I think, that the scattered remarks on freedom, quoted from the Kant interpretation above, were not throwaway comments but evidence of a growing interest: interest, that is, in a freedom that nevertheless takes its cues from without. We find here one through-line from Heidegger's fundamental ontological philosophy of the 1920s to his history of Being in the 1930s – from the being who makes metaphysics possible to the historical shifts that fill the gap between the fundamentally temporal beings that we are and the particular metaphysics that we adopt.

Conclusion

My preceding discussion has highlighted Heidegger's method of interpreting Kant. On the one hand, Heidegger engages deeply with Kant's philosophical questions, his conceptual machinery, and his arguments, in order to identify Kant's most compelling account of his subject matter. On the other, he considers the phenomena that Kant attempts to explain, in order to locate the strand of argument that does justice to that subject matter, and to dispute those arguments that do not. While Heidegger finds affinities between his own views and the arguments that he finds in Kant (at least the best, most innovative arguments), these findings are won through interpreting Kant's text. This interpretive work, indeed, allows Heidegger to make progress on his own theory of time – that is, to learn from Kant. Thus, I have maintained that even when Heidegger offers a novel interpretation of Kant, departing from the conclusions of the interpretations on offer during his time, Heidegger offers a genuine interpretation *of Kant*.

To reinforce my claim that Heidegger is, indeed, an interpreter of Kant, I would like to conclude by locating Heidegger's interpretation among contemporary Anglophone interpretations of Kant. I suggested already that Heidegger's interpretive *method* resembles some contemporary interpreters of Kant, who recognize the tensions in his texts and navigate these tensions by seizing on the most compelling line of argument. Here, I focus rather on the *results* of Heidegger's interpretation: the Kantian position that Heidegger's method of interpretation unearths. My work here will show that Heidegger's reading is legible within the broader landscape of Kant scholarship.

1   Metaphysics

Heidegger insists on a metaphysical or ontological reading of Kant. That is, he thinks that answering Kant's main question calls for an ontology – and not, as the Neo-Kantians would have it, an epistemology. This debate can be transposed onto contemporary conversations in Kant scholarship.

Kant's main question is: How are synthetic a priori judgments possible? Kant is specifically concerned with the judgments that we make about objects, independent of our encounter with specific objects – for example, that every event has a cause. According to Heidegger, inquiring into the universal and necessary judgments that we make about objects, this question asks about an ontology: the ontology of those objects that we encounter when we observe the world around us. But, moreover, in asking about the possibility of an ontology, this question, per Heidegger, asks after another ontology: the ontology of the human knower, who makes synthetic a priori judgments, and whose constitution indeed allows for the making of such judgments. Kant, therefore, in Heidegger's view, seeks a fundamental ontology, where one ontology (the ontology of the human being) explains the possibility of another (the ontology of observed objects). Though Kant does not complete this task – he hesitates to specify the ontology of the human being, failing to recognize that his characterization of our cognitive capacities gives insight into the sort of beings that we are – his inquiry provides direction on how to do so. Spelling out the interconnections at which Kant hints, between the cognitive faculties that Kant identifies, provides the ontology of the human being who forms a basis for other ontologies.

Heidegger rejects epistemological readings of Kant. Simon Truwant has argued recently that Heidegger's rejection of such readings can be mapped onto Heidegger's distinction between the ontic and the ontological (2022: 88) – that is, the so-called ontological difference between beings and Being. While the Neo-Kantians see Kant as attempting to justify our claims about *beings*, Heidegger sees Kant as, more fundamentally, inquiring into the ontology (i.e., the understanding of *Being*) that makes such judgments possible. Thus, the Neo-Kantians frame the Transcendental Deduction as a juridical question (are the categories valid, capturing the structure of beings?), whereas Heidegger focuses on the a priori syntheses that enable empirical cognition – syntheses that, taken together, provide an understanding of Being and that map onto the three equiprimordial capacities that constitute the human being.

In rejecting an epistemological reading of Kant, Heidegger concurs with some contemporary Kant scholars and opposes others. Notably, Heidegger opposes Henry Allison's epistemological reading even though (as I will review shortly) he agrees with Allison's discursivity thesis and two-aspect view.[1] The

---

[1] As Karin de Boer pointed out to me, the convergences between Allison and Heidegger might not be accidental. Allison was a student of Aron Gurwitsch, who was "deeply influenced by Husserlian phenomenology," and took Gurwitsch's seminar on the first *Critique* while studying at the New

disagreement between Allison and Heidegger on this particular score hangs, I think, on what counts for them as metaphysics or ontology: the "pre-critical" metaphysics that explains the ultimate nature of reality (Allison 2004: 16), or Heidegger's ontology of "the Being of entities," which is indexed to our (human) understanding of Being (BT 11). For Allison, Kant does not provide a metaphysics because he gives no final answer on how things are in themselves (2004: 16–17); indeed, Kant denies that such a metaphysics is possible for us.[2] Nevertheless, Kant does address the Being of beings in Heidegger's sense: what fundamentally characterizes the beings that we *do* experience – the Being that we *do* understand. Kant moreover provides insight into the sorts of beings that we are: not the immortal things at issue in rationalist metaphysics, but the capacities at the basis of any understanding of Being.

Following a rationalist understanding of metaphysics, Allison rejects the very notion of a fundamental ontology. He denies, that is, that a characterization of the human being would provide a basis for another ontology (e.g., the ontology of observed objects). Allison argues that Kant's "idealism is more properly seen as epistemological or perhaps 'metaepistemological' than as metaphysical in nature, since it is grounded in an analysis of the discursive nature of human cognition" (Allison 2004: 4). That is, because Kant's analysis is grounded on an account of human cognition, it cannot count as a metaphysics or ontology; it must rather be an epistemology. By contrast, Heidegger maintains that any ontology whatsoever must be grounded in the human being, the distinct kind of being who has "an understanding of Being" (BT 12). As Heidegger puts this point, "*fundamental ontology*, from which alone all other ontologies can take their rise, must be sought in the *existential analytic of Dasein*" (BT 13). We can see here that Heidegger operates with a definition of ontology that is squarely post-Kantian, taking it seriously that metaphysical claims are firmly tethered to the human standpoint.

Though his language sounds peculiar within the landscape of contemporary Kant scholarship, Heidegger makes a move that characterizes metaphysical readings of Kant: downgrading the expectations of rationalist metaphysics. For instance, Lucy Allais points out that

> Kant wants to show, for example, that we can know a priori that the spatial objects of our experience are in necessary causal connections with each

School for Social Research (de Boer 2022: 2). See also Serck-Hanssen 2015, who argues that Allison is "clearly indebted" to Heidegger's interpretation.

[2] Allison contrasts his epistemological reading to the metaphysical readings offered by Paul Guyer and Rae Langton (as well as their teacher, Peter Strawson), and also Jay Van Cleve and Karl Ameriks.

other and that they are made up of stuff which exists before and after they exist (that substance is conserved). Despite his rejection of transcendent metaphysics, it is not unreasonable to see this as giving us an account of metaphysical claims that we can establish: a metaphysics of experience, as opposed to a transcendent metaphysics. (2014: 6)

However, in holding that Kant spells out our metaphysical structure (without naming it as such), Heidegger also goes beyond typical metaphysical readings of Kant. That is, while metaphysical readings agree that Kant provides a metaphysics of the natural world, they do not suggest further that Kant provides a metaphysics of the human being; indeed, such a metaphysis seems to be precluded by Kant's Paralogisms. Again, this difference can be traced back to Heidegger's unique understanding of ontology. If Kant fails to characterize us as causally interacting substances, that does not mean that he fails to characterize us altogether. On Heidegger's view, we are beings of a different sort from those beings that we observe in the natural world; we are fundamentally characterized by capacities, not physical attributes. Heidegger pushes the metaphysical reading of Kant one step further: if we are giving up the pretensions of rationalist metaphysics by giving up insight into things in themselves, why not also give up the traditional idea that an ontology is only provided in the form of physical attributes like causality, substantiality, and so forth?

2 Discursivity

While many interpreters read Heidegger as prioritizing receptivity, and play up his claim that cognizing is primarily intuiting, I have insisted that Heidegger does justice to what Allison calls Kant's discursivity thesis. Intuition and thinking are both necessary for cognition. For Heidegger, intuition takes up what is given, while thinking determines what is given by way of universal concepts. Both elements are required for us to encounter a spatiotemporal being that, for example, persists across moments of time, and changes according to necessary laws. These elements, moreover, are qualitatively different; they perform reciprocal tasks, and cannot be reduced to one another. Heidegger does justice to the dualism of Kant's philosophical position, in agreement with many contemporary interpreters, and in contrast to the Marburg Neo-Kantians, who reduce intuition to thought.

However, Heidegger's interpretation also goes beyond the discursivity thesis, by inquiring into the "common root" that unites sensibility and understanding. Like many of his contemporaries, Heidegger believed that

Kant's own inquiry calls for this deeper story; while the Transcendental Deduction attempts to spell out the unity between intuition and thinking, it fails. On Heidegger's own account of this failure, Kant's Transcendental Deduction isolates two more specific elements that must be unified to secure the possibility of synthetic a priori judgments: time, the universal form of intuition (inner *and* outer), and apperception, the form of self-consciousness that employs the categories. However, since apperception is construed as atemporal, or removed from the condition of time, it remains a mystery how these two elements are united. Heidegger thinks that this problem can be resolved by disputing Kant's suggestions that apperception is removed from the condition of time. According to Heidegger, apperception is related to the future, comprising our adoption of an identity (i.e., an awareness of the sort of self that we are), along with expectations for the sorts of beings that we will encounter. This interpretation of apperception enables its unification with an intuition that takes in the present and an imagination that reproduces the past. Heidegger argues that these three elements are unified in the threefold structure of the transcendental power of imagination, which he identifies with original time or fundamental temporality.

While Heidegger exhibits a certain violence in regard to the Transcendental Deduction – disputing some claims and embracing others – he also reiterates the discursivity thesis at a deeper level. This move contrasts with the German Idealist account of the common root. The German Idealists trace Kant's dual faculties back to a single, simple source that is supposed to be capable of generating those faculties: a source that is spontaneous, allied with thinking. Heidegger, by contrast, insists that the common root is a pluralistic structure, composed of multiple parts. The empirical work of sensibility (taking in a particular located in space and time) and understanding (determining that particular by seeing it *as* something) is rooted in a diverse, a priori structure that is both spontaneous and receptive. The moments of this structure do not generate Kant's faculties – a claim that would seem to overextend Kant's category of causality, applying it to cognitive faculties to which it cannot apply – but fit them together in an interdependent, unified whole. If contemporary interpreters have given up the search for a common root, Heidegger nevertheless offers an interpretation of that root that does justice to a mainstay of contemporary Kant scholarship: the irreducible plurality of human cognition. Heidegger shows us that the search for a common root need not be accompanied by a denial of the plurality of cognition; it can recognize and do justice to that plurality. Thus, Heidegger offers an account of the common root that might be more palatable to contemporary interpreters.

3 Conceptualism

An ongoing debate in contemporary Kant scholarship concerns the conceptualism versus non-conceptualism of intuition.[3] Are intuitions informed by concepts, such that our having an intuition depends on conceptual processes? Or, conversely, are intuitions non-conceptual, making the procurement of an intuition and the conceptual processing of it distinct and separable moments of cognition? As Kant scholars have debated whether Kant qualifies as a conceptualist or non-conceptualist, other scholars have debated the merits of these positions more generally: Is human experience wholly structured by concepts? Prominently, Hubert Dreyfus presents Heidegger as a non-conceptualist who challenges John McDowell's Kant-inspired brand of conceptualism. To raise this challenge, Dreyfus appeals in particular to the "unthinking nonconceptual engagement" that in his view characterizes Heidegger's account of equipment use in *Being and Time* (Dreyfus 2005: 60).[4] However, Heidegger's interpretation of Kant tells a different story, offering a position that is conceptualist rather than non-conceptualist.[5]

Heidegger's account of the transcendental imagination, where the imagination is the common root of sensibility and understanding, locates the site where a priori intuitions and a priori concepts meet, forming two reciprocal components of a single, complex structure. Heidegger arrives at this meeting point by construing the categories not as abstract notions (i.e., removed from the condition of time, devoid of intuitive content), but rather as transcendental time determinations. The categories, that is, determine the form of time, such that it is taken to be, for example, something that endures despite the progression of moments (i.e., determined by the category of substance), comprising moments that progress necessarily in one direction (i.e., determined by the category of causality). The form of time sustains or takes up that determination, forming the unthematic horizon shaping our uptake of anything empirical.

---

[3] For a helpful summary of this debate, see McLear 2014.
[4] Dreyfus' 2005 address to the Pacific APA kicked off his debate with John McDowell, with Dreyfus defending non-conceptualism and McDowell defending conceptualism. Both agree, however, that Kant is allied with the conceptualist position. For the Dreyfus-McDowell debate, see Dreyfus 2005, Dreyfus 2007, Dreyfus 2013, McDowell 2007a, McDowell 2007b, and McDowell 2013.
[5] For a similar take on Heidegger's stance, see Golob 2014: 30.

Heidegger's interpretation of the categories puts them at the ground floor of empirical intuition, determining the form of time that shapes any empirical intuition. We intuit particulars at particular moments in time, and the categories form or specifically determine that time. Interpreting categories as time determinations leads to a conceptualism about intuition.

Given that some take Heidegger to be a non-conceptualist, though, I will briefly consider two objections to my claim that his interpretation of Kant offers a conceptualism – objections that, indeed, can be drawn from my foregoing analyses. First, one might appeal to my account of self-affection in Chapter 6 to argue that Heidegger does make room for something non-conceptual or pre-conceptual in his account of the transcendental imagination. Namely, the categories are supposed to interpret the time that we already are: the underdetermined temporal capacities of reaching-back, seizing, and reaching-ahead. However, these temporal capacities must be determined in order for us to have the particular sort of experience that Kant describes in the *Critique of Pure Reason* – that is, an experience where we observe some particular occupying a present "now." Arguing that the imagination is the common root of sensibility and understanding, for Heidegger, amounts to saying that the transcendental synthesis of the imagination (where time is determined as a sequence of nows, by way of three a priori syntheses) enables the empirical capacities assigned to sensibility and understanding. So far as we are talking about empirical intuition, the taking up of some particular, we are talking about something that is dependent on and framed by a conceptually determined form of time.

Second, one might appeal to the account of the Metaphysical Deduction and Schematism in Chapter 5 to object that Heidegger operates with a peculiar definition of concepts, and thus does not qualify as a true conceptualist. After all, Heidegger argues that the categories are time determinations, rather than rules lacking sensory content; that is, they are schematized, rather than being pure notions. However, notice that Heidegger's definition of the categories is in fact more robust than the latter definition; crudely put, categories are *rules plus sensory content*, rather than merely *rules*. Thus, on Heidegger's version of conceptualism, empirical intuition is not structured by anything less than a full-fledged concept. Further, Heidegger insists that his account of the categories does justice to their status as rules. That is, for something to be a rule, it must be taken up or submitted to; a receptive moment is required. An empty notion loses that receptive moment, lacking precisely what makes the category a rule. Insofar as rules are central to Kant's understanding of categories, and of concepts more generally, Heidegger can claim that he is a conceptualist in the only way that is tenable – that is, in the only way that does justice to a crucial feature of concepts.

Recently, Allais has drawn on a non-conceptualist reading of Kant[6] to defend the claim that Kant is something of a realist: intuition gives us "acquaintance" with objects that exist independently of our conceptual processing (Allais 2014: 14). So far as Heidegger offers a conceptualist reading of Kant, he would seem to block this particular route to realism, in keeping with my claim that Heidegger reads Kant as an idealist. I explore this further, returning to the idealism of Heidegger's interpretation, in the next section.

4 Idealism

Kant's transcendental idealism claims, crucially, that we have access to appearances and not things in themselves. In Chapter 2, I argued that Heidegger defends a two-aspect view of this distinction between appearances and things in themselves. That is, Heidegger takes these terms to capture two different perspectives on the same being, rather than capturing two different beings (i.e., the two-object or two-world view). Thus, Heidegger concurs with commentators like Allison and Graham Bird, and departs, for example, from Jay Van Cleve and Peter Strawson (as well as his contemporary Neo-Kantians, who he argues were led astray by this reading).

On Heidegger's own construal of the two-aspect view, the appearance is the being insofar as it is accessible to human cognition, which must receive content from without to cognize beings, and must make sense of that content by way of mediate concepts. By contrast, the thing in itself is the same being as it would be cognized by an infinite knower, who creates beings in the act of intuiting them, thereby cognizing them fully and immediately. Heidegger in the lecture series registers some resistance to this distinction, questioning the assumptions that the infinite being is essentially a maker and beings essentially made. Nevertheless, he takes up the finitude of the human knower as a running theme in his interpretation. Heidegger maintains that we appreciate beings from within a limited horizon; though we create that horizon (by interpreting the time that we ourselves are), our reliance on it – our "transcendental neediness"

---

[6] For a helpful account of the non-conceptualism of Allais' reading, see Newton 2016.

(KPM 165) – ensures the perspectival nature of our cognition. Thus, even this act of creation affirms the limits on human cognition.

Some commentators, however, think that Heidegger's interpretation of Kant does assign us access to things as they are in themselves. That is, they take Heidegger to offer a realist reading of Kant, where we are affected by independently existing beings, and we turn toward these beings in a way that allows us to appreciate their spatiotemporal natures. This reading resembles Allais' reading of Kant in that she also insists on the existence of independent beings. However, the reading goes beyond Allais' account in that it takes us to access how these independent beings really are; the spatiotemporal properties that we find in them captures their actual natures. Allais, by contrast, argues that we access only "manifest qualities" – "mind-dependent feature[s] of mind-independent things" (2014: 103). That is, though we are acquainted with independent beings, our appreciation of those beings is still filtered through our human ways of knowing; their spatiotemporal features are features that manifest to us, rather than features of what they are like in themselves, "independently of their perceptual appearing to us" (2014: 129).

However, on my reading, Heidegger's interpretation of Kant makes neither of these moves: it does not (more modestly, with Allais) commit to the existence of mind-independent beings, and does not (more radically, beyond Allais) suggest that we access their mind-independent features. Heidegger's opening discussion of intuition describes an experience of an independent object affecting us; Heidegger then proceeds recursively from that experience to the conditions that enable it, landing on our interpretation of time (i.e., our creation of a horizon) as what allows us to experience a being as an independent object. Heidegger's discussion does not attribute features like existence and causal efficaciousness to beings as they are in themselves.[7] It describes features of our experience of objects that are ultimately explained by the interpretation of time that we bring to those objects (indeed, that allows us to see them as objects).

Nevertheless, Heidegger's claim that intuition has primacy in this sort of experience allows him to meet one of the goals of Allais' own interpretation:

---

[7] Heidegger's claim that the categories are essentially schematized, as transcendental time determinations, blocks him from the particular path that Allais takes to arguing that we are given objects that independently exist. In particular, Allais thinks this "existential commitment" is "legitimate" insofar as we use "the unschematised category of existence" (2014: 69), rather than cashing out existence in terms of our sensible forms of space and time (which come from our perspective on things, rather than how they are independently).

"emphasising Kant's notion of intuition and the role of intuition in cognition" (Allais 2014: 13). Allais argues that "much work on Kant's transcendental idealism and on his account of cognition has failed to take sufficiently seriously the role of intuition in cognition" (2014: 146). Heidegger, however, does justice to the features of intuition that Allais charges others with missing. First, Heidegger captures that intuition is an "essential ingredient in cognition" (Allais 2014: 146) by maintaining that, in the sort of experience that when we cognize some object, intuition leads the other elements of cognition. What we take up in the present dictates the content of what we understand and reproduce; it drives the empirical concept that is applied, and the reproduction that is relevant. Moreover, since Heidegger attributes this leading role to intuition, he can acknowledge that intuition limits the bounds of "empirical reality" (Allais 2014: 146); if intuition kicks off any cognition, then cognition is limited to what we can intuit.

In my view, Heidegger does justice to the role that Kant attributes to intuition without giving up the idealism of his position. Heidegger retains this idealism by tracing the experience where intuition is primary (i.e., our cognition of some object) back to the human perspective enabling that experience. However, while defending an idealist interpretation of Kant, Heidegger admits to revising Kant's idealism in his treatment of time. According to Heidegger, time is not just one of the a priori conditions constraining and enabling human cognition; time is *the* a priori condition, the horizon that unifies the human perspective, sustaining the determinations of the categories. Further, Heidegger deepens Kant's idealism by arguing that this interpretation of time is created by three temporal capacities that constitute the human being. Thus, Heidegger develops an account explaining how the human being is the source of the a priori conditions framing the experience of beings. This revision comes at the cost of interpreting the understanding as related to time (specifically, the dimension of the future), in tension with some of Kant's claims. However, it has the benefit of unifying those capacities that must be unified in order for synthetic a priori judgment to be possible. Such judgments, on this reading, outline the temporal constitution of any and all of the beings that we encounter, on the basis of our sustained understanding of time.

5 Historicism

The historicism of Kant's account of cognition has remained a live issue in Kant scholarship. Kant embraces the Newtonian science of his day, but also claims to provide an account of human cognition that is a priori – necessary and universal, apparently holding despite a specific knower's historical location. Since science has advanced beyond the Newtonian paradigm, scholars of Kant have been forced to ask what is historically contingent and what is historically noncontingent in Kant's account – and whether the latter lines up with what Kant himself deems to be a priori. Heidegger's interpretation also weighs in on this issue.

To bring out Heidegger's distinct view of what is contingent and what is noncontingent in Kant's theoretical philosophy, I will set it into relief with recent work by Michael Friedman, which offers a reading of Kant's *Metaphysical Foundations of Natural Science*. Friedman notes that this work traditionally has been insulated from the *Critique of Pure Reason*; the *Metaphysical Foundations* are supposed to represent Kant's engagement with the science of his day, while the *Critique* provides an ahistorical account of human cognition (2013: x). This traditional reading preserves Kant's account of what is a priori, separating Kant's synthetic a priori principles from the laws of nature put forth by Newtonian science. Friedman, however, argues for a tighter connection between the two works. On Friedman's account, the *Metaphysical Foundations* helps us see that Newtonian science impacts the categories and principles presented in the first *Critique*. In particular, Newtonian science (more specifically, Newton's account of matter) provides them with "determinate *theoretical* content" (2013: 606), such that the categories can be applied to empirical objects. Nevertheless, Friedman distinguishes between the categories – that is, the "pure concepts of the understanding ... derived from the logical forms of judgment" (2013: 18) – and their historicized application to empirical objects. Per Friedman, the categories themselves are insulated from the Newtonian science of Kant's day, for other sciences could differently enumerate their application to empirical objects (2013: 592). Thus, the categories are ahistorical, even if the conditions governing their application are not.

We have seen Heidegger make rare comments affirming (though not further developing) Friedman's basic suggestion: the principles found in the first *Critique* are in some way historically contingent, undergoing a "transformation" over the course of history (KPM 162). However, Heidegger would disagree with Friedman that the categories offer a non-contingent part of Kant's system. Again, Heidegger denies that the categories are mere notions derived from the table of judgments. These notions are abstractions of the categories, and abstractions that lose what makes them categories: the receptive taking-up that sustains a determination as a rule. Heidegger resists the idea that the categories are independent from the form of time, but rather argues that the categories are developed as determinations of time (time "guides and sustains" them) (KPM 63). Going beyond Friedman's claim that Kant's (ahistorical) categories are historicized in their application to empirical objects, Heidegger locates historical contingency in the categories themselves.

For Heidegger, the necessary and universal core of Kant's account is time itself: not the succession of nows that smacks of Newtonian science, but the fundamental, temporal structure of the human being. The three interlaced temporal capacities of the human being provide the noncontingent ground for any conceptual scheme; we are beings who reach back, seize, and reach ahead. Interpreting these capacities means arriving at an interpretation of the time we expect to encounter out there, among beings – a time that is specifically determined, for example by way of categories. However, these three capacities underdetermine that conceptual scheme, admitting of multiple interpretations. Thus, the conceptual scheme that interprets these capacities is contingent, even though the temporal capacities are not.

Heidegger finds contingency where Kant, apparently, did not: in Kant's a priori form of time, as well as the a priori categories. Nevertheless, Heidegger does not retract his claim that Kant is laying the ground for metaphysics: a science of universal and necessary principles. Rather, Heidegger arrives at a sense in which these principles can be considered universal and necessary without being ahistorical. For Heidegger, interpreting time makes it possible for us to draw conclusions about the beings that we encounter within that horizon – that is, to make synthetic judgments a priori. However, for these principles to hold necessarily (such that the beings we encounter must be this way) and universally (such that they apply to every being we encounter), something is required of us. We must maintain this interpretation of time and, along with it, this interpretation of our own, underdetermined temporal capacities – this interpretation of ourselves. Metaphysics rests, then, on a sort of commitment: our holding fixed a historically contingent interpretation of time. This commitment is enabled, but not dictated, by the fundamentally temporal beings that we are.

Heidegger admits that this foundation for metaphysics – the underdetermined sort of beings that we are – lacks "the crystal clear, absolute evidence of a first maxim and principle" (KPM 26). That is why laying the ground for metaphysics, as Heidegger interprets it, "lead[s] us to an abyss" (KPM 117). Yet our findings ought not be dictated by a desire for stability, certainty, or finality; they must do justice to the phenomena under consideration. And Heidegger insists that Kant in his best moments recognized that our metaphysics can achieve no firmer basis than the beings that we ourselves are – and that these sort of beings are defined not by content but by capacity.

6 Concluding Remarks

This concluding chapter has argued that Heidegger's interpretation of Kant is legible within the broader landscape of contemporary Anglophone Kant scholarship. In particular, Heidegger offers a *metaphysical* reading of Kant that commits, further, to the *discursivity thesis*, the *conceptualism* of intuition, and a *two-aspect* view. Most radically – though still responsive to the challenges faced by Kant's account – Heidegger commits to the non-contingency of our fundamental, temporal structure, but the historical contingency of those categories that are used to determine it.

This book, more broadly, has argued that Heidegger's interpretation of Kant takes up Kant's main questions and seeks out Kant's best, most promising answers to those questions. Indeed, Heidegger's relentless pursuit of Kant's philosophical questions shows his adherence to an interpretive style that is well captured some years later when Heidegger turns to interpreting Nietzsche:

> It will be fatal if we, lacking the resolve for genuine questioning, simply "busy" ourselves with Nietzsche and take this "busyness" for thoughtful discussion of Nietzsche's unique thought.... Mere toying with philosophical thoughts, which keeps to the periphery right from the start because of various sorts of reservations, all mere play for purposes of intellectual entertainment or refreshment, is despicable: it does not know what is at stake on a thinker's path of thought. (N3: 9)

As with Nietzsche, Heidegger, in interpreting Kant, refuses to keep to the periphery by trying on his thought for novelty – a task that would perhaps exercise his philosophical acumen without carrying the danger of adopting new philosophical commitments. Heidegger rejects carrying out an interpretation that does not treat that thought as a live option – as something that could actually do justice to the question that it tries to answer, to the phenomena that it attempts to explain. Instead, Heidegger entreats us to engage in "genuine questioning" when we interpret texts: to take up the pursuit of the philosopher, and travel "a thinker's path of thought" to make progress on a shared question. Similarly, I hope to have laid out a convincing case that Heidegger's interpretation of Kant should not be read as a novelty – a strange exercise in particularly violent interpretation, which could perhaps be read for fun without the danger of commitment. Rather, Heidegger offers us a live option for interpreting Kant – for actually doing justice to the inquiry that Kant undertakes in the *Critique of Pure Reason*.

Coda

I officially embarked on the research that would one day become this book in June 2013, when I defended a prospectus promising a dissertation on the topic of Heidegger's Kant interpretation. Not one year later, in March 2014, selections from Heidegger's so-called Black Notebooks were published in his *Gesamtausgabe*. This material confirmed that Heidegger's philosophy could not be insulated from his Nazism and, indeed, from the anti-Semitism that he expressed in those volumes using his own philosophical vocabulary.

As with many who research and think with Heidegger, this material led to a lot of soul-searching on my part. I held myself in suspicion for finding so much insight, so much with which I myself agreed, in Heidegger's philosophical thought. As I researched Heidegger's method of interpreting Kant while grappling with the disturbing content published in the Black Notebooks, an idea began to grow that intertwined these two paths of thought: Could we turn Heidegger's interpretive method on Heidegger himself? The interpretive method that I have outlined in this book is a method designed to peel a philosopher's insights from their errors, in service of the questions that they themselves pursue. It is a way to isolate what is insightful and promising in a philosopher's thoughts, while leaving aside the errors that get in the way of a philosopher's best ideas. At the same time, this interpretive method does not sweep a philosopher's errors under the rug. It recognizes those errors as constituting a strand of argument; it inquires into the sources of those errors; it attempts to avoid those errors while reconstructing the best account of the phenomena under consideration. Could Heidegger's interpretive method tell us how to disambiguate Heidegger's philosophical insights from his own profound failures of thought?

Undoubtedly, Heidegger's method was not designed for this particular purpose. When Heidegger worried about the traditional prejudices infecting philosophical thought, he no doubt worried about the abstract, philosophical prejudices that he names in his work, such as the prioritization of thinking and logic, the forgetting of the question of Being, and so forth. He did not worry, that is, about how anti-Semitism could distort one's philosophical thought. But what better candidate could there be for interpretive violence? Perhaps, when he reads Kant, Heidegger unwittingly tells us how to read himself.

While I could not work out this idea in the foregoing study – applying the interpretive method to Heidegger himself would take me too far afield from spelling out how the interpretive method applies to Kant – I mark it here as the next frontier of my research. In this way, I hope to rise to the occasion of this critical moment in Heidegger scholarship.

Bibliography

Note: Works by Heidegger are included in the List of Abbreviations in the front of the book.

Adickes, Erich. 1924. *Kant und das Ding an Sich*. Berlin: Pan Verlag Rolf Heise.
Allais, Lucy. 2014. *Manifest Reality*. Oxford: Oxford University Press.
Allison, Henry. 2004. *Kant's Transcendental Idealism*. Revised and enlarged edition. New Haven, CT: Yale University Press.
Alweis, Lilian. 2015. "Heidegger's Black Notebooks." *Philosophy* 90.2: 305–316.
Banham, Gary. 2005. *Kant's Transcendental Imagination*. London: Palgrave Macmillan.
Barash, Jeffrey Andrew. 2012. "Ernst Cassirer, Martin Heidegger, and the Legacy of Davos." *History and Theory* 51: 436–450.
Barrett, William. 1968. "The Flow of Time." In *The Philosophy of Time*. Edited by Richard M. Gale. London: Macmillan, 355–378.
Beiser, Frederick C. 2014. *The Genesis of Neo-Kantianism, 1796–1880*. Oxford: Oxford University Press.
Blattner, William. 1994. "Is Heidegger a Kantian Idealist?" *Inquiry* 37.2: 185–201.
  1999. *Heidegger's Temporal Idealism*. Cambridge: Cambridge University Press.
  2004. "Heidegger's Kantian Idealism Revisited." *Inquiry* 47.4: 321–337.
  2006. "Heidegger's Appropriation of Kant." In *The Cambridge Companion to Heidegger*. Edited by Charles Guignon. Cambridge: Cambridge University Press, 149–176.
Brandom, Robert. 2002. *Tales of the Mighty Dead*. Cambridge: Cambridge University Press.
Carman, Taylor. 2000. "Review of William D. Blattner: 'Heidegger's Temporal Idealism.'" *Journal of Philosophy* 97.5: 308–312.
  2003. *Heidegger's Analytic: Interpretation, Discourse, and Authenticity in Being and Time*. Cambridge: Cambridge University Press.
  2010. "Heidegger's Anti-Neo-Kantianism." *Philosophical Forum* 37.1–2: 131–142.
Carr, David. 2007. "Heidegger on Kant on Transcendence." In *Transcendental Heidegger*. Edited by Steven Crowell and Jeff Malpas. Stanford, CA: Stanford University Press.

Cassirer, Ernst. 1967. "Kant and the Problem of Metaphysics: Remarks on Martin Heidegger's Interpretation of Kant." In *Kant: Disputed Questions*. Edited and translated by Moltke S. Gram. Chicago: Quadrangle Books, 131–157.

Cerbone, David. 1995. "World, World-Entry, and Realism in Early Heidegger." *Inquiry* 38: 401–421.

Child, William. 2006. "Interpreting People and Interpreting Texts." *International Journal of Philosophical Studies* 14.3: 423–441.

Cohen, Hermann. 1902. *System der Philosophie 1: Logik der reinen Erkenntniss*. Berlin: Bruno Cassirer.

Crowell, Steven. 2001. "Neo-Kantianism: Between Science and Worldview." In *Husserl, Heidegger, and the Space of Meaning*. Evanston, IL: Northwestern University Press, 23–36.

  2002. "Does the Husserl/Heidegger Feud Rest on a Mistake? An Essay on Psychological and Transcendental Phenomenology." *Husserl Studies* 18.2: 123–140.

Curtius, Ernst Robert. 1916. "Das Schematismuskapitel in der Kritik der reinen Vernunft." *Kant-Studien* 19.1–3: 338–366.

Cutrofello, Andrew. 1990 "Derrida's Deconstruction of the Ideal of Legitimation." *Man and World* 23: 157–170.

Dahlstrom, Daniel. 1991. "Heidegger's Kantian Turn: Notes to His Commentary on the '*Kritik der reinen Vernunft*.'" *The Review of Metaphysics* 45.2: 329–361.

  1994. "Heidegger's Kant-Courses at Marburg." In *Reading Heidegger from the Start*. Edited by Theodore Kisiel and John van Buren. Albany: State University of New York Press, 293–308.

  2010. "*The Critique of Pure Reason* and Continental Philosophy: Heidegger's Interpretation of the Transcendental Imagination." In *The Cambridge Companion to Kant's Critique of Pure Reason*. Edited by Paul Guyer. Cambridge: Cambridge University Press, 380–400.

Davidson, Donald. 1991. "James Joyce and Humpty Dumpty." *Midwest Studies in Philosophy* 16: 1–12.

  2001a. "A Coherence Theory of Truth and Knowledge." In *Subjective, Intersubjective, Objective*. Oxford: Oxford University Press, 137–157.

  2001b. *Inquiries into Truth and Interpretation*. Oxford: Oxford University Press.

de Boer, Karin. 2000. *Thinking in the Light of Time: Heidegger's Encounter with Hegel*. Albany: State University of New York Press.

  2020. *Kant's Reform of Metaphysics*. Cambridge: Cambridge University Press.

  2022. "Response to Morganna Lambeth, Finitude and Discursivity in Heidegger's Interpretation of Kant." Conference presentation (unpublished), Virtual Meeting of the North American Kant Society, March.

de Boer, Karin, and Stephen Howard. 2019. "A Ground Completely Overgrown: Heidegger, Kant and the Problem of Metaphysics." *British Journal for the History of Philosophy* 27.2: 358–377.

Declève, Henri. 1970. *Heidegger et Kant*. The Hague: Martinus Nijhoff.
Derrida, Jacques. 1988. "Afterword: Toward an Ethic of Discussion." In *Limited Inc*. Translated by Samuel Weber. Evanston, IL: Northwestern University Press, 111–154.
Dreyfus, Hubert. 1991. *Being-in-the-World*. Cambridge, MA: MIT Press.
   2005. "Overcoming the Myth of the Mental: How Philosophers Can Profit from the Phenomenology of Everyday Expertise." *Proceedings and Addresses of the American Philosophical Association* 79.2: 47–65.
   2007. "Response to McDowell." *Inquiry* 50.4: 371–377.
   2013. "The Myth of the Pervasiveness of the Mental." In *Mind, Reason and Being-in-the-World*. Edited by Joseph Schear. New York: Routledge, 15–40.
Dyck, Corey. 2014. *Kant and Rational Psychology*. Oxford: Oxford University Press.
Engelland, Chad. 2017. *Heidegger's Shadow: Kant, Husserl, and the Transcendental Turn*. New York: Routledge.
Farías, Víctor. 1989. *Heidegger and Nazism*. Philadelphia: Temple University Press.
Farin, Ingo, and Jeff Malpas. 2016. "Introduction." In *Reading Heidegger's Black Notebooks 1931–1941*. Edited by Ingo Farin and Jeff Malpas. Cambridge, MA: MIT Press.
Franks, Paul W. 2005. *All or Nothing*. Cambridge, MA: Harvard University Press.
Friedman, Michael. 2000. *A Parting of the Ways*. Peru, IL: Open Court.
   2013. *Kant's Construction of Nature: A Reading of the Metaphysical Foundations of Natural Science*. Cambridge: Cambridge University Press.
Gadamer, Hans-Georg. 2013. *Truth and Method* [TM]. London: Bloomsbury Publishing.
Golob, Sacha. 2013. "Heidegger on Kant, Time, and the 'Form' of Intentionality." *British Journal for the History of Philosophy* 21.2: 345–367.
   2014. *Heidegger on Concepts, Freedom, and Normativity*. Cambridge: Cambridge University Press.
Gordon, Peter. 2010. *Continental Divide: Heidegger, Cassirer, Davos*. Cambridge, MA: Harvard University Press.
   2013. "The Empire of Signs: Heidegger's Critique of Idealism in *Being and Time*." In *The Cambridge Companion to Heidegger's Being and Time*. Edited by Mark Wrathall. Cambridge: Cambridge University Press.
Grene, Marjorie. 1957. *Martin Heidegger*. London: Bowes and Bowes.
Guyer, Paul. 2000. "Absolute Idealism and the Rejection of Kantian Dualism." In *Cambridge Companion to German Idealism*. 2nd edition. Edited by Karl Ameriks. Cambridge: Cambridge University Press, 37–56.
Han-Pile, Beatrice. 2005. "Early Heidegger's Appropriation of Kant." In *A Companion to Heidegger*. Edited by Hubert Dreyfus and Mark Wrathall. Malden, MA: Blackwell.
Hegel, G. W. F. 1977. *Faith and Knowledge*. Translated by W. Cerf and H. S. Harris. Albany: State University of New York Press.
Heidelberger, Michael. 2006. "Kantianism and Realism: Alois Riehl (and Moritz Schlick)." In *The Kantian Legacy in Nineteenth-Century Science*. Edited by

M. Friedman, A. Nordmann, and G. E. Smith. Cambridge, MA: MIT Press, 227–247.
Henrich, Dieter. 1994. "On the Unity of Subjectivity." In *The Unity of Reason: Essays on Kant's Philosophy*. Translated by Günter Zöller. Cambridge, MA: Harvard University Press, 17–54.
Hoppe, Hansgeorg. 1970. "Wandlungen in der Kant-Auffasung Heideggers." In *Durchblicke: Martin Heidegger zum 80. Geburtstag*. Frankfurt am Main: Vittorio Klostermann.
Husserl, Edmund. 1997. *Psychological and Transcendental Phenomenology and the Confrontation with Heidegger (1927–1931)*. Edited and translated by Thomas Sheehan and Richard E. Palmer. Dordrecht: Kluwer Academic.
Kant, Immanuel. 1996. *Practical Philosophy*. Translated and edited by Mary J. Gregor. Cambridge: Cambridge University Press.
   2000. *The Critique of the Power of Judgment*. Translated by Paul Guyer and Eric Matthews. Cambridge: Cambridge University Press.
   2003. *The Critique of Pure Reason*. Translated by P. Guyer and A. W. Wood. Cambridge: Cambridge University Press.
   2004a. *Lectures on Logic*. Translated by J. Michael Young. Cambridge: Cambridge University Press.
   2004b. *Prolegomena to Any Future Metaphysics*. Translated by Gary Hatfield. Cambridge: Cambridge University Press.
   2006. *Anthropology from a Pragmatic Point of View*. Translated by Robert B. Louden. Cambridge: Cambridge University Press.
Kinkaid, James. 2018. "Phenomenology, Idealism, and the Legacy of Kant." *British Journal for the History of Philosophy* 27.3: 593–614.
Kisiel, Theodore. 1993. *The Genesis of Heidegger's Being and Time*. Berkeley: University of California Press.
Korsgaard, Christine. 1996. *Creating the Kingdom of Ends*. Cambridge: Cambridge University Press.
Kraus, Katharina. 2019. "Rethinking the Relationship between Empirical Psychology and Transcendental Philosophy in Kant." *International Yearbook of German Idealism* 15: 47–76.
Krois, John Michael. 2004. "Why Did Cassirer and Heidegger not Debate in Davos?" In *Symbolic Forms and Cultural Studies*. Edited by Cyrus Hamlin and John Michael Krois. New Haven, CT: Yale University Press, 244–262.
Lafont, Cristina. 2008. "Meaning and Interpretation: Can Brandomian Scorekeepers Be Gadamerian Hermeneuts?" *Philosophy Compass* 3.1: 17–29.
Lambeth, Morganna. 2019. "A Case for Heidegger's Interpretation of the Kantian Imagination." In *Proceedings of the 13th International Kant Congress 'The Court of Reason' (Oslo, 6–9 August 2019)*. Edited by Camilla Serck-Hanssen and Beatrix Himmelmann. Berlin: Walter de Gruyter, 1285–1293.
   2020. "Book Review: *Heidegger's Shadow: Kant, Husserl, and the Transcendental Turn*." *Journal of Transcendental Philosophy* 1.2: 257–263.
   2021a. "A Proposal for Translating Heidegger's Interpretation of Kant." *Gatherings: The Heidegger Circle Annual* 11: 20–57.

2021b. "A Tale of Two Faculties: Heidegger's Method of Interpreting Kant." *History of Philosophy Quarterly* 38.1: 57–80.

Lambeth, Morganna and Christopher Yeomans. Forthcoming. "Reconsidering Heidegger's Temporal Idealism: Finding a Successful Argument with the Help of Fichte and Hegel." *Epoché*.

Llewelyn, John. 2000. *The HypoCritical Imagination: Between Kant and Levinas*. London: Routledge.

Longuenesse, Beatrice. 1998. *Kant and the Capacity to Judge*. Princeton, NJ: Princeton University Press.

Lotze, Hermann. 1843. *Logik*. Leipzig: Weidmannsche Buchhandlung.

Löwith, Karl. 1995. "The Occasional Decisionism of Carl Schmitt." In *Martin Heidegger and European Nihilism*. Edited by Richard Wolin and translated by Gary Steiner. New York: Columbia University Press, 137–172.

Luft, Sebastian. 2011. "Continental Divide: Heidegger, Cassirer, Davos (review)." *Journal of the History of Philosophy* 49.4: 508–509.

Lynch, Dennis A. 1990. "Ernst Cassirer and Martin Heidegger: The Davos Debate." *Kant-Studien* 81.3: 360–370.

McDowell, John. 2007a. "Response to Dreyfus." *Inquiry* 50.4: 366–370.

2007b. "What Myth?" *Inquiry* 50.4: 338–351.

2013. "The Myth of the Mind as Detached." In *Mind, Reason and Being-in-the-World*. Edited by Joseph Schear. New York: Routledge, 41–58.

McLear, Colin. 2014. "The Kantian (Non)-Conceptualism Debate." *Philosophy Compass* 9.11: 769–790.

McQuillan, Colin. 2017. "Kant, Heidegger, and the In/Finitude of Human Reason." *CR: The New Centennial Review* 17.3: 81–102.

2021. "Comments on Lambeth, 'The Role of Receptivity in Heidegger's Kant Interpretation.'" Conference Presentation (unpublished), Central Division Meeting of the American Philosophical Association, February.

Mörchen, Hermann. 1970. *Die Einbildungskraft bei Kant*. 2nd edition. Tübingen: Max Niemayer.

Natorp, Paul. 1923. *Die Logischen Grundlagen der exakten Wissenschaften*. Leipzig: B. G. Teubner.

2015. "Kant and the Marburg School." Translated by Frances Bottenberg. In *The Neo-Kantian Reader*. Edited by Sebastian Luft. London: Routledge, 180–197.

Newton, Alexandra. 2016. "Non-Conceptualism and Knowledge in Lucy Allais's *Manifest Reality*." *Kantian Review* 21.2: 273–282.

Nir, Gilad. 2021. "Heidegger on the Unity of Metaphysics and the Method of Being and Time." *The Review of Metaphysics*, 74.3: 361–396.

Nordmann, Alfred. 2006. "Critical Realism, Critical Idealism, and Critical Common-Sensism: The School and World Philosophies of Riehl, Cohen, and Peirce." In *The Kantian Legacy in Nineteenth-Century Science*. Edited by M. Friedman, A. Nordmann, and G. E. Smith. Cambridge, MA: MIT Press, 249–274.

Philipse, Herman. *Heidegger's Philosophy of Being*. Princeton, NJ: Princeton University Press, 1998.

Piché, Claude. 2000. "Heidegger and the Neo-Kantian Reading of Kant." In *Heidegger, German Idealism, and Neo-Kantianism*. Edited by Tom Rockmore. Amherst, NY: Humanity Books, 179–208.
Poma, Andrea. 1997. *The Critical Philosophy of Hermann Cohen*. Translated by John Denton. Albany: State University of New York Press.
Reid, James D. 2003. "On the Unity of Theoretical Subjectivity in Kant and Fichte." *The Review of Metaphysics* 57: 243–277.
Richardson, William J. 1993. *Heidegger: Through Phenomenology to Thought*. 4th edition. New York: Fordham University Press.
Ricoeur, Paul. 1978. "The Critique of Religion." In *The Philosophy of Paul Ricoeur*. Edited by Charles E. Reagan and David Stewart. Boston: Beacon Press, 213–222.
Rousse, B. Scot. 2022. "Retrieving Heidegger's Temporal Realism." *European Journal of Philosophy* 30.1: 205–226.
Safranski, Rüdiger. 1998. *Martin Heidegger: Between Good and Evil*. Cambridge, MA: Harvard University Press.
Sallis, John. 1980. *Gathering of Reason*. Albany: State University of New York Press.
    1987. *Spacings – Of Reason and Imagination*. Chicago: University of Chicago Press.
Schalow, Frank. 1992. *The Renewal of the Heidegger-Kant Dialogue*. Albany: State University of New York Press.
    2013. *Departures: At the Crossroads between Heidegger and Kant*. Berlin: Walter de Gruyter.
    2016. "A Diltheyan Loop? The Methodological Side of Heidegger's Kant-Interpretation." *Frontiers of Philosophy in China* 11.3: 377–394.
Schopenhauer, Arthur. 2010. *The World as Will and Representation* [WWR], vol. 1. Translated by Judith Norman, Alistair Welchman, and Christopher Janaway. Cambridge: Cambridge University Press.
Serafin, Andrzej. 2015. "A Reception History of the Black Notebooks." *Gatherings* 5: 118–142.
Serck-Hanssen, Camilla. 2015. "Towards Fundamental Ontology: Heidegger's Phenomenological Reading of Kant." *Continental Philosophy Review* 48: 217–235.
Sherover, Charles. 1971. *Heidegger, Kant, and Time*. Bloomington: Indiana University Press.
Strawson, Peter. 1966. *Bounds of Sense*. London: Methuen.
Truwant, Simon. 2022. *Cassirer and Heidegger in Davos: The Philosophical Arguments*. Cambridge: Cambridge University Press.
Waxman, Wayne. 1991. *Kant's Model of the Mind*. Oxford: Oxford University Press.
Weatherston, Martin. 2002. *Heidegger's Interpretation of Kant*. Hampshire: Palgrave Macmillan.
Woodward, William R. 2015. *Hermann Lotze: An Intellectual Biography*. Cambridge: Cambridge University Press.
Wrathall, Mark. 2022. "The Question of Ontological Dependency." *British Journal for the History of Philosophy* 30.3: 547–559.

Index

abyss, 30, 34–35, 103, 203
Adickes, Erich, 115
affection, 55–57. *See also* self-affection
anthropology, 22
Anthropology from a Pragmatic Point of View, 60, 62, 89–90
anti-Semitism, 9, 43, 206
anxiety, 17, 28–36, 106
appearances, 75–78, 81, 86, 88, 101, 119, 163, 166, 199
Appendix, 86–91
apperception, 13, 29, 70, 85–88, 91, 133, 137, 147–148, 150–155, 158–160, 164, 177, 182, 184–185, 196
Aristotle, 24, 35, 104–105, 110
authenticity, 35, 171–173

basic power, 85, 88–93, 96, 98
Being, 38. *See also* ontology
  history of, 14, 163, 188, 191
  question of, 4, 207
  understanding of, 4, 51, 79–80, 105, 149–150, 193–194
beings. *See* ontic
bias, 29, 116, 118
Black Notebooks, 9, 206
Blattner, William, 16, 66–67, 71, 78, 163–164, 172–173, 180, 182–183, 190
Brandom, Robert, 15, 17–18

care, 27, 41, 70–71, 139, 171
Cassirer, Ernst, 16, 41, 43–44, 80, 82, 93
categories, 6, 12, 35, 39, 44–46, 59–61, 64–66, 71, 77–78, 84, 87–88, 91, 97, 99–102, 135–136, 150–154, 158–159, 164, 185, 188, 193, 196–203. *See also* causality, category of; substance, category of
  source of, 13
causality, category of, 6, 12–13, 56, 84, 92, 97, 99–100, 118, 164, 196–197
charity, 18–19, 28, 39, 159

cognition, 1, 5–8, 10, 12, 23, 38, 40–73, 75–80, 102, 110, 116, 134, 148, 175–180, 193–196, 199–202
Cohen, Hermann, 40–41, 43–46, 82, 137
communicability, 57–58, 167
comportment, 152–154, 171
concepts, 4, 6, 41, 45, 49, 58–59, 64–65, 76–77, 87, 98, 101, 116–124, 126, 135–138, 144, 148, 150–151, 155–156, 177, 195, 197–199. *See also* categories; determining
conceptualism, 197–199, 204
Copernican Revolution, 1, 5, 38
creativity, 57–58, 79–80, 180, 187
Critique of Judgment, 1, 116
Critique of Practical Reason, 1, 10, 191

Dahlstrom, Daniel, 2, 10, 16, 23, 29, 41–42, 48, 50, 69, 116, 133, 150, 159, 165–169, 179–180
Dasein, 4, 22, 27, 31, 34, 36, 38, 67, 69–70, 80, 100, 139, 160–163, 168, 171–173, 180, 185, 188–189, 194
Davidson, Donald, 11, 17–20, 22, 24
de Boer, Karin, 2, 41–42, 44–45, 67, 75, 81, 85, 133
decisionism, 9, 189
Derrida, Jacques, 33
Descartes, René, 86, 136
destruction, 36, 169
determining, 57–59, 62–63, 65–66, 77–79, 85, 98, 119, 126, 128–131, 143, 146, 164, 185–186, 195–198, 203
discourse, 172
discursivity thesis, 12, 40, 42, 45, 49, 58, 71, 193, 195–197, 204

ecstasis, 172–175, 182–185
epistemological reading, 48, 192–195
equiprimordiality, 41, 61, 69–70, 92–93, 157, 172, 183, 185, 193

Erdmann, Benno, 43
error, 11, 17, 19, 23–29, 31–32, 36–37, 39, 206
falling, 172
fear, 29–31
Fichte, Johann Gottlieb, 48, 82, 85, 92, 94
finitude, 5–6, 54–60, 75–81, 95, 102, 172, 174, 184, 199
for-the-sake-of-which, 171, 173
forms of intuition, 7, 44–45, 60, 63–64, 66–67, 84, 86, 97–98, 102, 116, 164, 166, 200
  form of space, 6–7, 61, 124–125, 164
  form of time, 7–8, 14, 61, 78, 97, 125, 130, 136, 163–165, 191, 196–198, 203. *See also* now-time; sequence of nows
freedom, 10, 182, 187–191
fundamental ontology, 4–5, 21–22, 24, 33, 36, 38, 51–52, 161, 168, 193–194

Gadamer, Hans-Georg, 11, 17–20, 22–24, 28–29, 31–32
German Idealism, 1, 6, 11–13, 48, 74–75, 80–86, 92–95, 103, 176, 196

Han-Pile, Beatrice, 50, 76–77, 163–164, 166, 180, 190
Hegel, Georg Wilhelm Friedrich, 82, 86, 93
Henrich, Dieter, 16, 31, 74–75, 81, 83, 85, 87, 93, 133, 144, 159, 176
hermeneutics of suspicion, 32–33
historicism, 187–188, 201–204
history, of Being, 14, 78, 163, 188, 191
horizon, 62, 78–80, 124, 127, 142, 146, 155–156, 158, 164–165, 169, 177, 179–180, 186–190, 197, 199, 201, 203
horror, 30, 34
Howard, Stephen, 41–42, 44–45, 67, 75, 81, 133
Husserl, Edmund, 2, 49–50, 140, 160

idealism
  ontological idealism, 164, 190
  temporal idealism, 7, 78, 161–191, 201
  transcendental idealism, 75–81, 136, 163–164, 167, 180, 199–201
imagination, 8, 10, 26–27, 34–35, 39, 41–42, 47, 72, 75, 79, 87, 101, 109, 113–114, 122. *See also* priority, of imagination
  as common root, 12, 92–99, 198
  empirical (reproductive), 60–61, 89, 146
  and German Idealism, 82–83, 85–86
  and time, 4, 14, 66–72, 107–109, 113–115, 119, 125, 129, 131, 133–159, 172–173, 187, 189

  transcendental (productive), 60, 63–66, 102, 112, 133–159, 164, 172–173, 196, 198
infinite cognition, 7, 56–58, 76–80, 85–86, 180, 199
interpretation
  interpreting time, 13–14, 79, 107, 125, 158, 163, 168, 191, 200–201, 203
  reconstructive, 3, 11–12, 25, 27, 32–33, 39, 140
  scholarly, 18, 37, 105
  two-strand, 2, 8, 11, 13, 23, 40, 95, 106, 132–133
intuition, 7, 41, 44, 135–138, 144, 155–156, 195. *See also* forms of intuition; priority, of intuition
intuitus derivativus. *See* finitude
intuitus originarius. *See* infinite cognition

Jacobi, Friedrich Heinrich, 55, 82, 94

Kinkaid, James, 165–167, 181–182
Külpe, Oswald, 166–167

Lafont, Cristina, 18–20
Lectures on Logic, 22
Leibniz, Gottfried Wilhelm, 86
logic, 13, 26, 29, 45, 89–91, 107–114, 128–131, 143, 202
  priority of. *See* priority, of the understanding
Lotze, Hermann, 26, 111–112, 130

magnitude, schema of, 125
Metaphysical Deduction, 10, 13, 17, 25–27, 106–114, 119, 128–133, 198
Metaphysical Foundations of Natural Science, 202
metaphysical reading, 192–195, 204
metaphysics. *See also* synthetic a priori judgments
  laying the ground of, 4, 10, 76, 83–85, 100, 102–103, 203
  metaphysica generalis, 105–106
  metaphysica specialis, 105–106
modality, categories of, 45
Mörchen, Hermann, 114–115

National Socialism, 9, 43, 189, 206
Natorp, Paul, 40–41, 46, 82, 137
Neo-Kantianism, 1, 6, 9, 11–12, 26, 40–63, 69, 71–73, 76, 78, 82–83, 93, 96, 111, 137, 166, 176, 192–193, 195, 199
Newtonian physics, 188, 201–203
Nietzsche, Friedrich, 32, 204
now-time, 69, 161–163, 165, 167–168, 170, 174, 179–186, 189–190. *See also* sequence of nows

ontic, 22, 51–52, 59, 80, 166, 180, 186, 193
ontological difference, 51, 193
ontology, 4, 20–21, 32, 51–52, 59, 61, 71, 79–80, 100, 105–106, 109, 129–130, 149, 165, 168, 180, 186, 190–195. *See also* fundamental ontology
original time. *See* temporality

Paralogisms, 87–88, 91, 100–101, 195
phenomenological reduction, 51
phenomenology, 49–52, 104–106, 131, 140, 160, 177, 193
philosophy, 3, 23–25, 50–52, 104–106
potentiality-for-being, 176, 179
potentiality-for-Being, 172–174
present-at-hand, 11, 52–53, 101–102, 162, 165, 167–168, 171, 179–180
priority
  of apperception, 177
  of the future, 139, 156, 172–174, 177–179
  of imagination, 11–13, 17, 23–24, 29, 35, 40, 48, 107–108, 131–132
  of intuition, 42, 46–47, 49–59, 175–177, 201
  of understanding, 12, 17, 23, 29, 34, 40, 48, 108, 131–132, 207
  temporal, 156, 168, 174–175
projection, 139, 152, 154, 156–157, 172–174, 176, 179, 185–187
Prolegomena to Any Future Metaphysics, 36
psychological explanation, 28–29, 31–32

quaestio juris, 135
quantity, categories of, 45

realism, 52–53, 55
  direct realism, 199–200
  empirical realism, 180
  temporal realism, 3, 42–43, 162–163, 167, 169, 180–181, 189–190, 200
receptivity, 6–7, 12, 40–72, 85, 95, 97–98, 143–146, 154, 160, 195. *See also* taking-up
Reinhold, Karl Leonhard, 82, 84, 89, 137
resoluteness, 36
retreat, 11, 28–31, 34, 36, 106
Rickert, Heinrich, 43
Riehl, Alois, 43, 53, 166–167

Scheler, Max, 181
Schelling, Friedrich Wilhelm Joseph, 82, 94
schema, 122–128
Schematism, 10, 13, 25, 31, 61, 70, 98, 106–109, 113–133, 158, 161, 164, 186–187, 198
Scholastics, 105

Schopenhauer, Arthur, 24, 31, 114, 119, 123, 130
second-rate thinkers, 24, 35
self-affection, 14, 62, 68, 162, 180–190, 198
sensibility, 40–42, 44–49, 54–60, 63–67, 69–75, 81–82, 84, 86–100, 109, 134–138, 140, 143, 145, 147, 151, 155, 158–160, 195–198
sequence of nows, 61, 67–69, 125–127, 129, 131, 138–139, 141–144, 158, 169–170, 176, 181–182, 184, 198. *See also* now-time
shyness, 29–30
spontaneity, 3, 6–7, 12, 34, 40–72, 82–83, 95–98, 103, 133, 143, 145–146, 150, 154, 160
substance, category of, 6, 63, 87–88, 100–101, 126–127, 129–130, 150, 164, 179, 183, 186, 195, 197
subsumption, 115, 118–120
synthesis, 55, 66, 86, 96, 99, 109, 112–113, 119–120, 125–126, 134–138, 148, 155–158, 164, 171–172, 177, 184, 187, 193, 198
  of apprehension, 140–145, 147, 150–155, 175
  of recognition, 155–156, 176–178
  of reproduction, 144–147, 150–155, 176
synthetic a priori judgments, 20–22, 25–27, 32, 51–52, 83–84, 92, 99, 105, 129, 131, 160, 193, 196, 201–203

table of categories, 26, 45, 65, 109–113, 125, 130
table of judgments, 26, 110–112, 129, 131, 202
taking-up, 11, 55, 63, 77, 179, 184, 195, 202
temporality, 8, 14, 67–71, 79, 130, 139–140, 145, 156, 159–164, 166–169, 171–175, 177, 179–191, 196
temporalizing, 154, 163, 174, 184
the they, 104
things in themselves, 75–78, 80–82, 86, 163–164, 166, 195, 199–200
thrownness, 41, 172
tradition, 2–3, 13, 29, 31, 36, 68, 71, 73, 84, 87, 94–96, 103–108, 111, 113, 115, 118–119, 124–125, 135–136, 169, 174, 179, 195
Transcendental Aesthetic, 10, 44–45, 51–52, 73, 95, 108, 116–117, 133, 137, 166
Transcendental Deduction, 4, 10, 13, 23, 25–26, 42, 44, 48, 50, 70, 74, 99, 108–109, 128, 133–159, 163–164, 170–172, 175–177, 181, 184, 187, 193, 196

Transcendental Dialectic, 10, 86–87, 96, 191
two-aspect view, 76–77, 193, 199–200, 204

understanding, 40–42, 57–59, 65–66, 73–75, 84, 86–100, 134–138, 147, 151, 155, 158–160, 195–198. *See also* priority, of understanding
unity, 8, 42, 44–49, 70–72, 155–158, 160, 172–174

vacillation, 23–24, 48
violence, 2, 16–17, 31, 35–37, 96, 108, 156, 159, 196, 205, 207

Windelband, Wilhelm, 43
Wolff, Christian, 85–86, 89, 91–94, 96, 99
world, phenomenon of, 170
world-time, 162, 168, 170–171, 175–176, 182–183

For EU product safety concerns, contact us at Calle de José Abascal, 56–1°,
28003 Madrid, Spain or eugpsr@cambridge.org.

www.ingramcontent.com/pod-product-compliance
Lightning Source LLC
LaVergne TN
LVHW020344260326
834688LV00045B/1529